Intervention for Human Rights in Europe

Also by Janne Haaland Matláry

EMU: A Swedish Perspective (*co-author with L. Calmfors et al.*)

ENERGY POLICY IN THE EUROPEAN UNION

Intervention for Human Rights in Europe

Janne Haaland Matláry
Head, International Politics Section
Department of Political Science
University of Oslo
Norway

palgrave

First published 2002 by
PALGRAVE
Houndmills, Basingstoke, Hampshire RG21 6XS and
175 Fifth Avenue, New York, N.Y. 10010
Companies and representatives throughout the world

PALGRAVE is the new global academic imprint of St. Martin's Press LLC Scholarly and Reference Division and Palgrave Publishers Ltd (formerly Macmillan Press Ltd).

ISBN 0-333-79424-9

This book is printed on paper suitable for recycling and made from fully managed and sustained forest sources.

A catalogue record for this book is available from the British Library.

A catalogue record for this book is available from the Library of Congress

10 9 8 7 6 5 4 3 2 1
11 10 09 08 07 06 05 04 03 02

Printed and bound in Great Britain by
Antony Rowe Ltd, Chippenham, Wiltshire

To the victims and survivors of the Balkan tragedy – that human rights be theirs

Contents

Preface

This study was started during my tenure as State Secretary of Foreign Affairs of Norway, 1997–2000. I was asked by Macmillan – now Palgrave – to write a book on my experiences of the role that human rights seemed to play in international politics, suggested by Norway's extensive engagement in this field – in human rights dialogues with Cuba, Vietnam and China; in our work in the UN Human Rights Commission; and in peace mediation in places like Guatemala, the Middle East and Sri Lanka; and not least in our work as chairman of the Organisation for Security and Cooperation in Europe (OSCE), which it fell to me to work on in particular.

I noticed that although traditional national interests clearly were important drivers in international politics, there was also an independent factor in the human rights discourse, as no one who wanted to be seen as a legitimate actor in the Western world could afford to be criticised on account of non-compliance with human rights standards. In short, all actors – governments and businesses alike – who aspired to a normal standing in Western international politics had to 'talk the talk' of human rights, democracy and the rule of law: and they also had to implement it for no other reason than to avoid being 'shamed' and exposed. This new 'logic' of soft power fascinated me, as it clearly had teeth, and was no longer simply something for festive speeches.

During our year in the chairmanship of the OSCE we had to deal with the very practical implementation of human rights and democracy in new states that aspired to membership and therefore good standing in Western international organisations – the Council of Europe (COE) and most of all, the European Union (EU); and we worked hard at specifying exactly how and by which standards one could 'remake' states into modern, liberal democracies. During this year we also had to deal with the Kosovo crisis, using first the normal 'soft power' approach of sending a field mission to Kosovo, the Kosovo Verification Mission (KVM); and then later, after having exhausted all the 'soft power' tools, resorting to hard power in a military campaign where human rights and humanitarian considerations did in fact play a significant role.

This study investigates the power behind human rights in today's open, public diplomacy, arguing that most actors adopt human rights standards and actually implement them for instrumental reasons, although persuasion and learning naturally may take place as well. My findings are, however, consistent with a view of politics where actors have instrumental interests, and where the role of power is just as relevant for 'value politics' as for other types of politics. I investigate the impact of what is termed the 'European human rights regime', which refers to the common values and definitions defined in the EU, the COE and the OSCE. The definitions of human rights, democracy and rule of law defined in the Convention of Human Rights, the Helsinki Final Act and later OSCE documents, as well as in the Treaty on Political Union (TEU) in the EU and its Charter, are all internally consistent, identical and together make up a whole – the *European human rights regime.*

The growth of public diplomacy introduces a new type of international politics where actors have to engage in human rights and democracy discourse where they have to accept and promote such values; and once engaged in this, they will be exposed if not compliant. The further a new state is from the centre of Western discourse and Western tradition, the less concerned it is with compliance. Some government leaders do not even 'talk the talk' of human rights, and even less, implement its content. However, there are increasingly fewer of those states. It is clear that states that seek membership of Western-dominated international organisations have to 'talk the talk', that is, adopt human rights rhetoric; but they are also forced to implement its contents as they proceed to work with these organisations. The EU has the most stringent standards in its pre-accession programmes, while the OSCE has field missions in place, observing state behaviour from within the state; and the COE has taken on a much more activist role after admitting very many new states from Central and Eastern Europe, and has the legal power vested in its court to impose rule of law and human rights as such.

This study looks at the *impact* that these central international organisations (IOs) in Europe have in the field of democracy and human rights. There is a *new interventionism* in Western foreign policy, we argue, one that employs soft power tools for the most part; and it is an interventionism which changes the norm of sovereignty. It is increasingly regarded as legitimate to intervene in states where human rights and democracy are endangered; and this also holds for Western states, although they usually do not engage in each other's internal affairs. However, the case of Austria's 'shaming' marks a new era in how the sovereignty norm is viewed by the international community.

In the field of international studies, one of the key questions is *whether* and *how much independent* impact international regimes and organisations wield. This is an important question in security and economic regimes. Here it has more or less been found that such non-state actors are important, sometimes as arenas, sometimes as actors. However, the question of whether these regimes and organisations also have an impact in the field of 'values and norms' such as human rights, has not been much studied. This book contributes to this debate by showing that the human rights regime itself has teeth – there are regime-specific powers in it, such as the supranational legal status of the European Convention of Human Rights (ECHR) and its court; the specificity and practical definitions of human rights and democracy in the OSCE texts; and the EU's stipulation of tailor-made demands on new entrants in this area. Thus, the human rights regime itself has various 'powers' built into it.

But the international organisations into which this regime is embedded also have 'teeth'. There are tools and powers that are specific to each organisation, and this makes for an independent impact of each one of them. Clearly states are the main driving forces and also 'owners' of international organisations, but the states do not account for the explanation of impact alone. In the OSCE it is the chairman who can influence the agenda-setting and often outcomes; in the EU both states and EU actors such as the Commission and the European Parliament have important roles. In the enlargement process, which is the key area where the EU has an impact in the human rights field today, the Commission has taken on the major role in defining demands and assessing progress vis-à-vis new entrants. Finally, in the Council of Europe the European Court of Human Rights clearly acts independently, but the new Commissioner for Human Rights also plays a similar role. Thus, in the analysis of impact in this study I seek to delineate not only the impact of human rights norms as opposed to other interests, but also the impact of regimes and international organisations as opposed to member states.

As State Secretary I was in charge of the OSCE chairmanship, the Council of Europe, and followed EU developments closely, although Norway is not a member. I also worked on the human rights politics and security policy in the UN system and in the Balkans, and led the Norwegian campaign to enter the Security Council in 2000. This gave me an opportunity to watch how human rights discourse and agenda-setting became central to public arenas, but also how *Realpolitik* met this new world of values. Nothing I experienced dissuaded me in my conviction of the primacy of *Realpolitik* in the international system, but the conditions for exercising *Realpolitik* are changing. Values matter in new ways, based on a purely self-interested, instrumental logic which will be analysed below; but values also matter in some cases as deep convictions, as what I here term 'value-based' interests. A lot of foreign policy is carried out for altruistic reasons, or at least for reasons where the so-called 'national interest' is hard to ascertain. For example, aid to Bosnia may be defined as long-term security policy for Norway as it contributes to regional stability, and everyone recognises that human rights and democracy are essential prerequisites for stability; but the link between the self-interested 'national interest' and the benefit is a long-term one, much money down the road. Thus, I think we can find that the values of human rights and democracy really do matter to some actors, but also that the adoption of human rights and the impact of human rights can largely be explained by instrumental factors.

But this, importantly, does not mean that values matter less, rather that they matter more: they are 'hard' values, like 'hard' interests, if they matter for real power reasons. They are powerful, like economic or security interests are powerful – under certain circumstances. This is the central thesis of this book.

As my practical political work in all these fields evolved, I managed to take notes and to gather material for the book that was to be written later. The intensity of practical work and travel during those years made it impossible to write much, but it gave me a unique opportunity to be on the inside of, and to influence, political processes that an academic would never have been able to access. I was a decision-maker in many of the situations described and analysed in this study, ranging from the Kosovo war to the human rights dialogue with Cuba, which I initiated. My general academic interest in 'soft power', agenda-setting power and the new public diplomacy existed prior to taking political office, and I now had the chance to assess the real importance of these factors in international affairs. I also managed to maintain a certain level of academic contacts, and am particularly grateful to Professor Joseph Nye of Harvard's Kennedy School and his staff where I tested my ideas in a seminar in November 1999; and to the then Foreign Minister of Canada, Lloyd Axworthy, with whom *inter alia* I discussed 'human security' on his aircraft back from Yerevan after the state funeral due to the awful killings of half the Armenian government in October 1999. On this particular plane trip the British Europe Minister Keith Vaz also partook in the discussion with very interesting contributions. Axworthy was also the architect behind the useful meetings of academics and practitioners in Ottawa on how to conceptualise and advance 'human security' – a security policy based on human rights. Now back in academia, he maintains, like myself, an acute interest in the practical usefulness of the academic work we do. I am grateful to these practitioners-cum-academics for the discussions we enjoyed on this theme.

From my time in political office I would like to acknowledge the importance of interaction and discussion about the problematic of this book with, *inter alia*; former Foreign Minister Knut Vollebæk, former State Secretary Wegger Strømmen; director-general Bjarne Lindstrøm, political directors Tarald Brautaset and Johan Løvald; OSCE director Kim Traavik as well as OSCE ambassador Kai Eide in the Norwegian Ministry of Foreign Affairs.

In the Council of Europe I had very useful meetings with the President of the European Court of Human Rights, Judge Luzius Wildhaber as well as his deputy president; with the Secretary-General of the Council of Europe, Walter Schwimmer and his deputy Hans-Christian Kruger; with the Human Rights Commissioner Alvaro Gil-Robles and with the President of the Parliamentary Assembly, Lord Russel-Johnston. The then Norwegian ambassador to the Council, Sten Lundbo, provided me with most of the written material on the COE in addition to setting up all the ministerial meetings I had in Strasbourg. His input has been very valuable for this book, and also for my interviews in the Polish Ministry of Foreign Affairs, as the current Norwegian ambassador to Poland.

During the year of Norway's OSCE chairmanship I was the deputy to the chairman, Mr Vollebæk. This gave me intimate and hands-on experience of the decision-making and impact of the organisation. Likewise, the OSCE staff in the secretariat in Vienna and the ODIHR staff in Warsaw, and in the various missions contributed a great deal to the information about OSCE's impact. I would like to mention in particular ambassador Robert Barry, head of mission in Bosnia; ambassador Gerard Stoudman, head of ODHIR; the High Commissioner for Minorities, Max van der Stoehl, and also the heads of mission in Albania, Kosovo, FYROM, Croatia and Kazakhstan. The OSCE is an organisation about which little is written and researched; thus, the field experience has been vital to procuring the input used in this study.

The role of so-called 'humanitarian intervention' was much discussed among policy-makers in NATO and at the UN during 1999. I am particularly grateful to UN civil servants in DPA and DPKO for fruitful discussions on peacekeeping and interventions under Security Council mandate; likewise I am indebted to former State Secretary Jan Eliasson of Sweden, now his country's ambassador to the USA, for his deep knowledge and also wisdom in these matters. A seminar in June 2000 at the Krusenberg estate outside of Stockholm gathered together the leading figure on the new value-based security policy, 'human security'; this was the result of Jan's initiative.

Finally, I have worked on the EU regularly for many years, and its human rights profile is now becoming a major part of its expanding foreign policy. On the question of its impact and on how to measure it, I have benefited from discussions with ARENA colleagues as well as with colleagues and students at the Department of Political Science at Lund University, Sweden, where I presented the arguments of this book in December 2000. Here in Oslo I also benefited from similar seminars in the autumn of 2000 at the Institute of Human Rights and at my own Institute of Political Science at Oslo University, where Professor Arild Underdal has been particularly helpful in his comments.

List of Abbreviations

CAP	Common Agricultural Policy
CFSP	Common Foreign and Security Policy,
CMEA	Council of Mutual Economic Assistance
CSR	Corporate Social Responsibility
DPA	Department of Political Affairs, UN
DPKO	Department of Peace-Keeping Operations, UN
ECHR	European Convention of Human Rights
ECSU	European Coal and Steel Union
EDC	European Defence Cooperation
EMU	European Monetary Union
EPC	European Political Cooperation
EU	European Union
FPÖ	Freiheitspartei Österreichs
FRY	Former Republic of Yugoslavia
FYROM	Former Yugoslav Republic of Macedonia
G-24	The EU states and like-minded states working as group to aid East-Central Europe
G-77	Group of 77, the UN grouping of developing countries, now comprising 144 states
HCNM	High Commissioner for National Minorities
ICC	International Criminal Court, UN
ICRC	International Committee of the Red Cross
ICTY	International Criminal Tribunal for Yugoslavia
IGC	Intergovernmental Conference
IO	International Organisation
JHA	Justice and Home Affairs
KFOR	Kosovo Force
KVM	Kosovo Verification Mission
NATO	North Atlantic Treaty Organisation
ODIHR	Office for Democratic Institutions and Human Rights (of the OSCE)
OHR	Office Of the High Representative
OSCE	Organisation for Security and Cooperation in Europe
ÖVP	Österreichische Volkspartei
PA	Partnership Agreement
SEA	Single European Act

SFOR	Stability Force
TEU	Treaty on European Union
UDHR	Universal Declaration of Human Rights
UNHCR	United Nations High Commissioner for Refugees
UNGA	UN General Assembly
UNMIK	United Nations Mission in Kosovo
UNPROFOR	United Nations Protection Force
WEU	Western European Union
WTO	World Trade Organisation

Part I

State Sovereignty and Human Rights in Europe

1
Towards a New Type of Sovereignty in Europe

It was argued in the debate following the Kosovo air campaign that there has been a shift from interest-based to value-based foreign policy. It was said that the West intervened militarily to protect human rights. Some called it a humanitarian intervention, a concept much in vogue at present, but with a long history. Yet others maintained that this was plain, old-fashioned interest-based policy, seeking to consolidate the balance of power of major states in the Balkans.

But they were hard pressed to identify exactly *whose* and *which* interests were being served by the risky and costly campaign. It was simply not plausible to maintain that the USA launched this intervention just in order to enhance its power in the area, or that other NATO allies had this intention. As a partial explanation it seemed right, but it was not the basic explanation. Also, how could 19 states have agreed on exactly the same national interests?

Values such as human rights appeared in this case to be more important as an explanatory variable. Massive violations of human dignity such as massacres, ethnic cleansing and deportations were seemingly impossible to contemplate. Media reporting on the internal situation in Kosovo did play a prominent part in NATO's decision-making. Exactly how much, will be discussed in Chapter 8. But the point of departure is that values also seem to play a major role in the exercise of hard power, or the use of military instruments.

So-called 'humanitarian interventions' – or hard power interventions that are justified and perhaps also really motivated by values – are not a new phenomenon in world politics (Finnemore, 1996; DUPI, 1999), but in the nineties we saw more violent intra-state conflicts than ever before. Between 1989 and 1997 there were 103 armed conflicts, out of which only six were inter-state (Wallensteen and Sollenberg, 1998).

Most wars in the present age are what used to be called civil wars; inter-state wars have become a rarity, especially in the Western world. Civilians are both protagonists and victims in intra-state wars. Modern media put the spotlight on these events in 'real time', and audiences all over the globe follow the same news. They naturally demand of their politicians: 'What are you doing about this?' The logic of this debate is very different from the traditional debate about national interests.

The mechanisms of foreign policy have thus increasingly come to resemble those of ordinary, domestic politics: non-govermental organisations (NGOs), media and citizens act and launch initiatives in posing questions and demanding accountability from foreign policy-makers. Thus, foreign policy-makers have to react and to act. They are no longer insulated from the domestic political process, while also simultaneously being subject to international pressures, constraints and persuasion. In a certain sense the distinction between domestic and international political processes is like a 'line in water', to cite Kjell Goldmann (1989), and it has long been known that there are profound mutual influences between the two levels (Gourevitch, 1978; Hanrieder, 1978; Hopkins, 1976). There can be little doubt that national interests are determined by both international and domestic variables, and that the foreign policy excutive is not always the 'gatekeeper' between the two levels (Putnam, 1998). Today there is growing evidence of transnational organisation of value-based advocacy networks (Keck and Sikkink, 1998), and of the role of global media in setting national as well as international agendas. In addition, it appears that values and norms are transmitted mostly *from the international to the national level* through the work of international organisations and advocacy networks (Matlary, 2000; Keck and Sikkink, 1998).

In the world of international business we are also seeing a new awareness of human rights and democracy. This is the result of the globalisation of NGO networks and media, and also of consumer and investor interest in issues such as the environment or child labour. There is a major effort on the part of international organisations to form partnerships with multinational companies: for example, Kofi Annan has introduced a 'Social Compact' which contains the major human rights, and to which an increasing number of companies subscribe.[1] There are various human rights and democracy standards presented by NGOs and churches, such as the Sullivan principles from South Africa which are voluntary commitments on the part of business.[2] Companies are increasingly expected not only to communicate their values, but also to have a substance behind this type of profile;

otherwise NGOs will easily expose them. For purely commercial reasons, companies increasingly seek to develop a corporate social responsibility (CSR) strategy for themselves where they develop a clear set of social and ethical values and communicate these to their stakeholders (Schierbeck, 2000). Thus, it has also become important for businesses to take human rights and democracy into account. Not least is this the case in foreign markets where corruption is rampant and social standards are low. But not only in the place of production is this an issue for the company; also in the larger political society business actors are increasingly called upon to develop support for and often fund projects that help in democratisation. The 'first-generation' expectation of internal business ethics is rapidly being supplemented by a 'second-generation' demand for socially responsible companies (Eide et al., 2000). It is important to note that even if these values are not genuinely adhered to, companies must, for purely economic and instrumental reasons, develop a 'value profile'.

With the 'democratisation' of foreign policy and transparency of business life, there has arisen a great interest in *human rights*. The *legitimation* and *justification* of foreign policy which are offered are increasingly those of human rights because the policy-maker has to address a constituency at home as well as abroad. Voters want to know how policy affects them and their fellows, not to hear about an often abstract 'national interest'. Further, the media focus on personalised stories, not on national interests. Political communciation cannot be about simple 'national interest' when the topic is human rights. It makes sense to talk about a 'national interest' in the security or economic field, but not in a debate framed around value questions. Granted, some public discourses operate with the concept of 'national interest', such as when an American candidate for the presidency talks about security policy, but once the agenda has been set around values, one cannot insert an interest-based discourse (Schimmelfennig, 1999).

Further, modern Western states 'intervene' in other states, for instance in terms of media support, human rights dialogues, party cooperation to develop multi-party systems, 'shaming' of recalcitrant states in international fora, economic boycotts or embargoes of non-democratic regimes, and so on. This 'new interventionism' is prevalent in the Cold War era, and is carried out by Western states and international organisations (IOs). There is a long list of such policy tools, and the list of states that do not claim to be democracies today, is short indeed. Foreign policy seems to gravitate more and more towards human rights and democracy, at least in terms of the *justification* policy given by policy-makers.

To put it simply: almost all states in the world today want to be accepted as democracies and as upholders of human rights. The states of the former Soviet Union and the Council for Mutual Economic Assistance (CMEA) also called themselves 'democracies', with the qualifier 'peoples' first. Today the few communist states left, such as Cuba, insist that they are both democratic and have a good human rights record.

But do such values as democracy and human rights *really matter*? Are we not rather talking about window-dressing on the part of states which all seek to enhance their relative power in the international system? Is the promotion of human rights and democracy not just a convenient Western approach, concealing other, more sinister motives – the quest for national power? Which role do these values play in setting in motion political action? Are they triggers that cannot be avoided or are they simply rhetorical justifications that carry little real weight?

In this book I seek to provide some answers to these questions. My argument, as an academic and as a former foreign policy-maker,[3] is that values are generally increasing in salience on the international agenda, and that these values are sometimes the real, moving forces of politics – they have independent explanatory power, as it were. They are, however, mostly adopted for instrumental reasons, but may later become internalised and promoted because they are thought to be morally and ethically right. The point is that even if instrumentality explains the adoption of human rights norms, this nonetheless shows that human rights have an impact. In short, the *Realpolitiker* of today must know his human rights and cannot afford to disregard them. *My assumption in this study is that instrumentality explains most of the impact of the human rights regime in Europe, but that this shows exactly how powerful this regime in fact is.* Traditional theories of international politics depend on an instrumental assumption, which implies that one does not take values into account for their own sake. If we can show that even on this logic of action the human rights regime has an impact, we will have shown that these theories fail to explain political action adequately. But even if one claims to act on a logic of appropriateness – doing the 'right' thing in the circumstances – this may in many cases be explained instrumentally: one does what brings advantage, given the social rules of the situation.

In Europe a human rights regime has developed which is particularly strong, and which is universal in terms of content. This regime contains democracy and the rule of law as the only form of government that is consistent with the implementation of human rights. This is a new development which we can date from around 1990, when the fall of communism enabled European states to dispense with this as an 'alternative' ideology and form of government. There has been a notable shift away from the view that the form of government is a matter for domestic policy choice to the view that only democracy is a legitimate form of government, to the extent that hard power intervention may contain an element of restoring democracy as a reason for such intervention: 'democracy may be emerging as an important criterion whereby a state's claim to be a legitimate member of international society is judged, but this is yet to be reflected in the body of international law relating to intervention' (Roberts, 1999: 107).

This study also documents how democracy and the rule of law have become intrinsic to the human rights regime and how democracy as a policy goal has an impact in Europe.

The values of human rights, democracy and the rule of law are embedded in different declarations and conventions. The UN's human rights *acquis* is authoritative, especially the Declaration of Human Rights and the two Human Rights Conventions of 1966. Later documents all correspond to, and are inspired by, the former.

In this study we look at the formation of what we call the *European human rights regime*, which ties human rights and democracy firmly together in the various forms in which it has been developed. This regime, in this respect consistent throughout, is embedded in various IOs: the Council of Europe (COE), the OSCE and the EU. The most interesting question is whether the human rights regime has an impact. This is basically the question of regime-specific tools and embeddedness: do the organisations in question, where the regime is embedded, have an impact? Does the regime, in its various forms, have independent tools at its disposal?

The new interventionism

The main part of this study is about *impact*. The argument is that values, as they are defined in the European human rights regime, have an impact on European states and states that seek membership in European IOs. This impact varies with the policy tools of the regime and the organisation in question, but there are similarities: all three organisations largely employ *soft* power tools in their work.

Soft power, discussed below, refers to non-coercive policy tools such as cooperation, persuasion and co-optation, but also to criticism and 'shaming' in public fora. Hard power tools are coercive, including sanctions and military intervention, while political and economic conditionality should be placed in the soft power category although they are 'tough' uses of power which often do not leave the state in question very much choice. Nonetheless these tools are not enforced; they are strong suggestions for compliance.

But is soft power *weak* power, as the term seems to suggest? In this study we argue this is not the case – it is increasingly becoming strong power. As hard power becomes more difficult to use – due to the relativisation of traditional state sovereignty and the growing importance of universal human rights standards, it is becoming less and less legitimate to coerce both within the state and between states. The use of coercive force to achieve foreign policy goals becomes less acceptable and much more visible than before. Therefore hard power is a power resource that will be used in its traditional sense only in extreme cases by Western states. Sanctions are used less today than before the reporting on their humanitarian consequences was high on the agenda. Also military power is very hard to use among Western states, usually requiring both a UN security Council (UNSC) mandate as well as strong public support. However, the incidences of using military power globally are increasing.

Soft power is being used in more and more intervention, both inside a state as well as in policy aimed at changing a state's form of government. The impact of the human rights regime through the organisations in this study takes place through various forms of intervention. Intervention here means active policy-making inside another state or aiming at fundamentally influencing domestic society and the government of another state so that it becomes democratic.[4] There is today a marked trend towards such interventionism, which for the most part is positive and benign, stressing help and assistance – 'carrots' – rather than 'sticks', in the form of threats and sanctions. But nonetheless we talk about transgressing traditional borders and about directly challenging the norm of sovereignty and its concomitant, the norm of non-intervention.

Further, values also seem to matter in the growing number of cases of hard power intervention since 1990. Security policy in the 1990s increasingly has had to grapple with the dilemma of massive human rights abuse in internal conflicts, and the hard power interventions authorised by the UNSC have increased in the present period.

Although not officially justified by reason of human rights abuse, the humanitarian situation clearly matters much in determining whether there is a situation of a threat to 'international peace and security', which is the formal basis for intervention by the UNSC. The old issue of 'humanitarian intervention' has again come to the fore of international security policy.

Thus, the role that the values of human rights, democracy and the rule of law play in foreign policy-making merits attention, both as regards soft and hard power intervention. When we focus on the human rights regime and its characteristics as embedded in IOs, in this study we choose to look at the impact of *regimes,* and not that of *state actors*. Clearly, states pursue human rights policies that have an impact as well, through their normal *bilateral* policy. It is an interesting, and not much researched, task to study the relative impact of these values as opposed to traditional national interests in such bilateral policy. However, this is not what this study does; its focus is exclusively on the impact of these norms through their embeddedness in the three IOs mentioned.

This serves a twofold purpose that is of interest in the literature on international relations in general and on regimes in particular. First, do norms and values matter as opposed to traditional national interests such as wealth and power enhancement; and second, do norms and values matter when they are pursued by IOs as actors? The first question is a major issue in all work on international politics, viz. that of realism vs. idealism in traditional terminology; the second question is highly topical in current research on regimes, posing the question of whether there is an *independent* impact of international regimes as they are embedded in various settings.

If we find that a regime such as the European human rights one has an independent impact, we find that not only do norms and values matter, but that the IOs where they are embedded in fact wield impact in and of themselves. This means that *non-state* actors – here international regimes and organisations – matter as actors, not only as arenas for states. It is admittedly difficult to isolate the relative impact of the member states in any given organisation from the impact of the organization itself, but this will be attempted here through a careful analysis of the policy tools that each organisation employs in its human rights and democracy policies.

In sum, this book seeks to contribute to the literature on regimes in an empirical way by testing the impact of the human rights regime against the mainstream approaches of neo-realism and neo-liberalism as the null hypotheses. The hypotheses and methodology are presented in Chapter 4.

Foreign policy decoupled from territory

Values also act as a veneer for military or economic motives, thus not invalidating a traditional realist's explanation. But what is new today, and what needs analysis, are the *mechanisms* whereby values come to matter more and more in world politics. They include new organisations embedding these values – such as new institutions like the tribunals for Yugoslavia and Rwanda as well as the International Criminal Court (ICC); they include the 'democratisation' of foreign policy and the growing importance of transnational NGOs; they include the globalisation of the media, and finally they include the growth of international and multinational regimes and institutions that are norm-creating and that to some extent can impose such norms and values on states.

As stated, in this study we wish to 'test' the hypothesis that values matter in world politics. This may seem unnecessary to some, but it remains true that realism's premise of military and neo-liberalism's premise of economic, power as the only real driving forces of world politics, are still well entrenched. We do not propose that there is a dichotomy between such power motivations and values – that either one explanation is true, or the other. In most cases there will be a combination of motives for action. What is new is rather that the values of human rights and democracy seem to play *independent* roles as both motives and triggers for action.

We wish to analyse *how* and *under which circumstances* these values matter, by exploring the mechanisms we mentioned above. Traditional national interests remain and are as important as before, but a new type of national interest is added: the important public diplomacy on human rights and values in general. Here non-state actors such as international advocacy networks and international regimes play important roles, but these roles have so far not been explored empirically to any great extent.

These factors – new actors, new institutions or regimes, new policy-making processes – seem to interact in typical ways; or in patterns. What happens to trigger these mechanisms, and how can policy-makers handle them?

We will examine some cases where values such as human rights, democracy and the rule of law seem to have carried the upper hand as real motivations for policy-makers, such as in the case of Kosovo, and before that, Bosnia. But mainly we will look at how the norms and values of three major European institutions, the OSCE, the EU and the COE, have an impact. In what sense do these norms play a role, and what are the policy tools of these organisations?

Sovereignty: the key principle

It is not news that there is a tension between human rights, by nature universal, and the central defining characteristic of the international system, which is the principle of sovereignty. Sovereignty means that no authority stands above the person or the state which is nominally and legally sovereign. The sovereignty of a state is 'supreme authority within a territory'.

Historically sovereignty has been tied to territory only since the Treaties of Westphalia of 1648, which ended the Thirty Years War by laying down the principle that the ruler decides within his territory. In a Europe where feudalism had defined power structures *non-territorially* and where the Catholic Church exercised both temporal and spiritual power, there had not been such a thing as the nation-state. Power or authority had been defined along *functional*, not *territorial* lines. But the long struggle between emperor and Church on the one hand and the Protestant princes on the other, was won by the latter.

As Krasner underlines in his study of sovereignty, there are several types of sovereignty: *legal* sovereignty, which means that all states are equal in the formal legal sense and which is established by mutual legal recognition between states; *domestic* sovereignty, which means that there is effective national control and governance in the form of policing and rule of law; *interdependence* sovereignty, meaning that there is effective border control and that a state really is independent from other states; and *Westphalian* sovereignty, which is 'the exclusion of external actors from domestic authority configurations' (Krasner, 1999: 9). All states that are recognised by other states enjoy legal sovereignty, but they may vary greatly across the other types of sovereignty: 'failed' states do not enjoy domestic sovereignty and are hardly able to maintain interdependence sovereignty, while repressive states may enjoy both, as well as Westphalian sovereignty. The weaker and the most repressive states, as Krasner notes, have always supported Westphalian sovereignty the most. This is what we observe when such states are criticised on human rights grounds: they respond by invoking the Westphalian sovereignty norm of non-intervention. Examples of such states today are Russia, China, Algeria, Cuba, Myanmar, North Korea, Mexico and Vietnam, to mention the most important. However, it is noteworthy that there are fewer and fewer states that respond to international criticism in this 'old-fashioned' way. Mostly governments engage in the terms of the human rights discourse when criticised, a sign that the state accepts the discourse itself as legitimate and universally valid.

The Treaties of Westphalia made it clear that

> to prevent for the future any differences arising in the politick state, all and everyone of the Electors, Princes and States of the Roman Empire, are so establish'd and confirm'd . . . that, by virtue of this present Transaction: that they never can or ought to be molested therein by any whomsoever upon any manner of pretence (art. LXIV)'.

In other words, the norm of *non-intervention* into a state was established. In addition it was made clear that these principalities had the right to close agreements between themselves and with other states, thus making the *territorial border the main political variable.* The theorists of the new order, such as Jean Bodin, referred to this as the fact that the sovereign or prince is not subject to any other's command. This is the main point; that no authority stands above the state, which means that states have to rely on themselves and their military power as the ultimate source of survival and security. The international system of states is a self-help system. As realists describe it: despite cooperation, regimes and alliances, the state is the ultimate unit of authority and self-protection. There is no 'world government' or world police to invoke.

Historically, intervention continued to exist in the form of war, which was until the twentieth century a recognised tool of foreign policy (DUPI, 1999), thus effectively limiting the realisation of state sovereignty of weak states. Further, as Krasner has shown, there were religious minority rights recognised by the sovereigns in the period after Westphalia. These rights mostly concerned the rights of Christians in Muslim states, yet they were clearly accepted by all parties, and as such, relativise the principle of sovereignty from its very beginning (Krasner, 1999).

The principle of sovereignty within the nation-state was consolidated with the state's monopoly on the use of military force to defend its territory, and with its monopoly on the use of force inside the state in the form of policing: 'The development of sovereignty is inextricably linked to development in the legal and political regulation of collective violence' (Rosas, 1993: 134). In fact, sovereignty was so closely linked to the concept of military power that if a state were attacked and conquered, its sovereignty ceased to exist (ibid.). The classical and medieval criterion that wars be just, that is, justifiable according to various ethical criteria, was superseded by a purely power-based criterion: if the state were so weak that it could not defend itself, its sovereignty was precarious to say the least. Thus, legal sovereignty was and is prey to power, although power itself is usually also dependent on legitimation and justification, perhaps especially in our time.

The principle of *concentration of power inside a given territory* became the cornerstone of the international state system, and in the 350 years or so since the Treaties of Westphalia the state system has become firmly entrenched and consolidated (Rosas, 1993, 1995; Rønnfeldt et al., 1999; Smith, 1999). After the Second World War new states have been added through decolonialisation, and the UN system now counts about 200 states. Although there are few states that still claim a traditional form of sovereignty which excludes international norms as universally valid, there can be little doubt that sovereignty remains a very strong norm. Intervention is still the exception to the general rule of non-intervention, but the gravity of the implications of a change in this norm is so important that any change in state practice here is significant. Scholars agree that we are witnessing an increased degree of interventionism in the present period (Chopra, 1994; Minear, 1994; Smith, 1997, 1999).

Non-intervention is laid down in the UN Charter and in other instruments of international law. Non-intervention is here made the central norm, as expressed in paragraphs 2.4. and 2.7 which state that the use of force against another state is impermissible, apart from the cases where military power is used in self-defence or where 'international peace and security' are threatened. The UNSC however, has in the 1990s defined several conflicts as such threats – Haiti, Somalia, Bosnia, and to some extent Kosovo, which signals a new practice in international relations. The extent to which human rights violations can be argued to be the reason for hard power intervention is discussed in Chapter 8.

If non-intervention is the key norm, how can we reconcile this with a politics based on *universal* norms and values? Human rights are by definition universal, and democracy and the rule of law are increasingly regarded as the only viable form of government. We see that some states will exclude any kind of intervention based on such norms, invoking the principle of non-intervention. But we also see that an increasing number of states accept such criticism by trying to justify that they are both democratic and that they respect human rights.

The norm of sovereignty has been changing over recent decades, especially since 1990 and the end of the Cold War. There is a growing body of scholarship that has addressed this development (Krasner, 1999; Hasmi, 1997; Lyons and Mastanduno, 1995; Rosas, 1993, 1995). Their main conclusions are that sovereignty is increasingly circumscribed, and that the norm of non-intervention in the classical sense is under siege. As stated, Krasner also makes the important point that Westphalian sovereignty has always been limited by minority rights, first for religious minorities and in the twentieth century by general human rights.

Summing up, it has become increasingly legitimate to criticise not only human rights failings but also lack of democratic government in other states. More and more states have developed their own bilateral human rights policies, as exemplified by the Carter government's stress on this in the 1970s, which marked a watershed in the development of national human rights policies. Later most Western states followed suit in designing such polices. The causes of this development are manifold, ranging from democratisation of foreign policy to the globalisation of media and interest groups. *Reputation and legitimacy* have therefore become a key variable for states, as for businesses. Intervention with soft power tools has become more acceptable, as part of normal foreign policy-making, and states often use NGOs and IOs to do this work.

Legal scholars have also analysed this development, and noted how legal norms change, and how the interpretation of norms change. It is clear that the UNSC has extended its interpretation of 'threat to international peace and security' in the 1990s to include massive human rights abuse towards a population – which does also have destabilising effects – but which has no legal status in terms of hard power intervention. It is also clear that so-called 'soft law', which is 'standards which are not legally binding in the strict sense' (Rosas, 1995: 69), has increased in importance (Abbott and Snidal, 2000), and that these norms often do not require state consent in an explicit way, but result from the political activity of international conferences and IOs.

The argument of this book is that the norm of sovereignty is changing because there is a growing acceptance in Western states of intervention in other states. These interventions ostensibly aim at improving human rights by establishing democracy. This is primarily true for 'soft power' intervention, but also seems to be true for much 'hard power' intervention.

An essential and persistent tension

While non-intervention remains an established norm that to a great extent defines what the international system is about, the notion of *legitimate* political order is another matter. What we mean here is how politics within the state is *regarded* by peer states and other actors like global media and NGOs, and how rulers can justify their claim to power.

The question of a state's legitimacy is thus not the same as the question of its sovereignty. The views on what is considered legitimate government have changed with time, and are changing. Despite this, relatively little attention has been focused on the ways in which legitimacy works (Hurd, 1999), perhaps because political scientists have focused on traditional types of economic and security power and resources.

There is growing evidence that norms influence the formation of state interests through diffusion of new standards and definitions of what is considered appropriate internationally (Cortrell and Davis, 1996). This has implications for how the norm of non-intervention is viewed. For public opinion today, it does matter whether a regime is authoritarian or not, democratic or not. It is increasingly accepted today that democracies will attempt to influence other states into becoming democracies, however with important exceptions and with a clear difference between the use of 'hard' and 'soft' power. Interventions with 'hard' power are reserved for the UNSC, and happen only in rare cases, although we have seen more interventions in the 1990s than ever before in the history of the UNSC. This body is the only one with a mandate in international law to use 'hard' power. But as the debate on 'humanitarian intervention' shows, this norm may also be changing. In an anthology with the telling title *Beyond Westphalia?* (1995), editors Lyons and Mastanduno conclude that 'constraints on state sovereignty not only have a long history, but have been increasing significantly in recent years as a consequence of both growing interdependence and the end of the Cold War' (p. 252).

The view of intervention, or seeking to influence within a state with 'soft' power tools, is also changing rapidly. There is now more and more acceptance of the need to establish a basis for human rights, in the form of democracy, in all states. This is a phenomenon that has become manifest in the post-Second World War period (Sikkink, 1993), and which seems to be strengthened with the globalisation of knowledge and the media as well as with growing multilaterism and the emergence of transnational advocacy networks. The link between democracy and human rights was only officially established in the OSCE texts in 1990, but is now firmly established in international human rights documents. Although the term 'good governance' is still used especially in UN texts because 'democracy' is sensitive in some states, the term is used more and more in connection with human rights.

The Westphalian principle says that the state has a monopoly on the use of force both *inside* and *outside* the state. On the outside, the state shall refrain from attacking other states and is obliged to protect its own territory, mostly by having an army. On the inside, the state has the monopoly on the use of force vis-à-vis its citizens.

Today an increasing number of states are democracies, and the state therefore derives its authority and ability to use force from the people. The rule of law secures that force is not used arbitrarily, and free and fair elections ensure that the state is not despotic. Thus, there is no central tension between non-intervention and human rights in a democratic system that respects human rights. The rights of the individual are in theory at least ensured by the state.

Thus one can argue that the individual right to security of person, for instance, entails an obligation on the part of the state to implement this right. If the state fails to do so, one may say that it is an illegitimate ruler, despite being an elected or at least de facto ruler. In the day and age of democracy – essentially in the twentieth century – this is logical. But there are many states that are so-called 'failed' states, which means that the government is too weak to do much for its citizens, or states that are anarchic or dominated by internal conflicts. In such states the rulers do not fulfil their duty to protect individual rights. One may thus argue that such regimes are *illegitimate*, despite the fact that they are sovereign states. This view is becoming increasingly accepted. The norm that only democracies are legitimate states is evolving. For instance, a global conference was held in Warsaw in June 2000 on how to consolidate and develop democracy, attended by foreign ministers from all over the globe. Here there was no debate about alternative forms of government for the realisation of human rights.

In the post-war period it was the human rights norm that was developed, challenging traditional non-intervention and sovereignty. In the post-Cold War period, especially in Europe, it is the democracy norm that is establishing itself. This can be seen both in the widespread foreign policy practice of 'soft power' intervention as well as in the growing acceptance of humanitarian factors in the determination of whether there is a 'threat to international peace and security' in the UNSC's decisions on 'hard power' intervention. In addition, post-war security policy is increasingly reoriented towards so-called 'human security', to be discussed below.

This book contributes to the documentation and analysis of how the norm of democracy as the only legitimate form of government is being consolidated. Democracy means not only the multi-party form of government, but also rule of law as well as the coexistence of a market economy. Human rights is the expression of the individual's political and other rights, moving the focus away from the state as the unit of analysis in world politics, to the individual. But for a long time it was also acceptable for communist and other non-democratic states to talk about their political system as being compatible with human rights as well as being a fully acceptable ideological alternative to democracy. The form of government belonged to the the sphere of non-intervention; the domestic sphere.

It is first and foremost the OSCE norms that illustrate the break with this. In what Thomas Buergenthal has called 'the democratic revolution' the OSCE laid down in its texts that only democracies were capable of implementing human rights (Buergenthal, 1990). This was an abrupt shift away from the traditional view that democracy and human rights were not linked explicitly. Further, in the norms of the COE there is an explicit link between human rights and rule of law, as laid down in the European Convention of Human Rights (ECHR); and in the EU there has been a similar link since 1995, when the so-called Copenhagen criteria came into power for agreements with third countries. They state that all new members must be democracies with a functioning rule of law, market economies, and fully implement human rights.

We can conclude that a tension exists between the principles of human rights and non-intervention, but that both human rights and democracy are becoming stronger norms at present. But the tension persists: the individual has rights that are universal and thus cut across borders; but we also accord the states themselves such rights, by accepting the Westphalian principle that the state has all power over citizens within its territory. How can these principles be reconciled if at all?

Logical inconsistency is no stranger to political life, and this is more true for international politics where there is no one legislator or polity. There are increasingly similarities between the domestic system of rule of law, and the international system of a growing number of regimes that also command enforcement and monitoring mechanisms, but the international system remains, despite this, essentially an anarchic system. But the degree of anarchy varies: the Western political system is the most institutionalised and thus resembles the domestic system the most; while regions like Africa and Asia, including the Balkans in Europe, remain little institutionalised. However, it is still usually left to states to implement international law, and failure to do so cannot usually be punished by means others than 'shaming'. The new feature of the Western system, however, is that 'shaming' and reputation matter relatively more now than before.

Thus, de Gaulle's dictum that 'treaties are like girls and roses, they last while they last' is undoubtedly still fairly accurate for the international system, and could be extended to norms: norms last while they last, and they change over time. Further, constructive ambiguity is often desirable, and therefore a result of deliberate design. It is therefore not a surprise that we operate with two sets of competing international norms – the state system logic and the human rights logic.

Finally, principles are one thing, practice another. The emphasis we put on principles gives them life and weight. Thus, what we observe in the present period is that the international community places relatively more weight on the human rights logic than on the state logic – albeit selectively, one may add.

This book will try to show that this is in fact the case, as well as to explain why this is so. The emphasis on values has not *replaced* geopolitics or the ultimate primacy of hard power. The international system is still made up of many states which seek to ensure their territorial integrity by traditional means of security. We still need military alliances, and we still use military power. The self-help system will remain as long as states remain the ultimate source of power. But what is new is that there are possibilities of other types of foreign policy as well, even in the realm of security policy where state sovereignty has traditionally been linked directly to territorial defence. As this book will show, contemporary Western security policy increasingly seeks justification from human rights arguments and increasingly deals with issues that are not tied to territorial defence. But also in general, when security needs are met and stability prevails, Western states in particular are able to pursue other policy goals. In the absence of war, the agenda is filled with other items.

Does this mean that power goes out when values come in? No. The change is that there are *new forms of power* that become more salient than old forms in specific circumstances where public diplomacy is the venue of politics. Hard power – military power – has become less usable and less attractive with the end of the Cold War. The thesis that values matter more now is therefore basically limited to the Western world, and to those states that desire to enter into Western-dominated institutions.

Values are not means, they are ends. Power is a means to an end, regardless of which one. Thus, before we discuss the values that we argue to be more salient now, we wish to discuss the new forms of power.

Power

Power is the key concept in any analysis of politics. It is the means to reach one's ends, but the ends vary greatly. Sometimes they are the values of democracy, rule of law and human rights. Sometimes they are quoted to be such, but this is just a cover-up for other, more sinister motives. And sometimes the ends are conquest or simply to achieve more influence internationally.

A great deal of confusion arises when we confuse means and ends. There is nothing negative about power – it is the necessary means to achieve any goal. Power is the ability to make others do what you want, a standard definition tells us (Dahl, 1961). But power is much more than this – it is also the ability to make others accept your own visions, values and goals. There are thus many types of power, and we need different types of power for different goals.

There is renewed discussion about power in the post-Cold War period. As Ingebritsen notes,

> international relations . . . have begun to focus on how states exercise influence in ways that do not conform to strictly economic or military capabilities. Instead of viewing the international system as fragmented and anarchic, a new wave of scholarship examines how states become socialized into an international community or society (Ingebritsen, 1999: 2).

Nye has developed this theme, coining the term 'soft power' as the power that persuades rather than coerces, and argues that the USA is the leading 'soft power' holder also in 'hard' fields like security policy. The future belongs to those that command 'technology, education, and institutional flexibility' (Nye and Owens, 1996), and in the military field it is the USA that leads because of its ability to process and gain knowledge through sophisticated systems of intelligence collection, surveillance and reconnaissance. This enables the actor to 'use deadly violence with greater speed, range, and precision' (ibid.: 23), as was evidenced in the Gulf War. The authors predict that with the leading edge in communication technology, the USA will be able 'without commensurate risk, to thwart any military action' (p. 24). Indeed, this is what we may be witnessing in the effort to create a shield against missile attacks.

Nye, the theorist of soft power, provides a very useful continuum of types of power (Nye, 1995). At the most familiar end, we find coercive power. This power gives you the ability to command others to follow your will. Military power is the key power source here, but economic power also counts. Sanctions are one instance of this. At the other end of the continuum we find co-optive power. This is the power to make others agree with you and desire the same things as you do. They may be induced to do so, through light pressure such as creating incentive structures that they follow, or through 'shaming' and open criticism, or threats of such. There are many diplomatic forms of arm twisting.

But as we move towards the right side of the continuum, we find 'agenda-setting' and 'attraction'. These power sources may be even stronger, for when you really manage to define a problem and set its agenda, then you have control of the decision-making process to a great extent. But your power may still be based on light coercion and pressure, although they are hidden as part of a 'democratic' decision-making procedure.

The most powerful situation is when you persuade others to think like you and strive for the same goals. When they accept your problem definition and the premises for the subsequent decision-making, you have exercised the most important power resource: the other person is *convinced* that you are right, and he/she internalises your views. You have exercised the power of persuasion.

With command power, you must assume that the other will turn against you and disobey you when you no longer threaten him. With co-optive power, you obtain your goal – to make the other do as you want – without pressure and threats. It is obvious that this type of power is much more effective than the former. Communists, like some Jesuits, have always known this. Indoctrination means to learn a doctrine; doctrine means the 'right view'. There is nothing new in this. Power has always come in different shapes. Throughout history women have often only been able to exercise power through their men, in an indirect and covert fashion. Today there are fortunately other power resources available to women.

Karl Marx's analysis of structural power is eminent: power that you need not exercise is more effective than active power use. If you own the town, you need not use the ballot to get elected – it is enough to throw your weight around. The Norwegian political scientist Stein Rokkan formulated this famously: 'Votes count, resources decide.'

Structural power is also embedded in social situations – everyone knows who is powerful, and they behave in anticipation of this. When journalists do not write about certain subjects, they exercise self-censorship because someone in that society has communicated that doing otherwise will lead to punishment.

Unseen power is hard to challenge. It may be personal power over others at the workplace, it may be power exercised over economic resources and jobs, and it may be military and economic power in the international system which determines who is a big power and who is not. When a big power moves a little, a small states jump. Some call it the 'dinosaur effect'.

But what is new today, says Nye, is the salience of co-optive or 'soft' power. He argues that the USA continues to be the most powerful state because it succeeds in exercising 'soft' power in addition to traditional 'hard' power:

> Soft co-optive power is just as important as hard command power. If a state can make its power *legitimate* in the eyes of others, it will *encounter less resistance to its wishes.* If its culture and ideology are attractive, others will more willingly follow. In short, the universalism of a country's culture and its ability to establish a set of favourable rules and institutions that govern areas of international activity are becoming more important in world politics today (our emphasis; Nye, 1995: 33).

Thus, the more the values of the human rights regime are seen as legitimate, the more impact they will have. Today these values are almost universally accepted as legitimate, and thus stand the chance of having much impact in the public arena where they are typically invoked. The new arena of global or at least Western public diplomacy implies that soft power is a key type of *policy tool* or power resource for any actor, regardless of his or her political goals. But it also means that the values of the human rights regime become *goals* of politics to the detriment of traditional national interests. Soft power therefore enhances the importance of these values, but the latter are also increasingly promoted by hard power. We must therefore distinguish carefully between the importance of soft power as a primary type of policy tool in public diplomacy; and the effect of this type of public debate which makes values key policy goals, even if they are only rhetorically adhered to at first. The terms of the debate in public diplomacy requires principled and value-based arguments. But these values as policy goals are promoted by both soft and hard power.

Can one have soft power without having hard power? This is a key issue for small states, like Norway, as well as for IOs and regimes. I will discuss this in more detail in Chapter 2; suffice it here to say that I think the answer is yes, but on certain conditions. A state with much hard power can more easily exercise soft power because of the 'dinosaur effect': everyone listens. But other actors – small states and NGOs, regimes and IOs – can also exercise soft power in particular areas where their knowledge and energy are applied. Finally, hard power does not translate into soft power. A big state which has no persuasive power will deter, not attract. Russia has much hard power, but little soft power. There is not much global attraction in Russian lifestyles, media, entertainment or ideas.

Soft power resources enhance the promotion of values such as human rights and democracy; in fact, soft power relies on an open society with free press and public discussion. This is because soft power is typically exercised in public, as part of public diplomacy. The actors using soft power are not only states, but also NGOs, media and IOs and regimes. The issues raised by the latter often concern international norms and issue areas such as human rights, the environment, humanitarian standards, 'detente' and so forth.

Keck and Sikkink (1999) provide a penetrating analysis of the phenomenon called 'advocacy networks', which are transnational interest groups. They can mobilise power on questions that are related to values such as human rights – typically issues where right vs. wrong can be easily defined, and where the public can identify with a 'just cause'. The point of departure for more and more foreign – as well as domestic – policy, is the individual and his rights, much more than states and their prerogatives. Multilateral diplomacy concerns itself with common interests or common problems, not with national interests in a narrow sense.

In the public sphere the *justification* offered for a policy stance cannot be just narrow national interest. It is not acceptable to argue that one is against an environmental measure because one's national industry will suffer losses. Another explanation must be given, preferably related to scientific reasoning. Thus, science as well as human rights can be the sources of soft power to a much greater extent than before, as has been shown by Haas's work on 'epistemic communities' (1992, 1993).

When discussing and negotiating in mulitateral diplomacy, the public explanation is never blunt national interest. As we shall see in Chapter 2, there needs to be justification for policy stances which is part of the general discourse. If an international treaty is not followed, there is an expectation for an explanation that refers to a general phenomenon. One cannot say that one simply does not care to implement it.

Thus, the logic of public diplomacy is such that principled and general reasoning – justifications – must be given. These must be relevant to the issue in order to be seen as legitimate by the other parties. Very often the real motivation is traditional national interest, but even so this has to be concealed to a great extent.

Values

Values are the ultimate moral standards an individual stands for, while norms are the behavioural rules in society that these values imply. For instance, if respect for life is the key *value*, the *norms* reflected in law and behaviour should forbid abortion, euthanasia and capital punishment.

The values we have mentioned are human rights, democracy and the rule of law. Human rights, one could say, are the values proper, the ends of politics. Democracy and the rule of law are political conditions or norms for the realisation of human rights.

Human rights is basically a phenomenon of the post-war period in the Western world, as will be discussed in detail in Chapter 3. They include traditional political and civil rights, as well as social and political rights: the right to life and security of person, the right to religious freedom, freedom of assembly, press freedom, freedom to own property and to marry and form a family, right to work and to a just wage, to social benefits and to political participation. In the major human rights document, the Universal Declaration of Human Rights of 1948, there is an explicit mention of the form of political system that corresponds to human rights, viz. democracy. The 'will of the people' is to be the basis of politics, and 'all are equal before the law'. This is the rule of law, the integral part of liberal democracy.

The connection between human rights and democracy, including the rule of law, may not seem obvious. When we examine the values underlying democracy, we find the central concept: equality. This is both an equality before the law as well as an equality in terms of rights to political influence and to social and economic benefits, thus corresponding to democracy as a political form.

Aristotle said that politics is the highest practical science where one learns to be a virtuous person, ready to serve others without self-interest in mind, because by nature man is a 'social and political animal' – in Greek, a *zoon politikon.* We can only realise our full humanity in social relationships, and politics is where we develop public virtues such as justice, which is about what is right and wrong.

Later Thomas Aquinas repeated this, in the thirteenth century, and laid the foundation for modern democracy by stating that all men are fundamentally equal. They therefore cannot be subjected to unjust rulers. Much later democratic forms of government developed in Europe, founded on this revolutionary equality. This is of critical importance for the question of values: equality means that people are equal before the law, but also that they have a certain economic equality. They cannot have dignity and freedom unless they also have some economic basis. For those who cannot work, or cannot find work, this places an obligation on the society to provide. We see immediately that democracy itself is founded on a value, equality, which implies not only rights, but duties.

Equality, to be realistic, means that the weak and the sick also have a right to participate and to live in society. These values correspond to what we call human rights in modern language. Thus, the political and the socio-economic rights that form the basis for equality are intimately connected, in national as well as international society. The UN passed two legally binding conventions in 1966: one on political and civil rights, the other on social and economic rights. The two sets of human rights hang together, and can only be realised in the form of a political system that promotes equal votes, press freedom, freedom of assembly, and so on. It thus makes sense to speak of human rights and democracy as part of the same regime as they are so intimately connected. Democracy without respect for human rights becomes an empty procedure, and human rights in a dictatorship hardly make sense.

Inside the nation-state of the West there has been democracy cum rule of law for more than 300 years; indeed, the Western state is built on the gradual evolution of this form of government. It is thus not news that human rights correspond to the current form of government, and that there is no essential tension between them in principle – albeit often in practice. The law-based international human rights instruments have therefore been compatible with national systems of governance in the West.

However, *national* policy has not often been thought of or discussed as human rights policy, which has mostly been the terms of discourse on the international, not the national level. In most states, governments have simply assumed that they fulfilled all human rights obligations. However, recently national governments have also appointed ministers of human rights, such as in Norway in the Bondevik government 1997–2000, in order to highlight the overarching importance of this concept. Not only do states have human rights policies as part of their foreign policy; they also have human rights monitoring for their own country. Norway, again as an example, publishes an annual 'human rights report' which details policies carried out both nationally and internationally.[5]

Human rights and security policy

It is a commonplace that the agenda of international politics has changed after the fall of the Berlin wall. The world may be increasingly unipolar, but it is also multipolar. There are new issues on the agenda, also in security policy. The threats have changed – from Russia there is no threat of invasion, but of poverty, anarchy, disintegration and mafia in addition to nuclear accidents, insurrections and armed conflicts. One should of course add that the nuclear arsenal of Russia remains in place as before, and that the Russians still see themselves as a superpower. But there is no doubt that the power balance has shifted dramatically, and that security policy has changed accordingly (Buzan, 1991; Gartner et al., 2001; Eknes, 1994).

There are of course national interests of a military and economic kind, and these are fairly constant. But a host of new issues have emerged that are truly common to many states: environmental problems, conflict resolution and peace implementation, terrorism and so on.

Here there is no zero-sum game, but a possibility for problem-solving that benefits many. The problems in the Balkans are common to Europe, and the many wars in Africa are a common problem to the whole world, and even more so to Africa. Environmental problems such as climate change are truly global, and require common solutions. Poverty, immigration, terrorism, resource depletion of the seas – these are all examples of the new type of issues where we can often not isolate any national interest.

The modern type of war is the internal conflict. More than 90 per cent of current wars are internal, armed conflicts, and in these conflicts civilians are the main actors – first and foremost as victims, but also as protagonists. Women and children suffer just as much as men. There are child soldiers in many of these conflicts, and they are fought with small arms and light weapons, with mines, and with guerrilla techniques. We have seen in Bosnia and Kosovo atrocities on a scale only matched by the Holocaust, and there have been and still are armed conflicts in the Caucasus, a region bordering on Europe.

'Human security' refers to this emerging security agenda where the point of reference is the *individual* person and his or her right to personal security. This is a human right enshrined in all relevant human rights documents.

It is symptomatic of the present-day concern for human rights that security policy is also defined in these terms. Traditional state security is not being supplanted by a new security policy, but is developing into new forms that complement state security as a result of the proliferation of modern-type conflicts. Both the EU and NATO are preoccupied with so-called 'out-of-area' operations, also called 'crisis management'. At the 1999 NATO summit it was this kind of security policy that was the object of most of the discussion in the new strategic concept of the organisation, and it is the same topic that engages the EU in the process of formulating a common security policy (Matláry, 2000).

The term 'human security' was first used in the Global Governance Commission in 1994 (Lodgaard, 2000). There the concept was used for a plethora of situations, broadening the security concept so much that it seemed to comprise everything. This, in our view, rendered the concept of 'human security' quite useless. But during the work on the landmine convention in 1996–97, the then Canadian foreign minster Lloyd Axworthy proposed to work with Norway on 'human security', and defined the concept in physical security terms, referring to all types of threats that could harm the person. The first meeting arranged by Norway and Canada took place at Lysøen outside of Bergen in Norway in 1998, resulting in a declaration from 14 countries on the need to form transnational cooperation on issues such as landmines, small arms and light weapons, child soldiers, civilians in war, and so on. These 14 states represented all regions of the world, but were selected because they were interested in driving this kind of agenda onto the international stage.

For instance, in 1999 Canada, during its tenure as chairman of the UNSC, launched a debate on 'Civilians in Armed Conflict' after the secretary-general had presented a report on the issue. In the spring of 2000, Norway, Canada and Switzerland again arranged a conference with like-minded states within the 'human security' network, focusing especially on improving legislation on non-state actors such as guerrilla movements and on preventing armed conflict. This 'like-minded' group has undertaken a large number of commitments to common policy in human security projects already. 'Human security' is thus becoming a standard term for security policy which evolves around a person's own physical security and integrity.

It is clear that the states that are hosts to modern armed conflicts are often either failed states, where governments cannot provide basic security for their citizens, or repressive ones, where citizens are endangered by the state itself. There is thus a need for international intervention, and this immediately raises the question of hard power intervention, i.e. the use of military means. Kosovo was a case in point, Bosnia another.

The issue of so-called 'humanitarian intervention' was widely discussed in the aftermath of the Kosovo campaign, illustrating the problematic raised by military intervention and values: could one intervene because human rights were violated? Ethically it seemed that this was acceptable and indeed necessary, but both in terms of political reasoning and international law there was not much enthusiasm for this concept.

The debate on 'humanitarian intervention' was one that combined all the elements of the 'values agenda' in foreign policy. It was felt that massive human rights violations could not be accepted, even if it meant hard power intervention in another state. Both governments and the UNSC rejected this notion, because there is no legal basis for intervention based on human rights argumentation. But the secretary-general nonetheless spoke to the UN General Assembly (UNGA) in the 1999 session about this issue, posing the dilemma of non-action by the UNSC. At the Hague Peace Conference he posed the same question more elaborately: if the UNSC is unable to act when it should act, what about its legitimacy?[6]

Human security in this book is debated in the chapters on the OSCE (6) and on hard power intervention (8), but it is in a basic sense the framework for the whole analysis. This is because security policy has always been seen as the cornerstone of hard power and high politics; an area where national interest and not values matter. However, if security policy also becomes more embedded in human rights discourse and justification, it means *that values have pervaded the very core of traditional foreign policy*. It is often thought that the values of human rights are more salient because the international agenda embraces more low-politics issues, such as the environment, women's rights and so on. Values in this sense are seen as appropriate there, whereas traditionally high politics – security – is thought to have nothing to do with such values. But this bifurcation may be wrong. The focus in this book on 'value-based' security policy thus has significance for the way we conceptualise foreign policy and power use. *If we find that values also play a key role where hard power is employed, it means that the mainstream, high-politics foreign policy agenda is transformed – certainly in terms of rhetoric, but perhaps also in terms of explanatory variables.*

'Soft power, hard values' – the argument

How likely is it that the values of human rights, democracy and the rule of law are becoming more prevalent today? Is there any difference between the world before and after the Cold War? How should we describe the international system today?

There are some that maintain that what decides in international politics is hard power, meaning military and/or economic power (Keohane, 1990; Krasner, 1999, Waltz; 1979). States seek to enhance this kind of power, and the most powerful states decide. 'The strong do as they want, the weak suffer what they must', says the old Greek dictum. This traditional realist view is simple, and therefore attractive as a model.

Yet most international actors today concede that even strong states are constrained by norms and rules, although they do not always abide by them. On what is often termed a liberalist view, such norms and rules – or sets of such, called regimes – exist and are created by states in their own interest, but they are not moving forces in and of themselves. These regimes and norms do not have an independent impact apart from constraining the pursuit of national interests.

The position we take in this book is a third one. On this view, it is normally states that create norms rules, and regimes in their own interest, but these regimes can in turn have an *independent* impact on the states, especially on the 'new' states in Europe that are as yet little developed as democracies, weak economically and dependent on IOs. How much of an impact a regime has on a given state varies from case to case, but in general we maintain that the regimes states create are not afterwards easily controllable by the same states. Once created, a regime in the form of a convention, or simply an international secretariat based on politically agreed norms, cannot be easily discarded and 'lives a life of its own'.

Apart from *constraining* state action, regimes may also influence interest formation within the state and impose their views on the state.

This is especially likely in the case of weak states that seek regime membership. But well-established Western states may also be influenced by regimes, to the extent of changing their national position through coercion or learning.

The regime 'tools' or powers, as they are called in this book, are typically 'soft power' tools: persuasion, scientific knowledge, aid programmes of both money and experts, agenda-setting skills in defining the interpretation of the regime, etc. However, some of the regime tools are 'hard', such as an ability to take legal action against non-compliance or conditionality tied to aid money as well as sanctions and ultimately military intervention.

Thus, we argue here that not only do regimes matter beyond constraining national interests, but they also matter in defining such interests. The norms of human rights and democracy matter in shaping what is defined as a national position or interest in states that seek to participate in the regime or which are already participants in the latter.

For instance, Klotz (1995) has shown that an international norm, that of anti-apartheid, influenced US foreign policy to the extent that the national US position versus South Africa changed. There is prima facie no reason why norms or values should not be able to influence national interest definition. Klotz and others (Finnemore, 1996; Risse and Sikkink, 1999; Risse et al., 1999) call their position a constructivist one, arguing that 'national interests are socially constructed in a global process of norm diffusion' (Klotz, 1995: 477). In this book we take issue with the constructivist position, arguing that national interests are real enough, but that values may influence politicians just as much as material interests, and that they may make for a third category of interests in addition to security and economic interests, which we term 'value-based' interests. This is developed in Chapter 4.

The debate about norms, values and interests is unecessarily bifurcated. There is no indication that *either* interests matter, *or* values. They probably matter in a mixture which varies from issue area to issue area. From my own experience in Norwegian foreign policy, it is quite clear that a modern Western state has both national interests of a strategic and economic kind, but also value-based interests, in the environment, human rights, gender issues – to mention a few areas.

Value-based interests do not normally enhance strategic and economic ones, and as such are not explicable as a *function* of the latter. There is no reason to doubt that these value-based interests are not sincerely held or adhered to, but they may also be adopted simply for instrumental reasons. This is for empirical research to determine. They can, and do, however, enhance the reputation of a state, and as such contribute to its general power and status in an indirect manner.

Value-based interests can be expected to increase in importance in a state's foreign policy. Public diplomacy, which must be argued in terms of values more than in terms of national interests, is gaining centre stage with the globalisation of communications and media, and the democratisation of foreign policy.

A caveat is in order here: I am not speaking about the whole world. There are many places where hard power is the only type of power, where the values of human rights, democracy and the rule of law make no sense and have no existence, and where state actors are not influenced by any external pressures. For instance, in states such as Algeria, Myanmar, Cuba, Vietnam, North Korea and China we see no pluralist power structure. In such states non-intervention is the only important norm, and universal human rights have no validity. In this book the scope is the Western world, including states that aspire to become Western-style democracies and to enter into IOs. This, however, includes an increasing number of states.

In sum, the central argument of this book is that values and norms matter in world politics, and that they matter to an increasing extent. Concretely, we argue that human rights and democracy have become stronger as motives for foreign policy. This does not mean that national interests have disappeared or that people have become more responsive to ethics. Human nature remains constant with its inclination to seek power and wealth, but also with a propensity for promoting values that one internalises and thus really believes in.

The premise of realism – that the international system is basically anarchic and that power distribution therefore matters relatively more internationally than nationally – remains true in a very basic sense today as before. Ultimately the international system remains a self-help system, and the power base of each state or alliance remains the ultimate source of security for that state. But the new logic of public diplomacy means that the legitimacy of the human rights regime is unchallenged, and that actors must be accepted as legitimate in order to exercise 'soft' power.

'Hard' power is only activated in very rare cases. The multilateral economic sanctions in place in the world today are few, and the sanction tool is becoming more difficult to use. The US government, which has a large number of unilateral sanctions, has signalled a review of its traditional policy in this respect.

Military might between states is used even more rarely, although used more in interventions. The point here is that even if these power resources remain the vital ones that underlie the whole international system, they are not used on a daily basis. The tools that are used in foreign policy are other ones: diplomacy, cooperation, criticism in bilateral and multilateral contexts, etc. These tools are called here 'soft' power tools. While the ultimate power base for the state is, as before, military power and the state's ability to protect itself from an aggressor, such power is less and less likely to be invoked, especially between democracies.

Thus, while 'hard' power remains the bottom line of the international system, it takes an extreme situation to activate and use this kind of power. 'Hard' power intervention needs a UNSC mandate in order to be regarded as legitimate, and economic sanctions also need this body's active approval. Unilateral use of military power is very rare, almost non-existent, in the Western world. This is especially true between states where cooperation is manifold and regimes many. Our argument therefore centres on the *normal* exercise of foreign policy, stating that the tools we use are increasingly those of 'soft' power.

But this does not mean that we 'intervene' less: on the contrary, there is more and more 'intervention' in the form of 'soft' power tools being used to promote democracy, rule of law and human rights, hence the title of this book. 'Soft' power is used more and more as a tool of foreign policy, while values such as democracy, rule of law and human rights are typically promoted by using such tools. Helping to form an independent judiciary, a political party, or a free press are the objects of 'soft' power intervention. The values sought seem to become 'harder', while the power used seems to become 'softer'.

In the following chapters we seek to substantiate that values matter. The argument is that there is much value-based intervention but that most of this is by using 'soft' power tools. But, we also argue, there is a major 'value' component also in 'hard' power intervention, such as for instance in Bosnia and Kosovo. Security policy is more and more widely defined in such places: it includes developing democracy and rule of law; conflict prevention and a human rights ethos. Thus, the regime impact of the OSCE and the COE, of the EU and of NATO are all important in a security policy sense.

In Chapter 2 we discuss which driving forces in international affairs make these values more salient. Here the role of global media, international advocacy networks, increased multilateralism, the democratisation of foreign policy, and increased power to supranational courts are analysed. We argue that together these trends interact and strengthen the role of values.

In the same chapter we also discuss which tools modern foreign policy employs. 'Soft' power tools include aid and assistance to forces in malign states that may help democratise those states, such as in kind and expert help to parties, NGOs and media; human rights dialogue with difficult governments, education of judges, exchanges of students and professionals, to mention some of the positive tools. In addition, there are tools such as criticism in international fora and media – 'shaming' – as well as pressures such as non-admittance into IOs and on the hard power end of the continuum, sanctions and even intervention.

In Chapter 3 we discuss which values we are dealing with, detailing the evolution of human rights and democracy after the Second World War in Europe. A key point of this is that this human rights regime is increasingly shared by most states and IOs, such as not only the UN, but also the COE, the EU, the OSCE and so on. The consensus on these values today is striking.

In Chapter 4 we discuss what it means to have an impact and how we can measure such an impact. First, what does it mean to have an impact with 'soft' power tools, and second, how can we measure the impact that human rights regimes have? This is a key issue in international relations research today, and we use regime theory as the framework for this analysis. By speaking about the impact of values, we imply that norms may matter as well as traditional interests of an economic or military kind. In the major debate in the literature some maintain that only interests matter, whereas values always serve only as justification. In this chapter we discuss the concept of national interest and how it is influenced by international norms.

In Chapters 5–7 we analyse the impact of the COE, the OSCE and the EU respectively: in what ways do their human rights regimes have an impact? In Chapter 8 we discuss the use of 'hard' power for human rights reasons in Bosnia and Kosovo. Does this mean that foreign policy has turned towards becoming based on these values also in the realm of traditional high politics?

2
Human Rights and Democracy: Driving Forces and Policy Tools

The more one works in international politics, the more one is struck by two insights, both of which are accurate. On the one hand, the system is very complex; on the other, it appears to be very simple. Sometimes state interests of a hegemonic kind overrule any opposition, and clear-cut national interests are brought to bear. Recalcitrant states are effectively disciplined. But often there are messy political processes with many actors – states, NGOs, multinational organisations and multinational enterprises – that all provide input into a policy process. Then even a hegemonic state may be overruled and sidetracked.

This was the case with the USA concerning apartheid (Klotz, 1995), the landmine convention (Price, 1998), and the creation of an International Criminal Court (ICC) in 1998, where the US delegation provided massive resistance to the very end, but was overruled. The ICC will come into existence when there are 60 ratifications, but of course its impact is small without the USA. However, there was much pressure on the USA to join in this new international legal regime, and the arguments to the contrary are not easily accepted.[1] Finally, before leaving office and some few hours before the time to add his signature, president Clinton signed the convention on 31 December 2000, along with Israel, another state wary of its sovereignty. This signals the importance of international norms and values, regardless of national interests. It carries a political and reputational cost to stay on the outside of important international regimes and organisations.

Today's international politics increasingly deals with value questions. Human rights discourse is becoming the major form of political argumentation, nationally as well as internationally. Human rights instruments have proliferated, both as hard as well as soft law. Legalisation as hard law, where there is a clear definition of states' obligations, is usually difficult to achieve in the human rights area, which normally requires consensus. For this reason those who want to change existing human rights norms mostly opt for soft law strategies, where one uses 'soft law to cast the normative net more widely, building as broad a coalition as possible. Strengthening the normative consensus and possibly the hardening of legal commitments is left to a more gradual process of learning' (Kahler, 2000: 679). This is also why those who want to change human rights seek an international strategy of soft law for the new norm above all else.

We should note that most soft law obligations are obeyed by Western states. Non-compliance is rare in all international regimes, even in the absence of coercive measures of enforcement. Chayes and Chayes (1995) investigated a number of international regimes where there were tenuous monitoring and implementation mechanisms, and found, like Koh (1997) in his major legal review, that international obligations are met by Western states, even in soft law cases. This indicates that the 'shaming' of non-compliance is feared, and that states do not want to be seen as unreliable international citizens.

We can also note that the political agenda is often set by professional interest groups that invoke more or less well-established international human rights norms as their basis of legitimacy. These actors we call 'norm entrepreneurs'. They are highly specialised, highly committed, and work exclusively for their cause. They are thus eminently equipped to succeed. Once an issue has been defined in human rights terms, it acquires a special legitimacy that is difficult to counter. No one is against human rights, democracy and the rule of law – at least not in public. The issue of being considered an actor in good standing, a legitimate actor in the international system, has attained a new importance in a world dominated by Western organisations and media.

The importance of norms, rules and regimes

How do the major theories of international politics deal with norms and values? Realism and neo-realism look at states and their interrelations: the world is made up of states as unitary actors and these actors are in turn embedded in structures that are geopolitical, economic, political and so on. These structures largely determine the scope of state action – its actor capacity – as well as its interests. International society is basically anarchic, and states seek to maintain a balance of power between themselves. This self-help system is premised on the primary importance of territorial defence, and was historically implemented in Europe and later exported elsewhere, through colonialism. On this view of politics, the state seeks security first and foremost.

Today this view of international politics is still relevant, although the nature of national interests has changed considerably: there are *national* as well as common, *international* interests. It is probably true that states remain the main actors in most international affairs, despite the prominence of global capital. And it remains true that the system is a self-help one in the end – no one takes care of the individual state but itself. The states are the ultimate building blocks in the system, whence emanates all power in a formal legal sense. But today there is an increased importance vested in non-state actors, be they economic or idealistic; the state is not alone in representing a country abroad, and interdependence is pervasive. Thus, in what is often referred to as the realist, Hobbesian view, states may still make up the system and its logic, but territorial interests and state actors alone far from *determine* outcomes in international politics.

The other mainstream conceptualisation of international politics is often referred to as the 'English school' or the Grotian tradition. These labels share the premise that there are *norms* that structure relations between states. The debate between realists and the promoters of a Grotian view is over whether there exist constraints on state action in the form of 'deep' norms; thus, essentially a debate about whether the international system is anarchic or constituted by norms. The empirical studies of 'norms' in this sense usually point to such norms as 'the balance of power', 'pacta sunt servanda' (agreements should be honoured), or 'non-intervention' as constitutive norms; that is, norms that define what a state is and can do in relation to other states. Anarchy is on this view a major feature of the system, and the states, which continue to be the main actors in international politics, act in their self-interests but are constrained by these deep norms in a real way.

Thus, if states are constrained by 'deep' norms that are constitutive rather than negotiated, we should expect norms and conventions to be more important as constraints on state interests than otherwise, viz. if the system is essentially anarchical. We should not expect states' interests to be different, but the conditions for realising them are different. States are genuinely constrained by norms such as 'pacta sunt servanda'. *The 'cost' of violating this norm will be great in terms of prestige and reputation.* Thus, if the norm in question is embedded in a regime, the state that does not comply with the regime incurs at least a political cost, and this matters. This entails a real loss of power. Thus, here norms or values constrain state interests, but the interests pursued remain geopolitical or economic. Value-based interests are not pursued for their own sake. Thus, in the 'English school' there are norms that proscribe and constrain state action, but this is compatible with realism. How one conceptualises the importance of state actors, their interests and the constraints on their action thus depends on the initial conceptualisation of the international system or society. Whether one assumes a Hobbesian or Grotian starting point evidently also bears on how one thinks about the importance and impact of values.

The disagreement in the international relations (IR) literature today is, however, not over the existence of non-state actors and international norms, but over the importance NGOs, international treaties and regimes have for states' sovereignty and freedom of action, and if and how they affect state policies and preferences.

In Holsti's analysis, '19th century international politics combined anarchical features and behaviours with those commonly found in loose systems of governance featuring norms, institutions, and authority structures that modify, constrain, and direct egoistic behaviour' (1992: 56). In Europe in particular there were norms that constituted a governance system: the norm of balance of power, the Concert of Europe, or 'pacta sunt servanda'.

Rittberger argues that there is no principled difference between domestic and international politics in this regard – in general, political behaviour is constrained by formal and informal legal and political norms – there are various forms of governance in various issue areas, and non-hierarchical politics is not specific to international affairs (Rittberger and Mayer, 1993: Introduction). There exists, argue these scholars, a *governance system* in the international system, at least in the Western-style democracies. Thus, egotisic and instrumental interest pursuit is compatible with normative constraints on such pursuit. Norms have power in this sense, and realism has to be modified as a theory of international relations to take this into account.

Governance is defined as different from anarchy in that 'states and other international actors recognize the existence of obligations and feel compelled . . . to honour them by their behaviour' (ibid.: 393). Governance may be hierarchical – one obeys laws in a state – or based on

> voluntary agreement to play by a set of rules which are binding in the sense that the compulsion exerted by the rules is not backed up by the threat or use of physical force . . . instead, it is the *legitimacy* of the rules and their underlying norms which make international actors comply (ibid.).

Thus, 'hard' power in the form of punishment is not needed in order to achieve compliance. It is enough that states realise that non-compliance violates what is considered legitimate in their particular society of states. This seems to hold as a general condition for Western politics: norms agreed to, for whatever instrumental or other reason, are basically honoured.

As stated, Abraham and Antonia Chayes, experts in international law, have examined a great number of international regimes and the reasons why states comply with them (1995). They found that 'the fundamental instrument for maintaining compliance with treaties at an acceptable level is an iterative process of discourse among the parties, the treaty organization, and the wider public' (p. 25). The regime – a set of issue-specific rules for a policy area – is often embedded in an IO, and thus has influence over states in ways that are non-tangible yet of ever-increasing importance, argue the authors. This conclusion is corroborated by Harold K. Koh's major survey of why states comply when there is no tangible punishment for non-compliance (Koh, 1997). Also he finds that *loss of reputation and standing largely explain compliance,* but that also what is termed the 'shadow of the future' plays a major role. The former reason is a 'soft' power explanation, while the latter is a realist reason. The 'shadow of the future' means that states comply so as not to be punished in the next round of political bargaining when other states know that they are unreliable and want to retaliate. However, both these authors claim that the 'soft' power reason for compliance because of fear of loss of reputation is gaining in importance. 'Shaming' is becoming more important in the Western world.

The major change that has taken place in international affairs in recent years is, as stated above, the growth in interdependence and complexity in interrelations, as well as the exposure made possible by the media. This amounts to no less than a new type of sovereignty, argue Chayes and Chayes (1995: 27; our emphasis):

> *In all but a few self-isolated nations, sovereignty no longer consists in the freedom of states to act independently, in their perceived self-interest, but in membership in reasonably good standing in the regimes that make up the substance of international life.* To be a player, the state must submit to the pressures that international regulations impose. Its behaviour in any single episode is likely to affect future relationships not only with the particular regime involved but in many others as well, and perhaps its position within the international system as a whole.

Thus, the soft power tool of 'shaming' is intimately tied to the 'hard' power tool of 'the shadow of the future', where compliance is based on every state's long-term self-interest. It is difficult to separate the effect of 'shaming' and the cost/benefit analysis of the 'shadow of the future'.

Applied to some organisations, such as the EU, one might add that if the so-called 'shadow of the future' is long in general because of the growth of international regimes and interdependence, it is almost permanent in the EU: no state has seriously thought of exiting yet. This also holds for the COE and the OSCE: states may be suspended or expelled from these organisations, but they do not leave willingly.

How is national sovereignty protected in such an interdependent international system? The authors argue that

> the only way most states can realize and express their sovereignty is through participation in the various regimes that regulate and order the international system. . . . Connection to the rest of the world and the political ability to be an actor within it are more important than any tangible benefits in explaining compliance within the international system'. . . . Sovereignty, in the end, is status – the vindication of the state's existence as a member of the international system (Chayes and Chayes, 1995).

The state's choice, given this, is often presented as the so-called 'integration dilemma', especially with regard to the EU; or as the 'dilemma of internationalization' (Jerneck and Gidlund, 1996; Jerneck, 1996; Petersen, 1996, Kelstrup, 1993). At issue is how much autonomy is lost and how much influence is gained by choosing regime participation. Jerneck argues that in general, and for small states in particular, the immediate gain in autonomy means little compared to a longer-term loss of actor capacity when a state chooses non-participation.

The reason for this lies in the typical features of international politics in Europe and the West today, which are multilateralism and increased internationalisation of much policy-making that was formerly domestic. The trend towards internationalisation is twofold: political problems are increasingly of an international scope and character; also, decision-making is increasingly internationalised, as evidenced by the proliferation of regimes and organisations (Goldmann, 1989; Hanssen and Stenelo, 1990).

In addition, so-called 'low-politics' issues have gradually entered onto the traditional foreign policy agenda of states – a phenomenon referred to as the 'domestication' of international politics. This is particularly important in the EU, where the state executive can subsume much if not all policy-making under the traditional 'foreign policy prerogative'. Thus, while the political issues themselves undoubtedly follow a trend towards more international problem-solving – a trend which is functional – politicians also set and manage the political agenda to their own advantage. Moravcsik argues that national executives relegate some issues to the international agenda in order to gain power domestically – 'exporting' difficult issues, and thereby also making policy-making about them opaque (Moravcsik, 1993). A sophisticated variant of this argument is Putnam's two-level game metaphor: state executives can use both the domestic and the foreign level to further their interests (Putnam, 1998).

A state must therefore review its foreign policy strategy in this context of interdependence, and the cost of non-participation in the long run is generally much higher than choosing to 'pool' sovereignty, these authors argue. 'Norms of reciprocity, loyalty and demonstrated willingness to adjust to other states' preferences are important factors . . . long-term national interests are not achievable at the expense of others in situations of complex interdependence' (Jerneck, 1996: 151).

On this line of thinking, it follows that *participation* is valued as a major political resource that allows a state to influence agenda-setting, which is of critical importance in an international regime. It also follows that small states and non-state actors like NGOs and IOs may develop skills at persuasion and problem-solving quite apart from consideration of their size and 'weight'. The 'integration' or 'internationalisation' dilemma for a small state consists in assessing 'what kind of power a small country can obtain and exercise in important international arenas, how this power is achieved, and finally, at what political price, externally and internally, this is accomplished' (p. 151).

Finally, this implies that isolation is no longer a viable international strategy for 'modern' states that want to be 'counted' in international society. Only the 'pariah' states isolate themselves: Myanmar, North Korea, Algeria, Cuba and some few others. Most states cannot 'afford' isolation and control of domestic press and NGOs – the loss of reputation in the case of criticism is too great. Currently we see many 'borderline' cases of states that seek to appear as democratic and open on the international scene while attempting to keep control in a traditional way at home. Russia's response to international demands for transparency about Chechnya is one case in point, to be discussed in detail in Chapter 5.

The importance of legitimacy

Thus, the powers that have gained in importance in interdependent Western and especially European politics are intangible ones, either as strategies for furthering traditional national interests or as 'real' developments in a region where even security policy means something very different in the 1990s than in the 1980s and before (Buzan, 1991).

In the assessment of the 'internationalisation' dilemma it is clear that intangible power resources are assumed to be crucial, especially for a small state which does not have 'weight to throw around'. The evaluation of the importance of such a loss of power varies according to one's main assumptions about power in modern international politics. While the literature on transnational actors challenges the state-centric actor perspective, and the interdependence literature likewise challenges the assumption that sovereignty can be retained by maximising national political and legal autonomy, there is, as discussed above, an emerging literature that emphasises new forms of political power.

The argument here is that 'old' forms of power – military and geopolitical power resources – are becoming less important in much international policy-making. These 'tangible' power resources count for relatively less, whereas 'intangible' or 'soft' power resources such as expert knowledge, brokerage ability, skills at communication and agenda-setting, framing of a political problem and so forth, matter more. As Nye argues, 'New power resources, such as the capacity for effective communication and for developing and using multilateral institutions, may prove more relevant' (1995: 184) because 'power is becoming less coercive, and less tangible' (p.188). Soft power carries more legitimacy than hard power, and reputation matters more in a political setting where legitimacy is a key factor.

Chayes and Chayes' main point is that regime compliance happens despite the lack of enforcement mechanisms or even the need to use enforcement. The reasons for this are to be sought in first, the condition of deep interdependence in the modern international system; and second, in the fact that international policy-making under conditions of complex interdependence is very much about *persuasion, justification and explanation.* If a state does not comply with a regime, the state is

> under the practical necessity to give reasons and justifications for suspect conduct. These are reviewed and critiqued not only in formal dispute settlement processes but also in a variety of other

venues, public and private, formal and informal, where they are addressed and evaluated (1995: 26).

Because of the very changes in the international system itself, away from bilateralism to multilateralism, national interests must be presented in terms of general arguments for solutions to common problems, not as a narrow, traditional interests.

They make the particular point that international political discourse is about *justification*. Justification not only means compliance with regime rules – something which gives regime actors great power as they often interpret the regimes – but justification can only be recognised as such when it is seen as legitimate.

Even though interests of a security or economic kind may underlie the discussions about human rights – or any other regime topic – the discussion itself is governed by rules and regulations that are not open to any kind of interpretation. If the regime is a legal one, international lawyers will know how to interpret it. Although there are disagreements about interpretations, there is nonetheless a certain logic to be followed: there are legal norms and standards, there are perhaps precedents; there is a context in which the specific regime is to be interpreted (Abbott et al., 2000; Keohane et al., 2000). One cannot pursue a national interest in the open; one must adhere to the regime rules and find a way to promote one's interests that way.

International lawyers of course know this; it is their very 'métier'. But political scientists have often not taken the importance of this sufficiently into account, thinking that the pursuit of national interests is all that matters, and that regimes are dictated by such interests. But even if national interests were the key movers in the creation of a given regime, the regime itself is cast in legal 'hard law' or 'soft law' terms, addressing a general problematic, often with scientific or normative content. 'Hard law' means that lawyers will interpret the rules of the regime and that participant states are bound by this interpretation, whatever their national interests. 'Soft law' regimes give more scope for political action, but here also non-state actors play a role that may compete with that of states (Abbott and Snidal, 2000; Matláry, 2000).

However, not only are regime actors forced to be skilled at and to adopt the rules and language of the regime, but state actors are often 'entrapped' in it. Returning to our case, the human rights regime in Europe, Schimmelfennig (1999) has a very interesting analysis of how what he terms 'rhetorical action' impacts on actors. His case is eastern enlargement of the EU, and he analyses how the commitment to the enlargement of Europe as a leading idea and value became established as the policy goal of the EU throughout the 1990s. There were clear national interests on the part of many EU states *against* enlargement, but none of these states could oppose enlargement in the public debate. Privately they could seek to slow the process in various ways, but they could not go against enlargement per se. Schimmelfennig shows how EU actors like the Commission managed to set the agenda for enlargement, and how opposing states simply could not risk their good standing and reputation by openly resisting this. It was not considered *legitimate* to oppose enlargement:

> Whereas the issue of EU membership is one of the principles and rights and thus belongs to the 'constitutional taboo zone' in which selfish bargaining and open opposition to the association and admission of European, liberal-democratic countries is regarded as illegitimate, hard bargaining on the economic and financial terms of enlargement and on the necessary institutional and policy reforms is legitimate practice in the EU governance system (1999: 51).

In this example we see how the discourse of public diplomacy is one of rights and duties, not of interests. The same applies to security policy in many cases when it enters the public and media arena. Issues are then 'translated' into stories about abuse and violence to groups and individuals.

The key here is that national interest pursuit is legitimate in some political fora, yet not in others, especially not in public diplomacy in IOs and regimes. Where values, principles, and norms are discussed – in particular human rights – it is not at all considered legitimate to contest them by selfishly pursuing one's own national interest. What is new today, as argued, is that the *question of legitimacy then has real implications for power politics*. Clearly those states which were against enlargement did not manage to keep it off the agenda, and thus enlargement will happen, albeit perhaps very slowly. But it is now considered unacceptable to try to veto enlargement as such.

Likewise, human rights and democracy matter in so far as being uncontested they gain status, and actors embrace them as policy goals. Once this is done, they cannot be questioned as part of the agenda, and are indeed often structuring it.

What drives the human rights/democracy agenda? What are the policy tools of this agenda? The general forces behind this development have been outlined above. Now we turn to the specific factors in this respect. They include the driving forces of *new actors, global media, legalisation of international politics and the creation of supranational courts, as well as the growth of multilateral diplomacy.* But states also create human rights and democracy programmes, and employ the tools of 'soft' power: political dialogue, aid conditionality, democracy and 'rule of law' assistance, and complex peace-building tools which integrate conflict prevention and resolution with aid and training programmes. In addition, states as well as IOs use 'shaming' and 'shunning' as 'sticks' when the 'carrots' do not work, often coupled with political conditionality in aid programming.

Below we specify the main driving forces behind the salience of human rights on the international agenda, and outline the major 'soft' power policy tools that both states and IOs employ.

New actors: the norm entrepreneurs

In the 1970s a literature on so-called interdependence developed in international relations (Keohane and Nye, 1972, 1989). It argued that states are interdependent to an increasing extent, and that there are important transnational actors in world politics. States are perhaps still the main actors, but not the only ones. However, the focus on transnational actors more or less disappeared in the 1980s and 1990s: a later volume was in fact entitled *Bringing Transnational Relations back in* (Risse-Kappen, 1995).

The focus on transnational actors was a focus on the role that non-state actors play in international politics, and thus challenged the realist and neo-realist exclusive focus on states as the salient actors. The focus on interdependence highlighted the interconnectedness of issues and the process towards more internationalisation in both economics and politics, through the globalisation of markets, capital and communications. The political 'response' to this development can be seen in the proliferation of international treaties and in the number of organisations in the present period. The international world is populated by a vast landscape of the latter. This is an empirical fact; what is highly contested is the extent to which regimes and institutions have an impact and what kind of impact they have.

There are many indications of such growth. Zacher reports that in 1909 there were 37 international governmental organisations (IGOs) and 176 non-governmental organisations (NGOs); in 1951 there were

123 IGOs and 832 NGOs, and in 1986 there were 337 IGOs and 4649 NGOs (1992: 65). In addition, there has been an exponential growth in the number of international conferences and international treaties, from 6351 in the period 1946–55 to 14 061 in the period 1966–75 (p. 66). Whatever measure we use, it seems clear that the extent of international policy-making and political ordering has increased especially rapidly from the 1970s onwards, and as a general phenomenon after the Second World War.

NGOs now play a major role in policy-making, nationally as well as internationally. They are transnationally organised and have a major impact on the policy-making of states. They are consulted and often asked to play semi-official roles in international conferences. In the OSCE's human rights review conferences NGOs participate on the same level as states, a unique phenomenon so far, but one that may become general. This indicates how the role of NGOs has become recognised in international politics.

What is considered legitimate is not always a function of it being a 'hard' law norm. Soft law norms may be politically powerful ones. New actors that are transnationally organised use whatever is convenient for their cause. For instance, NGOs that promote alternative family forms or abortion will use the Beijing Final Document from the Fourth World Conference on Women in 1995 instead of the Universal Declaration of Human Rights of 1948 when seeking texts that conform to their political agenda, although the former has no legal or authoritative status whatsoever. What matters politically is to find some international, preferably UN, document that can be invoked because UN documents carry legitimacy in most states around the world. The fact that most UN texts in the human rights area are not legally binding makes them a good basis for value politics. Human rights is a fluid area of international soft law, where transnational interest groups and advocacy networks often work to find a suitable text that can be invoked as authoritative in their own domestic context.

As mentioned above, the agenda-setting stage matters a lot to public diplomacy, and here transnational advocacy groups are experts. They usually concentrate on only one interest or in one issue area, and know the relevant international instruments, scientific experts and coalitions of 'willing' states. Because human rights is an area of increasing importance where the norm development is contested and subject to change, such non-state actors may play pivotal roles. The International Coalition of Ban Land-Mines (ICBL) played such a role in the making of the landmine convention, by the right timing, the right 'shaming' and the right coalition of 'willing' states. Together these factors set the agenda and defined the political process so that the convention became reality, despite strong opposition from the USA. The soft power of a non-state actor had prevailed (Price, 1998).

Further, the growth of transnational advocacy networks is very important to the understanding of value politics today (Risse-Kappen, 1995). The growth of national NGOs is to be found in single-issue areas, and these groups easily network in horizontal ways. Modern communications help this organisational form (Kamarck and Nye, 1999). NGOs typically seek out causes where it is easy to present the issue as a singularly good thing, as an improvement or progress, and use human rights language as mode of argumentation and as justification.

Keck and Sikkink (1998) and Risse-Kappen (1995) have done extensive analysis of such transnational advocacy networks. They describe the strategies of these actors as a *pincer movement*: first, the new or redefined norm is established at the international level. Here UN conferences are the best arenas because they carry most legitimacy, but other arenas may also be attractive in specific regions. The norm change sought is typically that of soft law, which does not require member state consensus.

Once a text change has been established, it can be invoked at the national level as authoritative. The national NGOs work at this level all the time, seeking to prepare the public debate and public opinion. The invoking of the norm from the international onto the national level is successful only if there is some preparedness for its reception (Cortrell and Davis, 1996). This can be created by the *elite policy level*, where civil servants incorporate SOPs (standard operating procedures) in bureaucratic routines that have political significance.

In order to succeed in doing this, one preferably needs both some scientific basis, which can be had for almost any argument today, as well as some text in an international document. The important role of scientific evidence has been studied especially under the aegis of the environment, in the case of climate change, which has been contested for a long time. Haas has shown how 'epistemic communities' – important groups of experts who agree on what the 'state of the art' in their field concludes – form to support a scientific viewpoint, and that such communities exert a major influence on both policy-makers and public opinion (Haas, 1992, 1993).

From Soviet history we know that all science can be manipulated, but the interesting question is to what extent political actors in

Western democracies try to create such epistemic communities in these areas today. It is clear that any position can find its scientific 'evidence' in the global marketplace, but it is politically significant if some actors, such as NGOs, actively seek to create scientific strongholds for their views. We know that the tobacco industry has supported medical research on smoking and there is every reason to believe that other types of interest groups also try to mobilise science on their side.

There are essentially three sources of legitimacy for political arguments about norms and values: *international approval; popular, domestic approval; and scientific evidence*. Thus, new norms can also be seemingly generated from below, through agenda-setting of the public debate. NGOs are, by their very nature, expert at this. Finnemore and Sikkink (1998) lay out how the invocation of the international norm happens while the same norm is being supported from below, so that one arrives at both democratic legitimacy as well as being 'told' by the UN or some other international body to follow the norm.

In the period after the norm has received some international recognition in some text, the advocacy networks work intensely to create a 'cascade': the norm should be seen and debated everywhere. Thus, one overcomes resistance to the norm by becoming familiar with it, and after a while one thinks that the norm is just, the result of progress, and natural. At this stage the socialisation process is under way. In this study we present an analytical framework which argues that most adoption of the human rights regime takes place for instrumental reasons. However, this may change once a new norm has been officially adopted and the process of domestic norm diffusion starts. Persuasion and learning may then occur as reasons for norm acceptance.

Thus, the interaction between the international and national level is an important one where the two levels consolidate each other: a norm invoked from the international level confers *legitimacy* (Hurd, 1999) – a key variable in modern transparent politics – and a norm seen to emerge from below likewise confers the most important source of legitimacy of all, viz. *democratic* legitimacy. A political process that can largely be managed typically displays how polls are taken at regular intervals, showing gradual increases in acceptance for a new human rights or a new policy concept. Once the numbers approach 50 per cent, the norm is well grounded. Politicians will then follow suit, based on their respect for popular opinion (or fear thereof!). The campaign is successfully completed when the new norm is embedded in national legislation and practice. At this point it is almost unassailable. Risse et al. (1999) have studied how norms are changed by strategic action on the part of transnational groups, arguing that once the new norm or values have reached the domestic level, a major process of socialisation is engineered by these groups, drawing on their international resources and their domestic organisation. Norms then gradually become accepted, or at least tolerated. Risse et al. attribute this to learning and persuasion, but the causal mechanisms may just as easily be instrumental, the results of pressures and public ostracism if one disagrees (Noelle-Neumann, 1993). The reasons for norm adoption and norm change are discussed in detail in Chapter 4.

Both national and international organisations and bureaucracies may be actors in norm change – they are 'norm entrepreneurs', as Sikkink call them. These strategic actors are often operators between the national and international levels, and we know that they wield important influence on negotiations in international conferences, working in networks of transnational civil servants. On this view, regimes based on norms can be expected to wield considerable influence. Norm diffusion is not dependent on traditional forms of power, but more on soft power resources.

As mentioned above, it is obvious that in order to succeed in such a norm change, one has to have a 'good cause' in the sense that it can be easily defined in terms of a human right, and preferably in terms of 'good vs. bad'. But in addition to a 'good cause' that easily persuades, one has to have a number of other political resources: a well-functioning transnational network, access to press and media, to the relevant international arenas and to favourable scientific knowledge when necessary, and an ability to stay the course during the period of international norm establishment and its domestic diffusion and embedding. In the case of the landmine convention, it was critical to the transnational NGO to get a core set of states on board. States are still the main actors of international politics. Once a 'coalition of the willing' has been established, however, this tends to attract other states which do not want to be seen as laggards. If bandwaggoning really gets started – as it was in the landmine case – then no state apart from those that really have a vital national interest at stake – wants to be left behind.

In sum, new actors in international politics – transnational advocacy networks of various kinds – play a major role when the issue is concerned with 'value politics', in the human rights area in particular where the appeal value of the word 'human right' is great and where interests for this reason get 'translated' into human rights language.

But there is also another type of non-state actor that has gained in importance in modern public diplomacy, and that is the IO.

New arenas: multilateral diplomacy and international organisations

Another characteristic of the 'new sovereignty' is that

> there are too many audiences, foreign and domestic, too many relationships, present and potential, too many linkages to other issues to be ignored. When a state's conduct is challenged as inconsistent with a legal norm or otherwise questionable, the state, almost of necessity, must respond – it must try to show that the facts are not as they seem to be, or that the rule, properly interpreted, does not cover the conduct in question, or that some other matter excuses non-performance. . . . The justificatory effort . . . is neither a logical nor an empirical demonstration, but an effort to gain assent to value judgements on reasoned rather than idiosyncratic grounds. It is an effort at persuasion (Chayes and Chayes, 1995:119).

If explanation, justification and persuasion are keys to international decision-making, then the ability to perform these roles is a key to state influence. As stated, much multilateral policy-making is both characterised by legality as well as by a discourse that is expert-based and specific to problem-solving. It is not acceptable to argue from national interest in such a discourse.

The number of *international arenas* for norm creation has increased significantly in the latest decade. A plethora of UN conferences on normative issues have been held: on the environment in Rio in 1992, on population and development in Cairo in 1994, on women in Beijing in 1995, on social policy in Copenhagen in 1995, and in 2001 *inter alia* on small arms and light weapons, and on racism. In addition, there are very many other fora where international norms are debated and developed: in the whole UN 'family' of organisations, in the OSCE, the COE, the WTO, OECD, etc.

Who are the interested parties here? The states, but only those states with a particular interest in an issue. Governments have far too much to do to invest major energy in such conferences apart from the states which take a particular interest in the issue area. Thus, the most interesting actors here often are the NGOs which drive single-issue causes.

In an IO, some states are leaders, others followers, and the rest often passive. At the UN, there are two Western leaders: the USA and the EU, and one non-Western leader, the G-77 (which now has 144 members). The USA is the only superpower in the world, and it is beyond doubt that the UN would amount to little without the USA. At the UN, the

EU has become a major power as well: it has 15 members, but is usually supported by all the candidate states (12), by the aspiring states beyond this, and by the EEA states like Norway and Iceland. The G-77 is an amorphous actor which is important because it gathers such a large number of states.

At the UN, the positions of these three actors basically determine an outcome. But the UN 'family' organisations and their bureaucracies also play a major part. These actors often have the expert knowledge that states lack, and influence the draft texts because they write these.

State power depends not only on size, but on staying power, engagement, discernment and ability to persuade. An IO will seek to enhance its own power, and state control is often very slack. There is evidence of regime impact from IOs on states (Rittberger and Mayer, 1993; Rosenau and Czempiel, 1992; Ruggie, 1993). Also, at the UN it is estimated that a very large number of ambassadors never ask for instructions from their capitals. In addition, democratic control of government mandates from national legislatures is largely an illusion. This means that IOs, international arenas, may also be actors in their own right, especially in human rights norm creation and change, where soft power means a great deal.

These arenas that host international conferences and public diplomacy have never been so prominent before. First, the sheer number of IOs has increased, and their visibility is shown in the policy-making they carry out; often in the form of public diplomacy, hosting a major conference, making a public appearance in the field or in taking an initiative in a topical area. IOs compete with each other in tasks, and mandates from member states are often slack and very general. Imaginative and clever management in IOs may be able to enhance their standing in the international community. We see this kind of potential rivalry in Europe when Javier Solana, who heads the EU's foreign policy secretariat, designs a security and defence policy for the EU after leaving the secretary-general's job at NATO, knowing the ins and outs of that IO. The question is suddenly but not unintentionally raised: what is the division of labour for this policy area in Europe? Similar rivalries existed between the OSCE and the UN in Kosovo, and exist between the COE and the OSCE in general.

IOs today have to build a role for themselves, and in order to do so, they need international attention and recognition. The member states, as the ultimate arbiters of the fate of IOs and of their budgets, both assess their performance and need the arenas they provide. But in day-to-day politics states cannot control the IOs.

If one doubts the importance of public diplomacy and multilateral arenas, one need only look to the key roles that the big UN conferences in the 1990s have played. The Rio conference in 1992 set the agenda on the environment for the entire world by getting both press attention and providing an arena for states' own description of themselves as environmentally sound; the Beijing Fourth World Conference on Women in 1995 did the same for women's issues, and so on. Although one cannot always point to *direct* policy effects of such events, it is clear that the *agenda-setting and the problem definitions* are very much decided in such fora. They are also arenas for states' own public diplomacy, where NGOs and the press gather along with state actors.

Other IOs also have important arena functions of public diplomacy: the OSCE gathers member states, NGOs and the press to its human rights review conferences, as well as to its ministerial and summit meetings. The WTO ministerial meeting in Seattle in 1999 ended in chaos as a result of NGO action, something which was widely reported on and paradoxically enhanced the visibility of the WTO in international politics despite the fact that the proposed agenda for the meeting had to be abandoned.

It is likely that both NGOs and the press will continue to focus on international arenas in such a manner, and that the arenas themselves will become more important. Meetings of state parties to existing conventions often attract major media attention and become the arena for further agenda-setting, such as the Climate Convention's meeting in The Hague in December 2000 which gained the attention of the world's press when it ended in failure.

Also states sometimes take the initiative in making so-called 'coalitions of the willing', where they seek to set the international agenda. The Canadian–Norwegian initiative on 'human security' is an example of this. Here 14 states sought to launch policies of 'soft security' in a global context, making it possible to put some of these issues onto the UN agenda in the UNSC.

The typical issues for multilateral diplomacy involve common problems and issues, and are therefore often dealt with in human rights and/or scientific language. National interests also exist here, but cannot be voiced as such. The emphasis is on problem-solving, not on bargaining.

New transparencies: globalised media and internet

There are many effects of the development of global media on international politics, and here we can only enumerate some of the most important mechanisms. They include the *global* character of media coverage through the internet and TV, the *'democratisation'* of foreign policy through media coverage in the domestic setting of events far away and the consequent engagement of the *ordinary voter in affairs that he/she formerly would not even know about; and finally, the very logic of the media* as opposed to the interest-based logic of traditional foreign policy.

All these mechanisms are relatively new, and impinge on foreign policy in important ways. They contribute to making human rights a major focus of foreign policy. We will briefly outline why this is so.

First, the *global* character of modern media: this means that events are reported in real time, often with simultaneous coverage of the event itself. One salient example is the attack by government troops on the East Timorese in the bloody fights in 1999 which led to the eventual acceptance of a UN peacekeeping force and to East Timorese self-government. The attacks on the population in Dili were covered both by a few foreign reporters as well as by local aid workers and members of the population who had direct contact via mobile phones to the outside world. One could follow, often tragically, the fate of those who were trapped by government soldiers. Some of them were killed just after they had been in contact with Western media.

There are many, many other examples of live coverage of major political events like the above, where the whole world's attention is drawn to a specific place for some days or weeks. This leads to political engagement and to pressure on one's own foreign policy-makers, thus activating what we have called the *'democratisation'* effect. Foreign policy is suddenly not about this or that 'national' interest of one's own country, but about human rights for this or that group or person. What do you do about the situation in East Timor? What pressures do you bring to bear? Do you boycott Indonesia, shame Indonesia; travel to Djakarta to meet with political leaders? Can you raise the issue at the UN? In short, your voters at home demand that you act, and you have to become engaged.

One should also note that here the *logic of the* media is basically *opposed* to the political logic of foreign policy. There is a demand for instant political action in the light of human rights concerns, where the question of procedure, interests and consequences of action is left on one side. The latter concerns are important in foreign policy, and often override human rights concerns, but are not seen as legitimate in a situation of urgency where an issue is on the public agenda. The media portray personalised stories as part of their presentation, whereas foreign policy-makers analyse possible tools, the cost of action in terms of interests vis-à-vis the state in question, how to proceed and, not least, short-term vs. long-terms effects. But when an issue is defined by the media, it is cast in terms of good vs. bad, of personal rights versus state power, of a moral duty to act. Then politicians cannot respond with 'we think immediate action will bring no results' or 'we shall consider the issue in all its aspects, but there is little our small country can do to really change anything'. The media set the agenda for political action once an issue has been sufficiently politicised, and no politician under public pressure dares opt out of action. One cannot be seen as defensive and reactive.

At this point NGOs will also be active, accusing politicians of compliance in the case of passivity. As discussed above, these groups are often part of transnational advocacy networks where their communication ensures real-time knowledge of the situation and a profound 'domestication' of a foreign policy issue. If a Norwegian NGO starts to pursue such an issue, it becomes part of Norwegian public debate and policy.

It is not only wars, armed conflicts and crises of various sorts that are 'translated' into human rights issues. Also long-term conflicts like the case of the Indians in Chiapas in Mexico were put on the international agenda by journalists and transnational NGOs in combination, and persisted on the agenda for a long time. In my bilateral meeting with Mexican policy-makers they were very upset about this, pointing out that they had done very much in Chiapas, but that the agenda-setting in a negative light continued.[2]

The globalisation of the media means that information is available in real time everywhere where internet, mobile phones and TV exist. This serves to strengthen NGOs which are in particular need of such information, but it also makes it possible for ordinary voters to check on the official version that their own policy-makers present them with. The actual agenda-setting is quite another matter, however; few pieces of news are important enough to make it to the headlines. They need to be dramatic, shocking, often violent and full of suspense. In addition, they need to have footage. Without picture material there is usually little chance of making a top story. In addition, where there is the possibility of full coverage, it is also a question of selection of which issues to cover. The so-called CCN-effect refers to the selectivity of issues.

Low-intensity conflicts are not dramatic enough to be covered, and thus get little or no political attention. There was harassment of Kosovars for ten years under Milosevic's rule, but it was not dramatic enough to be high on the media agenda. Only when several massacres were recorded, the worst of all in Rajak in January 1999, was there full attention from the world's press, and with it full political attention. The subsequent NATO threats to use force created a drama which sustained media attention.

The general implication for human rights is that most foreign policy events that make it to the top of the media's agenda concern persons and *personal stories*. They are often about the *rights of persons or groups* – to independence, to justice, to freedom. They are about suppression, dictators, armed conflicts and violence to attain rights. They invariably contain strong prescriptions about right and wrong.

Traditional diplomacy, however, is based on *Realpolitik* and a careful attention to the norms of the international system: a new state is not easily recognised, at least not unilaterally, and one does not interfere in the so-called 'internal affairs' of another state. The logic of the media and of human rights, however, is the very opposite, transcending national borders, interests and careful analysis of consequences. The demand is to be just and opt for good vs. evil.

We are not suggesting that either of these foreign policy 'styles' is right or wrong; simply pointing out that they are very different, and that *modern media go well with the human rights logic*. Public diplomacy is cast in terms of right and wrong, of doing something to help someone; not in terms of the status quo or one's own interests. We can conclude so far on the note that the media, transnational advocacy networks and proactive governments use human rights logic as the very definition of foreign policy. These drivers are important explanations for the prominence of human rights and democracy on the international agenda.

Even international business actors pay a great deal of attention to the power of human rights: 'Globalisation and the age of the internet mean that . . . multinational companies . . . are subject to increasing scrutiny at home. They cannot escape the attention of pressure groups seeking to impose moral standards on their activities.[3]' As discussed in Chapter 1, companies are increasingly adopting human rights codes both internally as well as vis-à-vis the countries where they operate, no doubt in order to hedge against unpleasant exposure and risk to their reputation.

New supranationality: courts and juridification of human rights

The process by which human rights logic – international, based on the person, not on the state – advances at the expense of state logic, based on territorial sovereignty, is also evident in international law and in the erection of international adjudication mechanisms.

First, there has been an expanding use of 'soft law' in international politics. Abbott and Snidal (2000) notice that 'soft law' – non-binding international documents – often carry much weight and are in fact treated by interested actors as if they were 'hard law': this applies directly to the UN conferences in the last decade. In fact, aiming for soft law bases for new norms is a preferred strategy because their status in the international political system is so ambiguous.

Soft law instruments as well as legalisation at the international level have increased greatly in recent decades. Legalisation is a strategy to create binding norms which carries more weight and legitimacy than the creation of 'soft law', but which is harder to achieve and which requires member state approval and often consensus (Keohane et al., 2000). Thus, soft law is the preferred tool for those who want to change norms (Goldstein et al., 2000; Abbot et al., 2000).

Second, there has also been an expansion in the use of 'hard' law', or law proper. More and more international regimes are legal conventions, and there are courts and adjudication mechanisms for many of these. Goldstein et al. (2000) argue: 'the world is witnessing a move to law', and this is particularly noteworthy for human rights. The number of international courts has increased, and action against individuals who are wanted for war crimes, genocide and crimes against humanity is now taking place outside of his or her national borders. The legal definitions for these types of crimes are fairly clear and have developed to become more comprehensive in the post-war period, but it has been a major problem that enforcement mechanisms for these crimes have been largely lacking: 'Existing mechanisms for implementation tend to rely on consent of a state with custody of the offender or a belligerent authority' (Chopra, 1994: 44). However, after the internal genocide in Cambodia from 1975 to 1979 there was a sustained effort to create a tribunal. The UN set up UNTAC in 1991, a mission with major powers for prosecution of criminals inside Cambodia. Although not entirely successful, this mission signalled the new trend of intervention-cum-law enforcement. The later case of genocide in Rwanda resulted in an ad hoc tribunal (UNSC res. 955/94) which exclusively judges cases in this theatre, and there is also a tribunal for Yugoslavia, the ICTY (International Criminal Tribunal for Yugoslavia) (UNSC res. 808/93), both erected by the UNSC. The next and logical step was the creation of the long-discussed International Criminal Court (ICC) in 1997. The court is not yet operative, as the number of ratifications has not reached the required 60. Further, the USA is not likely to ratify. However, the trend towards supranationality in crime persecution is evident in the erection of these courts and tribunals, as well as in the increasing willingness on the part of nation-states to extradite criminals and to accept universal norms instead of insisting on national jurisprudence.

For example, a key politician in the Kremlin, Pavel Borodin, was arrested for fraud in the USA on the demand of the Swiss authorities,[4] much to the protestations of Russia; and the infamous Pinochet case began when UK police arrested him in London at the request of a Spanish judge, against the enormous protests of Chile. However, a little later Pinochet was in fact facing trial in his home country. Milosevic is awaiting trial in The Hague, and the government in Croatia is extraditing people indicted for war crimes to The Hague. The idea of supranational norms and also supranational law enforcement in crimes against humanity has rapidly become accepted in Western public opinion, but this would have not been the case just a few years ago.

There are similar cases which need not be mentioned here, but the trend is clear: those who may be charged with crimes, especially war crimes and crimes against humanity, cannot feel protected by diplomatic immunity – the hallmark of traditional sovereignty – any longer.

Nuremberg was the first case of a supranational tribunal which laid down the principle that there is a higher law than that of one's superiors and state. This vindication of natural law, that each person is obliged, but also able, to judge for himself whether an action is right or wrong, implies that it is not one's national laws, commanders or governments who can absolve the individual of his choices and actions. There is a higher law, which only a higher court than national courts can pass judgements on.

After Nuremberg the whole corpus of universal human rights was elaborated, starting with the Universal Declaration of Human Rights of 1948 (Glendon, 2001), much inspired by the need to prevent the atrocities of the Second World War from reoccurring.

But it was not until recently that supranational human rights tribunals were again erected. The tribunals for the FRY and Rwanda were established as ad hoc tribunals in the wake of the massive human rights violations there, and the former especially is gaining an important role in international affairs. In addition, the decision to create an international criminal court, the ICC, marks a watershed in the attitude to state sovereignty. It is no longer absolute. Human rights logic is gaining ground over state logic not only in terms of intervention, but also in terms of enforceable law, at least in the Western world.

In addition, more and more states are being compelled to establish their own truth commissions in order to arrive at an accurate account of what happended in their particular crisis. In South Africa[5] there was an extensive process in this regard, painful but useful in getting to the truth; in Guatemala another such national process; and after the excavation of bodies in Peru, the authorities have agreed to set up such a commission.[6]

Truth commissions are often alternatives to courts, and do not provide any punishment. They aim at national reconciliation and forgiveness, but are premised on the idea that there can be no peace without justice. Justice can only prevail when the truth of what really happened, is known. Thus, internationally renowned experts have to partake in such commissions to ensure impartiality.

It is remarkable that we are witnessing this prominent degree of human rights concern, both 'above' states, in the form of courts and tribunals, but also inside states where respect for human rights has often been at its lowest ebb. No major intra-state conflict today can be resolved without some sort of such procedure. Argentina, Guatemala, Chile and now Peru are recent signs of this trend. The demands for such processes by those affected and by human rights groups can no longer be silenced inside the state.

Policy tools of human rights and democracy

Human rights policy tools include the development of bilateral human rights policies, a phenomenon that has taken place mainly from the 1980s onwards. In developing a human rights policy, states as well as IOs have developed specific tools for this field.

Taking Norway as an example of a well-developed human rights policy, the typical features can be largely summed up in 'soft power' measures: *development cooperation* combined with help in developing democracy, rule of law and human rights; *cooperation with NGOs* towards third countries in bringing about human rights improvements, such as Amnesty or the Helsinki Committee; establishing *human rights dialogue* with selected countries in order to persuade and teach through cooperation; *developing specific human rights soft and hard law* through international instruments and organisations; use of praise as well as *shaming,* and sometimes even *shunning,* in isolation or in combination with aid conditionality.

These are some of the most frequent tools for promoting human rights, and if we look at the Norwegian example again, we will find that a 'snapshot' of its human rights policies in 1999 included the following: shaming and praising at the UN Human Rights Commission in Geneva, where Norway was displeased with the weakened language of some resolutions (Sudan, Myanmar, East Timor, Rwanda, Burundi, Nigeria and Colombia), but pleased with the strong denunciation of the FRY in the Kosovo resolution. However, displeasure was expressed at the 'non-motion' action by China, which also in 1999 managed to prevent a resolution being passed on its human rights situation, and it was also recorded that Cuba got a critical resolution passed, albeit with a small margin. In addition to country resolutions, Norway promoted the human rights defender work based on a declaration by the United Nations General Assembly (UNGA) after many years of work, a long-term project to get a special rapporteur named on the issue of protection of NGOs and other human rights defenders. Another positive development, Norway noted, was the adoption of a resolution, for the first time, on the right to development.[7]

There is naturally a coordinated approach to the employment of multilateral and bilateral tools. There is always extensive lobbying in national capitals before the March session of the commission, both from the USA which promotes in particular the China, Sudan and Cuba resolutions; and from states subject to criticism, especially China and Cuba. As we will see in Chapter 7, the EU has been wary of sponsoring the China resolution after Denmark did this and was promptly punished by cancellation of business contracts. Cuba has also used tough retaliation: the 1999 Cuba resolution at the Human Rights Commission in Geneva got Norwegian support, but this was seen as criticism by the Cubans and they cancelled the bilateral human rights dialogue with Norway. The same was the result of open Canadian criticism of Cuba in 1998. The only two countries with such human rights dialogue with Cuba have thus been cut off, a move the wisdom of which one certainly may question.

The international arenas for *shaming* and *shunning* are very much seen and noted, first and foremost by other states, but also by companies and the press. A state's standing here matters a great deal for its international standing and reputation, hence the major activity undertaken to avoid having a critical resolution passed. There are basically two such arenas that are global; the UN Human Rights Commission in March–April each year, and the UN's Third Committee, which meets in the autumn in New York. Prior to these meetings a lot of consulation goes on, and states receive their 'grade book' on both these occasions. There are traditional resolutions that are repeated each year, with slight changes in a positive or negative way. The imaginative national policy-maker will keep the 'shaming' pressure up through public diplomacy in these meetings so as to have some leverage in a bilateral context with specific policy programmes, thus drawing on the power wielded in the public forum for traditional or 'classic' diplomacy.

Again drawing on our example of soft power human rights work in public diplomacy, we notice that the Norwegian human rights policy contains a number of human rights dialogues, a new policy tool used by more and more states and IOs. Norway's extensive engagement now includes dialogues with China, Cuba (suspended in 1999), Turkey and two new states where the dialogue is in the making: Vietnam and Indonesia.

The dialogues are used by the 'problematic' country to justify their human rights work, while the 'donating' state may use them to justify the lack of international criticism, such as often alleged in the case of China and the EU: closed rooms instead of the open forum are chosen for criticism. These dangers are certainly part of any human rights dialogue, but they do not invalidate the importance of such dialogues. From my own experience in developing the Norwegian human rights dialogue with Cuba, it is clear that human networks and sympathy play a major role in learning and persuasion. The participants in such dialogues often become close associates, to the point where they can discuss 'how far' each side can go without losing support at home. Thus, they can become real motors for change because they can rely on trust built up gradually. Human rights criticism is such a senstive matter that open shaming usually does not lead to results, only to rejection and anger. At the same time it is important to retain the corrective of open fora, as they also work as a deterrent.

Conclusion: how strong are the driving forces?

We have explictly confined ourselves to the Western world and to states that desire to become members of Western and international organisations. There are clear differences between regions in terms of the importance of 'shaming' in the human rights area. The importance of human rights and democracy is also spreading to other regions, but we expect that a state's reputation with regard to such values will vary quite a lot. The Western world participates more or less in the same public diplomacy and reads and listens to the same news. The 'public opinion' which is formed here therefore affects all the states in question.

However, there is reason to believe that this dynamic will spread rather quickly to the global arena. Multinational and increasingly global companies adopt CSR strategies as a hedge against risk to their reputation, and this becomes company policy worldwide (Schierbeck, 2000). Further, NGOs are global and communicate globally, so that events are reported in real time. This extends transparency to all places under scrutiny. Finally, investment does not come unless the human rights record is acceptable. An illustrative example of the necessity of adopting human rights talk, for what is a purely instrumental reason, is China's sudden embrace of human rights and democracy in their campaign to get the Olympic Games.[8] Hitherto China had rejected the coupling of business and human rights, but learning has been fast in this case.

Thus, although our hypotheses and analysis in this study are confined to Europe, we think that the public diplomacy dynamic we describe will also extend to other regions of the world. There they will soon be forced to 'talk the talk' of human rights and democracy. There is of course a long road to be travelled between rhetoric and reality, but that road begins with adopting the concepts as valid ones.

3
The Formation of the European Human Rights Regime

In this chapter we outline and establish what we term the human rights regime in Europe. A regime is a set of rules, norms, regulations and decision-making procedures that regulate an issue area, as a standard definition of the term goes.[1] A regime can be legally binding, or just politically binding; it can be loosely embedded in an IO, or have its own IO as a secretariat: these factors are important for determining its impact, discussed in the next chapter.

The reasons for calling the values in this study a 'regime' is that it is internally consistent, containing the same elements, summed up as human rights, democracy and the rule of law. The *consistency in terms of content is remarkable,* although there is some difference in emphasis. The European Convention on Human Rights (ECHR), which is the first development of the regime in Europe, stresses in particular rule of law, while the OSCE's Helsinki Final Act and other documents emphasise in particular democracy. The EU's Charter on Fundamental Rights contains both rights as well as elaborations on the form of government to achieve and sustain them.

The ECHR was completed in 1950, and entered into force in 1953, with a full set of institutions to implement the convention. About 20 years later the then CSCE convened its conference in Helsinki, which was to last for three years, ending with a politically binding document, the Helsinki Final Act. This was a breakthrough for the idea that there were universal human rights also in Eastern Europe and the Soviet Union. After this the CSCE/OSCE continued its work on norm development and practical implementation in collaboration with the COE. These two IOs prepared the ground for the EU's late arrival on the scene: only in the SEA in 1986 is there any mention of human rights and democracy as goals of EU policy. However, after this time the EU has rapidly expanded and consolidated its normative basis in this area, and even saw it necessary to have its own charter of human rights.

The background to the importance of human rights in the post-war period is the Second World War. The Nuremberg trials had established that there are higher laws than those of the state, and that the individual both enjoys such rights, and is obliged to live by them. Hence, one cannot blindly obey orders, even if they are legally sanctioned in one's own country. This vindication of natural law was a tremendously important impetus to the movement for codifying human rights.

The League of Nations of the inter-war period had failed to prevent another war, and illusions about world government were recognised to be such – just illusions. Sikkink notes that

> human rights ideas entered policy debates in the US and Europe at the same time – in the period immediately after WWII . . . in Europe, international human rights policies have been present constantly since WWII, gradually increasing in comprehensiveness throughout the period. In the US, after a flurry of activity around the drafting of the UDHR and the covenants, human rights policies virtually disappeared for twenty years, only to resurface in the early 1970s (Sikkink, 1993: 139).

Thus, it is primarily in European regimes and IOs that we find the major development of human rights as relevant, practical and enforceable parts of foreign policy.

The precursors

The traditional concern for the rights of individuals in Western history was not called 'human rights', but there was nonetheless a provision for rights beyond state borders in most international treaties even from the times of the foundation of nation-states. As Krasner (1999) has shown, the Treaties of Westphalia contained rights for religious minorites. Such rights were very important in Europe, and continued to figure in most international treaties as well as in the multinational and multi-religious empires of Europe. Thus, there were always exceptions to Westphalian sovereignty. In the period before 1648, there were well-defined universal principles of natural law *(ius naturale)*, although they were not termed rights as such. The ruling system of temporal and spiritual powers was, however, based on universal, and not on territorially limited concepts of legitimacy and rule. The 'rights' in this system were balanced by duties of inhabitants of each state – the peasantry, the artisanry and the nobility in terms of society and politics, although Christian 'rights' in spiritual terms were based on equality. The classical and Christian tradition was not based on any limitation of territory.

Thus, there is not much that can be said about human rights as a field within international relations in the twentieth century, indeed, prior to the Second World War. The Geneva Conventions were promoted by the International Committee of the Red Cross (ICRC), and there was a sustained and prolonged popular movement to recognise humanitarian rights in armed conflict. Finnemore has shown how Henri Dunant's ideas were gradually adopted as an international politial norm (Finnemore, 1996). There was also a long-term recognition of minority rights, both ethnic and religious, which hark back to the practices involved in the sovereignty norm as defined by the Treaties of Westphalia (Krasner, 1999). Also, several military interventions had been justified in the nineteenth century by the argument for minority religious rights, such as the intervention in Greece in 1827 by the UK, France and Russia in order to stop the massacres of Greek Christians; the French intervention in Lebanon in 1860 in order to stop the massacres of Christian maronites, the European Great Powers' intervention in the Balkans in 1873 to protect Christians against the Turks, and finally, the intervention in Turkey in 1903–8 in order to help the suppressed Macedonian Christians. All of these interventions were *justified* and *legitimated* as humanitarian interventions, although *Realpolitik* probably ruled in most of them. The European balance of power system was visible as the motivating forces of Balkan interventions.

The point here is that there were a few elements of human rights argumentation in international affairs prior to the Second World War, such as the concept of humanitarian intervention and religious rights, but they were not codified in any systematic manner. Some topics, like rights of the civilian population in war and armed conflict, and the abolition of slavery, were codified in the Geneva Conventions and the 1926 slavery convention. However, human rights as such were not a unified whole, and were not defined as such.

Human rights in international politics

The Second World War brought it home that something had to be done at the international level to prevent atrocities like genocide from happening again. The UN was to be a realistic attempt to create a world governance system, and the idea of a human rights charter was promoted by NGOs as well as by politicians such as Franklin Roosevelt and Winston Churchill. However, it was the NGOs, churches and individuals that secured the human rights charter, later named the UDHR: '[These groups] conducted a lobby in favour of human rights for which there is no parallel in the history of international relations, and which was largely responsible for the human rights provisions of the charter.'[2]

The core of this was the UDHR of 1948 and the two later covenants on civil and political rights, and economic and social rights of 1966. These, like the UDHR, have no monitoring and compliance mechanism.

The UN system was set up in order to create a forum for all states that would hinder major wars and crimes against humanity. Although the UN Charter explicitly recognises non-intervention as a key norm of the international system, it also defines and bestows the only mandate there is for hard power intervention in armed conflict, viz. the Security Council (UNSC). Chapter VII of the UN Charter grants this mandate in cases where there is a 'threat to international peace and security'. As we shall see in Chapter 8, there has been increasing hard power intervention in the 1990s under this mandate, which has linked human rights and security policy in unprecedented ways.

The UNSC is admittedly non-democratic and exclusive, granting veto power to the five permanent member states. But it is nonetheless the only body which has a mandate to use force, however unrepresentative it be.

In the USA, the creation of the UN and the formation of the UDHR represented the high point of political interest in human rights. Afterwards the Cold War dominated the foreign policy agenda. The parting of the ways between the USA and Europe after the Second World War in the human rights field meant that it was only in Europe that one 'moved quickly and consciously to build a regional human rights regime' (Sikkink, 1993: 148).

In Europe, the major shift towards the convergence of human rights and democracy came with the demise of the communist system of government. This demise was abrupt in 1989 onwards, but had been gradual in coming. There had been a gradual dissemination of knowledge about democracy along with the evident malfunction of the economic system of the communist world.

But other forces also helped this development. In Chapter 2 we analysed the driving forces of the contemporary emphasis on human rights, democracy and rule of law. The globalisation of the media and the consequent dissemination of common norms are one explanation; another is the triumph of capitalism and its demand for predictable and stable government where rule of law is a necessity. International investors as well as financial institutions all demand political stability and democracy as key criteria of investments. This has simply to do with investors' predictability. But we can note, at this point, that there is a convergence between the consciousness of the population about their rights and the need of investors. This undoubtedly leads to synergies in terms of the promotion of these norms as the only viable ones.

The European human rights regime: the ECHR and later instruments

The UDHR is not legally binding, but is considered the Magna Carta of human rights. As stated, its rights were, however, developed into the two legally binding covenants on political and civil, economic and social rights, dating from 1966. Thus, in the period up to 1970 the major international human rights instruments were drafted.

Around the same time the Europeans drafted their legally binding convention, the European Convention on Human Rights (ECHR). Again NGOs spearheaded the notion of a convention and a court to implement it, and this was taken up by the newly formed Council of Europe (COE). The ECHR was, as stated, created in 1950, and entered into force in 1953. The powers of the European Court of Human Rights, created in 1959, and its Commission on Human Rights which reviewed cases, were far-reaching.

There is a remarkable consistency in the human rights as they are defined in the major human rights instruments. The core human rights are well defined. In the Universal Declaration, they include the right to 'life, liberty and security of person' (art. 3), equality before the law and due process (arts. 7–11), right to privacy and a good name (art. 12), right to freedom of movement and nationality (art. 15), right to marry and to form a family, and special protection of the family on the part of the state (art. 16), right to freedom of thought and religion, to public worship and conversion (art. 18), freedom of opinion and expression (art. 19), freedom of assembly and association (art. 20), and the right to political participation (art. 21).[3]

These fundamental human, civil and political rights are complemented by social and economic rights: the right to social security (art.

22), the right to work and to fair pay (art. 23), the right to an adequate standard of living (art. 26), the right to education (art. 26), and finally, the duty to contribute to the community as well as the right to do so in order to realise one's full human potential (art. 29).

These rights and duties form a whole, as Glendon brings out in her work (Glendon, 2001). But not only that: the rights defined in the Declaration presuppose both a democratic form of government as well as the rule of law. In art. 21 which states that 'everyone has the right to take part in the government of his country', there is a specification in para. 3 which states that 'the will of the people shall be the basis of the authority of government; this will shall be expressed in periodic and genuine elections which shall be universal, and equal suffrage, and shall be held by secret vote or by equivalent free voting procedures'. There is no doubt that this is the definition of a democracy, however without the specific mention of its name.

Further, in the article on equality before the law (arts. 7–11), there is explicit mention not only of equality, but also that arbitrary detention, exile or arrest is forbidden (art. 9), that tribunals must be independent and impartial and that everyone has the right to a fair and public hearing (ibid.), that a person charged is presumed innocent until found guilty and that his trial should be public with the appropriate defence. These provisions correspond to what we normally call the *rule of law:* objective and transparent application of the law in equal measure to all, fair trial, defence as appropriate, and independent courts.

There is thus a clear provision for both democracy and the rule of law in the UDHR.

Turning to the ECHR, the convention refers to the UDHR, 'considering that the universal declaration aims at securing the universal and effective recognition and observance of the rights therein declared' (preamble), and contains the same rights: the right to life (art. 2), the right to security of person (art. 3), detailed provisions on the rule of law as regards both arrest, imprisonment and trial; the right to privacy and family life (art 8), freedom of thought, conscience and expression (art. 9); freedom of expression (art. 10), and freedom of assembly and association (art. 11). In the exercise of all these rights and freedoms the frame of reference is explicitly that of a 'democratic society'.

The convention is especially detailed on aspects of *rule of law*: on the conditions for arrest and detention, the prohibition of torture and punishment without law, the rights to a fair trial, the right to an effective remedy, and so forth. It is the individual and his rights vis-à-vis society and governments that form the major part of the convention, but the classical civil and political rights are also included. One can safely say that the convention's special competence is the rule of law.

The statutes of the COE make membership conditional upon the respect for human rights and the rule of law, and there is a clause on suspension for breach of these conditions. The court is supranational and accepts petitions from individuals of member states, an unprecedented degree of direct effect in this area. The convention itself was drafted and opened for ratification within a short timespan of 15 months in 1949–50, and granted strong powers to a Commission of Human Rights within the COE machinery in monitoring. [4] The right of individual petition[5] to the court and its supranational jurisdiction was adopted throughout the 1950s by the major member states, and the court came into operation in 1959.

Since the convention entered into force, more than 170 additional treaties under the COE have been created. The most important ones include the European Social Charter, which refers to social and economic rights and which entered into force in 1965; the European Convention for the Prevention of Torture and Inhuman or Degrading Treatment or Punishment ('The Torture Convention'), entering into force in 1989; the Framework Convention for the Protection of National Minorities, which entered into force in 1998, and the European Charter for Regional or Minority Languages, also entering into force in 1998.

These special conventions complement the ECHR in specific areas, and have different enforcement mechanisms. The Social Charter, whose protocols were merged with the charter in a new convention entering into force in 1996, now covers the rights to housing, health, education, employment, social protection and non-discrimination.

This convention, however, has a much weaker implementation mechanism than the ECHR, which has a supranational court. However, it has a monitoring machinery, a secretariat which collects national reports on a biannual basis and sends these to the European Committee of Social Rights, which is composed of independent experts. They examine the reports, and make recommendations to a so-called 'governmental committee', consisting of national representatives. They in turn may suggest that the Council of Ministers make individual recommendations to states, asking them to change policies and/or law to make them comply. In 1998 a complaints procedure was added to this convention, making it possible for trade unions, employers' organisations and relevant NGOs to complain to the expert committee. By the end of 1999 three such complaints had been received.[6]

The Torture Convention, however, has more 'bite' in its implementation procedure. The convention establishes a committee, called the Committee on the Prevention of Torture (CPT). It is entitled to inspect any facility in a signatory state on an unannounced basis – prisons, mental hospitals, police stations – and can interview any person in these states. The main aim[7] is to ensure that detained persons enjoy at least minimum standards in custody, that prison conditions are good, that foreign nationals receive proper treatment when under arrest and in prison, and that involuntary placement in psychiatric establishments is according to the standards of the convention. The inspection visits by the CPT, often highly publicised, have become central preventive measures in this field. For instance Norway, where I hosted a visit by the commission in 1999, has received sustained criticism by the latter on account of its use of custody.

The CPT makes a confidential report on its findings after the visit, asking the state in question to act according to the criticisms made. Recently the practice of publication of both report and state response has increased,[8] so that the shaming effect in the national press can be used to the full. The impact of the CPT is assessed to be important in case studies of the visits and follow-up of recommendations (Morgan and Evans, 1999).

A third important convention is the 'Framework Convention for the Protection of National Minorities'. This convention is often quoted by the OSCE as the standard for its extensive work on minority issues. This convention is the first legally binding instrument in this field worldwide, and the problems of minority rights are increasing. Monitoring and implementation are based on the submission of state reports to a committee. These reports are public and will be examined by an advisory committee which in turn makes its recommendations to the Council of Ministers, which makes individual recommendations. The implementation of these will in turn be monitored.[9] Although this convention is very important, there has not yet been extensive integration of the work done by other IOs in this area with the COE's own work.

The role of the COE is thus a complex one: while its main convention, the ECHR, has a supranational court, its specific conventions rely on various weaker enforcement mechanisms. Some of these conventions also fall outside the human rights regime proper, such as those dealing with culture, education, standards, etc.

The COE's human rights regime has developed throughout the postwar period when new conventions have been added to the ECHR.

Some of these are highly topical for human rights that are especially conflictual, and their legally binding character means that they also are the firmest reference point for invoking them in political debates. However, many of these approximately 170 conventions lack efficient implementation mechanisms, and it is thus largely left to the power of shaming whether a state will comply, although suspension from both the Council of Ministers and the Parliamentary Assembly (PA) is a possibility. Some of the most important of these conventions are so new that we do not yet know how well they will be implemented. Much will depend on how eager the COE's committees are to ensure implementation, and on whether they will be ratified by the new member states that have problems in the human rights area.

Thus, the main part of the human rights regime is made up of the ECHR and its implementing body, the court. However, the Council of Ministers as well as the PA have also taken on much more active roles in regime implementation over the last few years. A public monitoring procedure has been established for the assembly, and a similar procedure based on confidentiality for the Council of Ministers.

The way these work and their impact are discussed in Chapter 5. The court itself has become much more prominent in European politics over the last few years, something which also highlights the importance of human rights in the domestic politics of Western democracies. For instance, each time Norway has been judged in the court there has been much media attention, and an immediate response by policymakers that they will implement the judgement, in law as well as in politics. The legitimacy of the court's supranational role is by now very well established, and its work is followed with much more interest in the general press than previously.

The European human rights regime: the Helsinki Final Act and later documents

The OSCE's human rights instruments are not legally, rather politically binding. The OSCE was not an organisation – the O in the acronym – only a conference – the C in CSCE – until 1992. The CSCE was the meeting point between East and West during the Cold War, and resulted in the famous Helsinki Final Act in 1975 which put human rights – or the 'human dimension' as it was dubbed diplomatically – above sovereignty in declaring them to be universally valid principles.

This was not achieved overnight. The CSCE was originally convened after several Soviet suggestions to hold an all-European security conference. This suggestion was motivated by the Russian interest in securing, and having recognition for, the borders of the Yalta division of Europe, while Western interest was in securing some liberties and freedom of travel for the populations of Eastern and Western Europe. In the 1950s, the Soviets held 'security conferences' which were only attended by the Eastern satellite states, resulting in the Warsaw Treaty of Friendship (Bloed, 1993).

However, a renewed Soviet effort was made in the 1960s. The German *Ostpolitik* was adopted around this time, and a new era of détente started. SALT I had been agreed, and NATO ministers declared that a conference on security and cooperation in Europe would be convened. They also insisted that force reductions would be a topic of negotiation, thus from the very beginning linking security and other cooperation.

The 32 states that convened in Helsinki in November 1972 spent more than half a year in agreeing on the modalities and the agenda for the conference. This is, however, not surprising, given that this was in the middle of the Cold War. Every aspect of both issues was important.

There could be no direct talk about human rights, democracy or the rule of law – all conceived by communist ideology as Western inventions. The agenda reflected the need for careful language, involving security, economic, scientific and technological cooperation, and then 'cooperation in humanitarian and other fields'.[10] The three themes of this agenda were referred to as 'baskets', and everything related to the human rights regime was simply called 'the humanitarian dimension', which is still the official name for it.

The decision-making procedure was consensual, which meant that progress would be very slow on all the issues, which were inherently very conflictual. The Helsinki conference in fact lasted for two years, 1973–75. It ended, however, with the adoption of the path-breaking Helsinki Final Act.

In the first 'basket'[11] the major principles agreed upon were presented: there was the statement of support for traditional sovereignty: non-intervention, respect for the rights inherent in sovereignty, but also the important principle VII on the 'respect for human rights and fundamental freedoms, including the freedom of throught, conscience, religion or belief'. On this latter point the Holy See, a full member of the CSCE, had played a pivotal role.

The inclusion of principle VII was, in the words of Arie Bloed, the foremost expert on the OSCE, 'a major achievement . . . it meant that in the Final Act the human rights principle has become just as important as other fundamental principles of international law, such as the sovereign equality of states and non-intervention in internal affairs' (Bloed, 1993: 6).

Here the two principles – sovereignty and human rights – were pitted against each other, logically mutually exclusive, but a major victory for human rights logic because it was the very first time the Soviets had accepted such a principle. Thomas, who has investigated how this event empowered and inspired NGOs in Eastern and Central Europe, mentions how the Soviet leaders tried to downplay their acceptance of human rights: Gromyko asserted principle VII on non-intervention, and stated that 'we are masters in our own house' (cited in Thomas, 1999: 209).

The Soviets accepted this text simply because it was a necessary compromise. They probably never thought it would mean a great deal, much less have any impact. But it was nonetheless necessary for Eastern and Soviet leaders to suppress the text as much as possible: In Poland under Gustav Husak only 500 copies were printed, for use of the elite only, and in Czechoslovakia the copies were never distributed after printing (Thomas, 1999: 209).

The Final Act was agreed to be only politically binding, but there were references to legally binding instruments, such as the UN Charter and the 1966 Covenant on Civil and Political Rights. But as Bloed concludes: 'The fact that the Helsinki Agreements are not legally binding agreements has not affected their political authority. The opposite is true' (1993: 11). He argues that the impact of the norms is seen in their frequent invocation as authoritative, and in the fact that they enjoy high status since they were signed by leaders from 35 states. The Helsinki Principles were a major achievement in the Cold War climate, and this made them so important. They are so frequently referred to that they should be counted as customary or soft law, argues Bloed.[12]

After the Act was adopted, there were follow-up conferences. The work of wording in the third basket, the humanitarian one, was piecemeal and difficult. Progress was achieved on family visits and contacts, on cultural cooperation and on educational measures. But these were cautious steps.

At the time of the Belgrade follow-up meeting in 1977, there were human rights persecutions in Eastern Europe, especially in Czechoslovakia and the USSR. At this time the human rights NGOs had become established as domestic challengers to the communist control of power, and these groups were severely repressed, such as Charta-77, and later in Poland where the newly elected Pope John Paul

II sparked off mass resistance to the regime. The Holy See, a full member of the OSCE, had drafted much of the texts on human rights, especially concerning freedom of religion. The Pope knew the Helsinki texts well, and demonstrated this when he wrote a letter to Brezhnev to avert a Soviet invasion of Poland in 1980. He invoked the principles of the Helsinki Final Act, but not human rights this time, rather the principles of state sovereignty and non-intervention![13] Citing the Helsinki Principles, his letter states in very direct language that Poland is a sovereign state where the principle of non-intervention was applicable.

The Soviet strategy had been to uphold this principle as the key one, and it was now being used against them. As the US negotiator Thomas Buergenthal concluded,

> for the Soviet Union and its then allies the adoption of the Helsinki Final Act was a major political blunder. The resultant CSCE process provided the West with a powerful diplomatic tool and ready-made platform for exposing the brutality of the Communist system and for challenging the Soviets to implement the human rights commitments established by the Final Act (Buergenthal, 1990: 5).

At Belgrade there was sustained conflict over these issues, with mutual accusations about human rights violations. It is interesting that the Helsinki Act had become the reference point for NGOs in the East, and their very activity based on the latter became the major bone of contention. Soviet acceptance of human rights principles was already beginning to have an adverse impact on the states in their sphere of interest and control. In the poor East–West climate, nothing was agreed at Belgrade, only the dates for some expert meetings and a new follow-up meeting in Madrid in 1980.

The Soviet invasion of Afghanistan in 1979 intervened and made for a major setback, as did repeated human rights violations, and the Madrid preparations took almost three years. The follow-up conferences were intended to monitor compliance with commitments and to refine and develop these further. Now the Soviet side did not want substantive time at the conference for discussing monitoring, and the disagreements led to prolonged time for agreeing on the agenda. When this was finally agreed on, the conference itself lasted almost three years, in a climate of hostility and persistent Cold War.

However, the results were interesting: there was agreement to convene a disarmament conference in Stockholm, and in the human rights field there was adoption of many measures that 'counterbalanced' the concessions made to Soviet interests in the security field;

their main interest. Importantly, the right to form trade unions was established, and there were improvements on freedom of the press, family reunions and freedom of religion.

The third follow-up meeting took place in Vienna, and also lasted for three years, 1986–89. This was the time of *perestroika,* and human rights discussion was very different from before. At Vienna, there was 'as far as human rights are concerned', a 'dramatic breakthrough beyond anything that could have been reasonably anticipated at that time' (Buergenthal, 1991: 349). The typical pattern of Soviet refusal to discuss human rights at home by invoking the principle of non-intervention, did not recur. Instead there was a Soviet acceptance of human rights as a legitimate field of discussion, which was a novelty (Bloed, 1993: 22).

At this meeting the OSCE human rights system was established in all its fullness, notes Buergenthal, an expert in international law. Using the example of freedom of religion, which was prominent in this conference, he cites the final text from the meeting in full. It contains the most detailed and precise obligations for governments to carry out in this field that exist in any international document. The states are to formulate many types of policies to implement this right, and the general human right of freedom of religion thus becomes a specific, well-defined right that is difficult for member states to ignore. This is the 'OSCE method' that from this point on became the way in which states are increasingly obligated to implement policies.

The Vienna document not only developed freedom of religion in detail, but also new human rights commitments, such as the right of the individual to both know and act upon human rights, as well as to organise NGOs in this field and even disseminate information about international human rights instruments in schools. In addition, new rights on equality between the sexes and rule of law were adopted, rules about leaving and returning to one's country, and finally, some institutional reforms such as biannual human rights conferences were agreed to.

Buergenthal remarks that the detailed provisions that were elaborated for each human right – the OSCE method – were initiated by the West 'to reduce arguments about non-compliance, which was being excused by assertions that the meaning of a given right was unclear' (1991: 352).

But the real change in the OSCE's human rights regime came with the demise of communism. At the Copenhagen meeting in 1990 the

Russians no longer insisted on communism as their ideological system. When they ceased to demand that human rights and communism were compatible, democracy then became firmly wedded to human rights. The concluding document states that we 'recognise that pluralistic democracy and the rule of law are essential for ensuring respect for all human rights and fundamental freedoms'.[14] Now the OSCE had shared values and ideology, and there was no room for major disagreement over the interpretation of either democracy or human rights.

This document contained more details about what a democracy is: it is pluralistic, based on a multi-party system, where 'democracy is an inherent element of the rule of law'(ibid.). There is a plethora of other specifications about the relationship between the executive, the judiciary and the legislature – *all according to the Western liberal tradition*: all states are to hold periodic elections, to allow parties and to give all citizens the vote, and so forth. The whole Soviet alternative – 'people's democracy', human rights in a totalitarian state – disappeared almost overnight in Europe, and the OSCE could capitalise on these changes. It very quickly moved to consolidate democracy and rule of law as the basis for the realisation of human rights, and at the same time deepened and broadened the human rights already agreed to. There were new rights as well, such as the right to own property, and a detailed elaboration of minority rights, a minefield in most eastern OSCE states.

The normative development of the OSCE reached its peak in the so-called Charter of Paris of 1990, which is usually cited along with the Helsinki Final Act as the normative basis of the organisation. It reaffirms what was agreed the same year at Copenhagen, and adds more body to the institutional side: a secretariat, a Conflict Prevention Centre, an Office for Free Elections – all these institutions were erected to implement the regime.

The last OSCE document to be included in this chapter is the so-called Moscow document from 1991. The paradox of its name becomes clear when one learns that the document, written and adopted in the capital of the former USSR which had denied intervention based on universal human rights and postulated the primacy of non-intervention, now contained the most far-reaching rewriting of this very norm in any international instrument. The Moscow conference took place in the aftermath of an attempted *coup d'état* in Russia, something which is evident in the text itself. Here there is the construction of a new OSCE commitment, viz. the 'collective determination' of the states to 'consolidate democratic advances in their territories'. The states in fact have a 'common commitment to countering any attempt' at overthrowing 'human rights, democracy, and the rule of law'. [15] There is further condemnation of anyone who tries to seize political power illegally and undemocratically. Thus, this document prescribes *a collective duty to intervene in each other's states* if such a situation should occur. This means that the norm of non-intervention is extremely circumscribed, and that a new norm of intervention had been established, based on the notion of legitimate government, i.e. a *democratic* government.

In sum, the OSCE documents provide the most comprehensive 'coverage' of the three elements of the human rights regime: human rights, rule of law and democracy. They state in great detail why and how human rights can only be realised with democratic political institutions, and why a democracy has to be based on rule of law. But each human right is also expanded upon to the point of detailing which policy measures must be taken to implement it. In our example of religious freedom, the documents gradually grow in size and precision as to how exactly a new state is to create conditions for religious freedom: by allowing for public worship, but also by encouraging churches and belief communties; by allowing them to register and in fact to welcome their activity, by respecting their autonomy, and so on.

Likewise, we find the same detailed prescriptive method for other rights, in particular the right to minority culture and language which is a sensitive and conflictual issue in many OSCE states.

The point has been made that such a detailed 'vade mecum' is necessary because one is dealing with states with little or no democratic tradition. The 'clientele' of the OSCE is vastly different from the traditional membership of the COE and the EU. The COE had to become much more involved in training, education and fieldwork once it admitted new states from the former Soviet Union and the Balkans as members. Thus, there is a good reason why the Western states especially insisted on such detailed commitments.

But one effect of this didactic purpose is that the OSCE now has the most detailed human rights regime in the world. It goes far beyond conventions on human rights in the description of policies to be undertaken to implement the rights – in fact, conventions usually do not mention policy at all – and it also commits the states in a very practical and verifiable sense by defining what exactly implementation means. The question of implementation or regime effect is an empirical one to be discussed in Chapter 6, but the point of departure for this impact is a strong one because the 'instructions' are so clear. The human rights regime in the OSCE is precise and detailed, but not legal.

Buergenthal discusses whether the non-legal character of the OSCE human rights regime implies that it is less powerful than a legally binding instrument, such as a convention. At the outset one would assume that this is so. But this is also a question for empirical analysis. He notes that creating a legally binding convention takes more actors and compromise on the text – not only must the government in each state negotiate and sign, but the convention must also be ratified in the national parliament, a procedure that may entail resistance which will either slow down the ratification procedure and therefore make the process towards the entry into force of the convention much longer, and/or make for an anticipated carefulness on the part of the government in negotiating the text. Logically one may therefore achieve a 'stronger' text when the agreement is not legally binding.

But in what senses are the OSCE documents binding? Buergenthal makes the point that the OSCE documents may gradually acquire the force of customary law, although the specific condition for this is that the states themselves treat these obligations as if they were legally binding for a sustained period of time (1991: 378). However this may evolve, one can at least determine that these obligations are 'soft law' – rules and prescriptions that are regarded as commitments to be honoured. It is obvious that 'soft law' may be as important as 'hard law', especially in international affairs where the mechanisms for enforcement are weak as such. Recalling the empirical work by Chayes and Chayes (1995) and Koh (1997), we know that most obligations under international regimes are honoured in spite of the difficulty of punishment and strict enforcement. To be seen as non-compliant is a great liability in a transparent world where reputation is a growing political asset; and non-compliance can also be punished by other states in the future – the problem of the 'shadow of the future'. The importance of these factors in our analysis is laid out in more detail in Chapter 4; suffice it to state here that the fact that the OSCE documents are not legally binding in the form of treaties or conventions does not per se mean that these norms have less impact on states.

A factor that makes it likely that there will be much impact is the detailed and prescriptive character of the rules and norms. In addition, they are based on many international legal human rights norms, so that the OSCE texts are full of norms that have a definite legal standing and also a legal interpretation according to the canons of international law. This means that 'international law plays a major role in the interpretation of the OSCE instruments' (1991: 379).

The OSCE process amounts to nothing less than a new type of international rule-making. Since there is no court to interpret the rules authoritatively, they have to be made as specific as possible so as to secure a common understanding. This makes for tight rules and little scope for defection. This is, in our view, a major regime-specific power.

The European human rights regime: the European Union's texts and its charter

The EU is a latecomer in terms of human rights. The first reference to this concept is found in the Single European Act (SEA) of 1986, where it is mentioned in passing. Prior to this other human rights instruments had been invoked, especially the ECHR, as well as the constitutional obligations of the member states.

The European Court of Justice (ECJ) in Luxembourg has, however, taken human rights into account in its rulings, thereby de facto as well as *de jure* incorporating these into the case law of the EU. The EU's annual report on human rights is quite explicit about this practice by the ECJ:

> Although the EEC Treaty contained no specific clauses on human rights, the ECJ has consistently recognised that fundamental rights form an integral part of the Community legal order, thereby ensuring that human rights are fully taken into account in the Community legal order. This case law of the court was gradually built up from 1969 onwards.[16]

Here we touch upon the very important practice of the ECJ: as will be further discussed in Chapter 8, the court has consistently built a supranational role for itself without any clear basis in the treaties. It established its doctrine of direct effect and legal supremacy in the 1960s, and few states have protested at this development. For now it suffices to note that there has been a consideration of human rights and case law on human rights despite the lack of any explicit human rights instrument in the treaty basis.

But the need for more explicit human rights policies has made the EU intensify its work in this field during the last ten years. It is the Treaty on European Union (TEU) which for the first time includes detailed human rights commitments. In art. 2 one of the objectives of the EU is to strengthen the 'rights and interests of the nationals of its member states', and in art. 6.1 we find the key sentence on the political foundation of the EU: it is 'founded on the principles of liberty, democracy, respect for human rights and fundamental freedoms, and the rule of law'. In the amendments made in the Amsterdam treaty, which came into force in 1999, there was an inclusion of a suspension clause in the case of breaches of human rights commitments (TEU, art. 7), and the provision that candidate countries must respect these principles in order to join the EU (TEU, art. 49). In art. 46 it has given the ECJ the role of ensuring that EU institutions comply with these requirements. At the Nice Inter-Governmental Conference (IGC) in December 2000 this paragraph was amended to make the procedures for suspension clearer and more applicable. This move was supported by Austria which demanded clear criteria for this kind of 'shaming' after its own experience earlier that year.

The TEU also moved important parts of justice and home affairs (JHA) into the treaty, such as asylum and immigration policy, thereby increasing the scope of EU policy mandates in the human rights field. Also in foreign policy, as will be discussed in Chapter 8, human rights conditionality has made important progress and impact.

Copenhagen criteria of conditionality

With regard to third countries, the EU had already formulated conditionality in the form of a conclusion from the European Council meeting in Copenhagen in 1993. The so-called 'Copenhagen criteria' stipulate that all applicant states must have achieved 'stability of institutions guaranteeing democracy, the rule of law, human rights and respect for and protection of minorities'. This last reference to the issue of minorities is important, as this is often the problem in Eastern and Central Europe where the borders decided at Yalta and before that, at Versailles in 1918, in no way correspond to ethnic groups or 'nationality'. We note also that the OSCE paid a great deal of attention to this issue in the Concluding Document of Moscow and in the establishment of the Office of the High Commissioner for National Minorities.

The EU's conditionality in the human rights field covers not only enlargement, but all third-party agreements, both in trade and aid. The record in terms of impact of this is analysed in Chapter 8. The conditionality is in the form of a demand for compliance with the International Labour Organisation's (ILO) standards for child labour in addition to the human rights, democracy and rule of law clause when the EU grants GSP (generalised system of preferences) conditions. Also, in the Lomé agreement with developing countries there has been such a clause since the early 1990s, and in Europe such agreements are also prefaced by the need to comply with OSCE documents – thus showing how there is in fact *one* European human rights regime.

There are also two important regional European political processes that deal with the promotion of democracy, rule of law and human rights at large, in Eastern Europe and in the Balkans. These EU-initiated political processes are called the 'Royaumont process', launched in 1995, and the Stability Pact for South Eastern Europe from 1999. In both these processes the EU builds policies around its human rights regime.

But in 2000 the EU acquired its own textual basis of the full regime, viz. 'The European Charter of Fundamental Rights'.[17] The Commission and the ECJ intended this charter to be legally binding and thus give the EU its 'constitutional basis', so much needed in order for the court to have a clear basis for its case law in this area, as well as for the federalists of the union to find a logical basis for a federal entity. This strategy has so far been delayed, after massive resistance from the UK and Denmark, but has only been deferred. The status of the charter will be discussed again at the next IGC in 2004.

The charter, like the OSCE's documents, is 'only' politically binding, and refers to and is inspired by other human rights instruments, especially the ECHR. It started as a German initiative, and former president Herzog led the drafting group which also had representatives of the COE in it. The charter was resisted by the COE[18] as being superfluous – indeed it threatened the very *raison d'être* of the latter, especially if it becomes part of the treaties – and it duplicates the work of the COE.

In terms of content, the charter sets forth all the traditional human rights, saying in the preamble that the 'Union is founded on the indivisible, universal values of human dignity, freedom, equality and solidarity; it is based on the principles of democracy and rule of law'. In fact, one may say that it reads like a shorter version of the ECHR, but with less detail on rule of law and with some new rights on children and the right to reconcile work and family life. Its tone is as solemn as any human rights declaration, and it clearly aims to provide the EU with a type of constitution.

However, the charter is invoked as if it were a constitutional text with legal status. It was promulgated as if it were a constitutional text at Nice, and has been invoked in the same manner, first by the Groupe des Sages that investigated Austria, and then by the advocate-general

Tizzano in his opinion on the BECTU case.[19] The importance of this lies in the use that EU officials make of the charter: the advocate-general states that the charter contains references to the major legally binding texts, and is therefore to be considered the major source of these rights. We see a practice emerging here that is not dissimilar to that of the use of the OSCE documents: although not formally legal texts, they contain references to the major legal texts and as such, carry an authority that is also legal in a way.

Complementarity of the European human rights regime

Looking historically at the evolution of the European regimes in human rights, one clearly sees a historical chronology where the COE was first and took its inspiration directly from the UDHR and the foundation of the UN in 1948. Also the European experience of the Nuremberg trials led to the search for foundations of human rights beyond the nation-state, and this directly led to the work for another European organisation than the failed League of Nations to deal with this theme. It was Europe that had witnessed the atrocities of the Second World War and the holocaust of the Jews. Against this background it is not surprising that it was in Europe that supranational human rights were developed more than anywhere else.

The ECHR puts its main stress on the rule of law and on how to define it, while it also gives ample room for other political and civil rights. Its strength lies very much in its system of compliance, viz. the court. As we will see in Chapter 6, however, new instruments have been added in the last decade, both in terms of conventions and of policies and institutions.

The OSCE is historically the second human rights regime. It appeared from 1975 onwards, and the so-called CFSE process negotiated the Helsinki Final Act which became a major human rights reference for both East and West. The inclusion of the concept of human rights, gradually developing to become all the political and civil rights of the UNHR and the ECHR, was nothing less than revolutionary in 1975, at the height of the Cold War. The Charter of Paris ended the main OSCE norm-making process in 1990, with the end of the Cold War. At this point, for the first time ever in any international human rights text, there is an explicit recognition that human rights can only be realised within a democracy, and that a democracy means the rule of law, not a type of 'socialist democracy'. It is in the OSCE documents that we find the most detailed and specific elaboration of what this means, and also about how states should implement human rights, democracy and the rule of law.

In the EU we find the ECJ using international human rights as its basis for case law, but the judges do this outside of the purview of press and politics. They do not have to rely on political decisions in this field, so if we only look at the ECJ, we find that the EU has had a tradition for taking human rights into account, and indeed for interpreting human rights, right from the mid-1960s when the court made its judgements on direct effect and legal supremacy. This history of 'constitution-making' is related in more detail in Chapter 8, but here it is interesting to note that the ECJ has acted on a non-existent 'constitution' all these years – it was only in 2000 that the EU acquired its own 'constitutional charter', but this is not legally binding.

But the official EU human rights policy only started in the 1990s, with insertion into the treaties of paragraphs on human rights, democracy and rule of law. However, in a very short time the EU has expanded its human rights and democracy basis to all policy areas, and in particular to policies towards third countries and enlargement. The textual basis here is small, and the regime is usually only defined as 'human rights, democracy, rule of law' with the 'addition' of 'market economy'. But as we shall see in Chapter 8, considerable impact lies behind these few words.

The texts of the human rights regimes in Europe – in the COE, the OSCE and the EU – are different in certain respects, but in terms of content they are identical. They all contain the basic elements 'human rights, democracy, and the rule of law'. This warrants the use of the term 'the European human rights regime'. The OSCE's texts are the richest, but the impact this regime has cannot be extrapolated from the texts alone. We need to look at how the regime is embedded in each IO, whether there are regime-specific powers and whether the IO in question has general powers and tools that strengthen regime compliance.

In conclusion to this chapter one may state that it is in Europe that the most developed human rights regime is found, and that this regime is embedded in three of the central European organisations that admit new states as members and that generally have a major impact on the development of those states.

We now turn to the major task of this study, viz. to analyse the actual impact that this regime has in Europe.

4
The Impact of International Organisations and Regimes

In order to study the impact of the human rights regime, we have chosen the vantage point of regime theory, whose 'specific object . . . is voluntarily agreed-upon, *issue-area specific* normative institutions created by states and other international actors' (Rittberger and Mayer, 1993: 393). It thus seems a natural point of departure for the study of how human rights and democratic norms matter.

Regimes are, in the standard definition to which there is general agreement, 'sets of implicit or explicit principles, norms, rules and decision-making procedures around which actors' expectations converge' (Krasner, 1982: 2). Young notes that the principal difference between regimes and other international orders often called international institutions is the *issue specificity*: 'international regimes are . . . specialised arrangements that pertain to well-defined activities . . . and often involve only one sub-set of the members of international society' (Young, 1992: 13).

Some scholars use the term 'institution' in much the same manner as 'regime'. However, issue specificity remains the major criterion of differentiation, and it is often confusing when the term 'institution' is used in several different ways as well. Some refer to institutions as general norms of society, whereas others reserve the term for IOs. Keohane defines *institutions* as 'persistent and connected sets of rules (formal and informal) that prescribe behavioural roles, constrain activity, and shape expectations' (Keohane, 1990: 3). We have previously defined institutions as the 'deep' norms of societal ordering, such as 'pacta sunt servanda', 'international diplomatic rules', and so on. We thus distinguish between regimes, which are issue-specific and are embedded in governance systems, and institutions, which are the general and constitutive norms in IR and which sometimes vary from region to region.

Status of regime theory

Much regime theory has been applied to studies of the *formation* of regimes; however, so far relatively little attention has been focused on the *impacts* of international regimes. As Rittberger concludes in his anthology on the 'state of the art' in regime theory,

> the third main task of international regime analysis [is] the study of regime consequences or effects ... *regime analysis has yet to develop plausible hypotheses guiding systematic empirical research. Moreover, the conceptualisation of what may be taken to be a consequence or effect of an international regime remains underdeveloped.* Also, the methodological problems involved in studying regime consequences are far from being solved. Yet the virgin nature of this segment of regime analysis holds the promise of rapid advance in the near future'(our emphasis) (Rittberger and Mayer, 1993: 392).

The end of this quotation may be too optimistic, yet it should be possible to develop ways of studying regime impacts systematically. In this regard Oran Young has made a significant contribution (Young, 1992). He asks how regimes can be said to have an impact. Regimes, in Young's view, may be both *independent* and *intervening* variables, and may have important effects as both. Assessing regime impacts on states means looking at *implementation, compliance* and *persistence* (1992: 162). In order to make the test of regime strength as reliable as possible, we should seek 'hard cases'. A 'hard case' is one in which regime participants have no incentive to comply with regime requirements, and also have an opportunity to disregard them. Three conditions for a 'hard case' are suggested by Young: major regime participants are predisposed to dislike the regime requirements, it is relatively easy to violate regime rules, and the regime is not strongly embedded or very 'solid'. The more of these conditions obtain, the more robust the test. As Young puts it, 'If international institutions . . . play significant roles in shaping behaviour in hard cases, we can conclude that they will be influential under more benign conditions as well' (1992: 166).

What evidence of regime impact exists from such 'hard cases'? Young reports on three: the Svalbard (Spitsbergen) Treaty from 1920; the regime for whaling in the International Convention for the

Regulation of Whaling in 1946, and the GATT trade regime from 1947. In his conclusions about the empirical evidence from various studies of these regimes (cited in Young, 1992: 166–75), he says that the evidence 'does suffice to demonstrate that the argument of those who assert that international institutions are mere epiphenomena, is wrong' (p. 175).

Which factors contribute to regime impact? Both Young (1992) and Chayes and Chayes (1995) highlight *transparency* as the key to ensuring compliance and exposing non-compliance. Both sets of authors stress that it is not the magnitude or severity of sanctions that make states comply, but the fact that they will be exposed for non-compliance. In fact, Chayes and Chayes make this the main conclusion of their book.

A second important variable that contributes to regime impact is *robustness*. This is twofold: internal robustness and robustness as the ability to change and adjust to other circumstances.

As for general conditions for regime impact, *diffusion of power* in the international system is an important precondition: 'a marked trend towards the diffusion of power within international society during the last several decades has produced a significant decline in the asymmetry characteristic of the immediate post-war era' (Young, 1992: 187).

Impact and how to measure it

Neo-liberalism and neo-realism

How can a regime have an impact? In which sense, and by which regime characteristics? In a neo-realist model, states are the main actors, non-state actors do not have any impact, and anarchy obtains in the international system. Conflict is assumed to be essential, i.e. to be the rule of politics rather than the exception (Cornett and Caporaso, 1992). Neo-realism or intergovernmentalism has no place for international regimes that have an independent impact. It is thus of no interest to this inquiry except in the form of a 'null' hypothesis: if the regime is found to have no impact, this model is vindicated. The interesting theoretical (as well as empirical) discussion in the field today is, however, centred on *which roles regimes or institutions play*. There seems to be agreement that they play a role, but about whether this is an independent role and how it is to be studied and assessed there is little agreement.

The outgrowth of neo-realism usually called 'neo-liberalism' (or neo-institutionalism, neo-liberal institutionalism) modifies some of the central assumptions of neo-realism and is the mainstream model of the relationship between states and international regimes today. In the words of Cornett and Caporaso, 'neoliberal institutionalism accepts neorealism's emphasis on anarchy, state interests, and power, but seeks to introduce an institutional component to systemic-level analysis' (1992: 232). Cornett and Caporaso remark that 'the decisive difference between neorealism and neoinstitutionalism has to do with the relative significance each attributes to international institutions'(1992: 233).

To the neo-realist, regimes simply reflect the power of strong states. Neo-liberalism claims that rules influence behaviour in ways that cannot be accounted for by actor capabilities and preferences. Thus, the basic anarchical character of the international system is modified by regimes and institutions. Cornett and Caporaso define the neo-liberal hypothesis on the role of institutions thus:

> Institutions not only constrain or empower states in systematic ways, but may also shape the perception of self-interest ... they may significantly change the means through which states pursue their interests. States' power is defined increasingly in terms of the ability to work with, not against, numerous rival sources of power and influence in world politics (1992: 233).

There seems to be general agreement, however, that regime theory has made it clear that regimes matter. In the words of Risse-Kappen,

> After more than ten years of empirical research, regime analysis has established that international institutions have substantial effects on government practices, both on policies and definitions of interests and preferences. State autonomy and control over policies are affected by the degree of the state's embeddedness in international structures of governance (1995: 29).

For instance, Muller has shown that an international security regime changes the parameters of the domestic discourse of security policy (1993).

Thus, there is agreement on the general fact that regimes matter, but there is less agreement on how deeply they matter, and in which ways. This is the central theme of this book: the empirical findings from this study will tell us something about the viability of the neo-liberal, mainstream model of IR.

Constructivism

There is, however, a third 'school' of IR theory today which is usually introduced along with neo-realism and neo-liberalism. The widespread use of the constructivist label among scholars suggests that it warrants scrutiny: Finnemore, Risse and Katzenstein all call their approach constructivist. Two of these scholars, Finnemore and Risse, have published extensively on the impact of human rights norms within this analytical approach. We will therefore discuss their definition of this approach as the third way of analysing regime impact, in addition to neo-realism and neo-liberalism.

Recent work in IR on the importance of norms has often been cast in what is termed a 'constructivist' or 'reflectivist' analytical mode. While constructivism is a philosophical metatheory making both ontological and epistemological claims, it is often also proposed as an analytical approach to the empirical study of international politics (Kratochwil, 1982). As Finnemore remarks, constructivism is the least specified theory of politics of these three, something which makes it difficult to evaluate as the basis for an empirical research design:

> Constructivism is the most amorphous and least defined of the perspectives emphasising the causal nature of social structure. . . . Conceptually, the relationship among principles, norms, institutions, identities, roles, and rules is not well defined so that one analyst's norm might be another's institution and a third scholar's identity. Substantially, similar problems exist' (1996: 16).

Constructivism as a metatheory postulates that ontological realism is impossible, as meaning and reality are created by the subjective interpretation of the individual himself. Intersubjective and empirically verifiable knowledge is thus *logically* precluded. This, it seems, must do away with empirical social science as a possibility, with its demand for intersubjectively verifiable knowledge.

Further, the claim on the part of some constructivists is that structure determines agency, akin to Marxist theory, and that all facts are 'constructed'. It remains unclear whether this construction simply means something like interpretation, in which case constructivism says nothing new: epistemology concerns itself with hermeneutics as well as positivist epistemology, and in the IR field works on perception and misperception are well known in the debate on deterrence theory and in security studies in general (Jervis, 1976). There is a large literature on political psychology which deals with how individual actors interpret political facts.

But the constructivist claim seems to be much more radical: that structure *determines* agency, and that this structure is constructed in the eye of the agent. Finnemore thus argues that 'Material facts acquire meaning only through human cognition and social interaction . . . material facts do not speak for themselves' (1996: 6). This is clearly the case for many facts, such as ideological statements and most political debates: they are in need of interpretation, and this interpretation cannot claim to be objective. But this act of interpretation does implicitly refer to a correct, intended meaning: did he mean this or that? We are not at all interested in what your or my interpretation is, but in finding out what the speaker's intention was: what is it that he wants to say? What did he really mean? Thus, even political statements refer to some facts or intentions that are objectively present; and we need interpretation in order to unearth them.

With other types of political facts is it easier: their meaning is very clear and they do not need much interpretation. Nuclear warheads in the Kola pensinsula and the Chernobyl nuclear power plant certainly do not need much 'interpretation' in order to be recognised as objectively real. The political meaning of the nuclear warheads is very clear indeed: deterrence and defence. Thus, in many cases the facts do indeed speak for themselves; in other cases they need interpretation, but this does not mean that they do not carry an objective meaning which we can determine.

Thus, the epistemological claim of constructivists seems to be very different from both neo-realism and neo-liberalism, and to rest on an ontological claim which we think is fallacious. Granted, facts need interpretation, and some political facts leave much more room for subjective interpretation than others. Military capabilities and threats are among those facts that are most clear and unambiguous, whereas human rights are among those items that can mean a variety of things. But this is not to say that ontologically they do not exist, or that they can be interpreted at will. Human rights, like properties of other regimes, are to be interpreted according to certain canons. These canons are most clearly determined in the case of legal regimes where lawyers interpret the meaning of the regime.

Finnemore further argues that 'states are socially constructed entities' (ibid.: 4). She supports this argument by saying that 'there is nothing immutable about the state-as-actor' (ibid.). This is of course true: the nation-state came into existence in the sixteenth century, and is as such, historically a new type of polity. Empires, monarchies, aristocracies, city-states, oligarchies and papal states have preceded it, and all these are polities. But the fact that the nation-state is but one among many types of possible polities does not make it 'socially constructed'.

It exists *objectively* as a nation-state from the moment it is thus recognised in international law – which is why so many aspiring states ardently try to achieve diplomatic recognition, such as Kosovo and Taiwan. Statehood is a dichotomous variable: a territory either is, or is not, a nation-state. For instance, in the jungle of Colombia there are two large territories where the two major guerrilla groups FARC and ELN have all command and control in agreement with the Colombian government, but despite this these territories are not states. Other examples can be mentioned: Kosovo has tried every means to gain statehood, to the extent of opening an 'embassy' in Oslo in 1999. The Norwegian MFA pointedly refused any contact with this office, underlining its non-recognition. Further, East Timor is not yet a state, but is not a province of Indonesia either; Montenegro is not a state, but may become one.

While it remains true that much about a given state is constructed, such as the national identity, its national symbols, even language and customs, the physical territory over which the government has exclusive authority, in Weber's famous definition, does exist physically and objectively. The state's government has exclusive power to stop any transgressor of its borders, and has the exclusive right and duty to use force inside the state. These, along with diplomatic recognition, are the objective criteria of statehood.

As Rosas (1995) remarks, the traditional theory of legal sovereignty meant that a state ceased to exist if it were invaded and could not muster enough military resistance to throw the invader off. Military power one-sidedly determined whether a state existed or not. Today this is no longer so in the Western world, but the primacy of military power still holds in many parts of the Caucasus and Africa. Here we need to talk about the importance of military power, not of social construction. When Milosevic was to be arrested by the Kostunica government in late March 2001, he was able to command the loyalty and physical force of the army. This posed the most critical challenge to the existence of the Serb state: if Milosevic had managed to retain the upper hand in terms of physical force, he would have reinstated his regime, thereby overthrowing the new Serb regime. When we talk about statehood, control of physical force and legal recognition by others continue to be the key variables. These are objective variables that do not lend themselves to much interpretation one way or the other.

Risse, in his study of the impact of human rights, similarly calls his approach 'social constructivism', defining this as being a situation where interests are defined by an agent's identity. However, in his work there is no argument for the determination of agency by structure, but an openness to empirical investigation of how interests are formed (Risse et al., 1999). Constructivism, in his definition, means by his own account that interests are shaped by *identity* of the actors, but in his 'spiral' model of regime impact in human rights he also argues that human rights norms are accepted for purely *instrumental* reasons. What he calls constructivism simply seems to refer to the impact that is wielded by internalisation and learning in the actors, which in his model takes place *after* rulers in a given state have adopted these norms for instrumental reasons.

This use of the term 'constructivism' is very different from the claims of those who propose this as a metatheory with both ontological and epistemological claims. Risse's model is empirically testable, in its generation of hypotheses about the conditions under which human rights norms have an impact: first, they are adopted for instrumental reasons; second, and depending on the presence of transnational interest groups, they may become internalised domestically. It remains, however, unnecessarily confusing to call this approach constructivist when the term in empirical analysis simply refers to the ability of actors to learn and internalise new norms which in turn lead to changes in their interests.

Below we will discuss the formation of interests and the relationship between norms and interests, key issues for the determination of regime impact. Those who call themselves constructivists rightly point to the deficiencies in the neo-realist and especially the neo-liberalist conceptualisation of interest formation. Here there is much need for theoretical as well as empirical work on how interests are formed, and on how the international level and IOs have an impact. In pointing to the weakness of existing theories of interest formation, the constructivist criticism of other IR theory is useful.

Two models of regime impact: neo-realism and neo-liberalism

Above we have outlined the main features of both realism and liberalism. We have stated that the main difference between neo-realism and neo-liberal regime theory lies in the assumption that international regimes may have an autonomous impact. It is, however, unclear what is assumed in this respect, and the empirical work on regime impact is only in its infancy (Rittberger and Mayer, 1993).

In neo-realism, there are assumptions about anarchy as the main condition prevailing in the international system and the consequent lack of any impact stemming from norms or international institutions; about the state as the predominant actor in this system and the consequent lack of impact from non-state actors; about interests as exogenously formed, prior to international policy-making and thus only subject to change under new calculi on that level; and about the content of 'national interests' as being determined by geopolitical factors such as territorial defence or national economic expansion, and actor strength as being likewise determined by these factors.

Neo-realism assumes that there is no power vested in international institutions and organisations. Neo-liberalism, which today can be described as the mainstream approach in IR, assumes that international institutions (both 'deep' norms, organisations and regimes) play some role in constraining states' choices, freedom of action and even the way they define their interests. However, central assumptions of this model remain as the state as main actor, exogenous interest formation and material interest contents, as well as the consequent influence of the regime as being mainly that of providing a new calculus for states' interests: 'Until quite recently, regime analysis was confined to the study of inter-state relations, took state power preferences and interests as given, and largely ignored the role of non-state actors in the processes of international institution-building' (Risse-Kappen, 1995: 15).

This study is an attempt to develop and add to this theory inductively. We contest the view that interests need always be material and that they are always formed at the domestic level. This does not disprove the theory, but will be an indication of where and how it should be qualified and improved. The central assumptions – states as the only actors, interests as exogenously formed, and the open-ended view of the impact of international regimes – need empirical testing in order for us to say something about the two main assumptions and the degree to which the third aspect – the role and impact of regimes – is important. As Keohane has formulated the latter hypothesis: 'international regimes perform the function of establishing patterns of legal liability, providing relatively symmetrical information, and arranging the costs of bargaining so that specific agreements can be more easily made' (1990: 88).

However, we stated above that many regime theorists allowed for some regime impact beyond that of being an arena for a changed calculus. This suggests that regime impact goes beyond a simple arena for a new calculus and adds something more. Here we touch on two central assumptions in the neo-liberal variant of regime theory: one, that preferences are exogenously formed – the *locus* of interest formation; and two, that they change only as a result of a new calculus on the international regime – the *contents and causes* of change of preferences.

Regime impact

There is no theory in the literature of when and how there is generally autonomous regime impact, as there is no theory of the role of international institutions in general. There are, however, studies of cases that are worth noting, such as the studies of the impact of the EU in areas where it has only a shared competence with the member states. These studies, specified below, are generally useful because they deal with an IO where there is some legal power embedded. They show that a legal competence does not mean that a regime has an impact on states, but that it is a powerful precondition for such impact. Sometimes legal competences are used, sometimes not. Likewise, a shared competence or even lack of any legal competence in an EU regime may mean that it nonetheless has an impact – when conditions are favourable for EU-level policy in general; when the Commission is able to exert effective leadership; when policy areas can be subsumed under the umbrella of competition or trade policy; where there is legal supranationality, to mention some of the examples from the literature.

It is obvious that the EU has impacts in areas where it has an exclusive legal competence, such as in competition, trade or agricultural policy, but even in these areas it is *not at all obvious that legal supranationality is a necessary condition for regime impact.* The Commission will only be bold in using its legal powers when it has general support for EU-level policy-making; and conversely, it may not even need such legal powers when it has such 'backing'. The point here is that legal supranationality may not be the main variable in explaining why states comply with a regime or are in other ways influenced by them. This ought to be an obvious point, but is not. It is, however, the main argument of Chayes and Chayes who investigated why states comply with international legal as well as non-legal regimes. Compliance has mostly to do with the wish of states to be participants of good standing in international regimes and organisations – reputation plays a major motivating role – and with the recognition that power is enhanced by good standing.

Power in this view is less and less structural power in the military, geopolitical or economic sense, and increasingly intangible powers such as knowledge and expertise, mediating and brokering ability, and skill at persuasion. These authors argue that this is the 'new' way to assert sovereignty and we may add, this is the new way of furthering 'national interests'. On this logic, non-participation means marginalisation.

The implications of the above for the question of regime impact is that *if political power is increasingly intangible, then also regimes may wield it.* Non-state actors in regime settings, such as an international secretariat, may in fact possess greater powers than states in terms of intangible powers. The secretariat of the EU Commission may easily possess the best knowledge available in an area, and it may use this power to set the agenda in certain ways and thereby influence the outcome of negotiations that are formally intergovernmental. For instance, a study shows that the staff of the World Health Organisation (WHO) were the main actor in influencing the politics of the WHO. This was done through the use of expert knowledge and the using this as a pretext for defining the policy agenda in a certain way as well as influencing the implementation of policy through coalition-building in recipient countries.

What is not covered by the neo-liberal model, in the words of Chayes and Chayes, is the 'active role of the regime in *modifying preferences, generating new options, persuading the parties to move toward increasing compliance with regime norms and guiding the evolution of the normative structure* in the direction of the overall objectives of the regime' (1995: 229; our emphasis). The latter consist of international bureaucrats, secretariats and/or transnational alliances consisting of the former, along with national experts and representatives. These regime networks may be extremely important in both the interpretation of regime rules and thus, in its implementation.

We may now return to a renewed appraisal of the importance of legal powers of a regime. It is mostly not the threat of sanctions that makes legal power important, but the general norm of 'pacta sunt servanda': most of the time one obeys because one feels obligated to do so. This is the reality in most Western nation-states, and also in the regime compliance cases examined by Chayes and Chayes, which cover an impressive array of international legal regimes and treaties in various issue areas. But this point is not only relevant for the question of compliance; it is also a key to understanding regime impact.

The importance of legality

The international regime's secretariat interprets and applies the legal rules of the regime. In this process they are engaged with member states in an ongoing and extensive process of *justification:* they justify their interpretation and consequent application while the states offer their interpretation. The logic of the discourse is that of justification – what is the *correct* and *reasonable* understanding of a given rule? In this process states cannot simply invoke a 'national interest', but must argue strongly for their interpretation in a major effort at persuasion. As Abbot and Snidal remark,

> legal discourse largely disqualifies arguments based solely on national interests . . . this discourse imposes some constraints on state action: governments will incur reputational costs within the legal community and often beyond if they act without a defendable position or without reasonable efforts to justify their conduct in legal terms (2000: 29).

Thus, legalisation increases the reputational costs of non-compliance. However, some states disregard reputation: as discussed in general above, states outside the remit of Western public discourse may do so without much loss to reputation, but also hegemonic states, such as the USA in the present period, may elect to carry such a reputational cost. The US rejection of the Kyoto protocol on greenhouse gas emission reduction in March 2001 caused outrage among Western states. But the powerful position of the USA enables it to violate the norms of international society more easily than other Western states.

Regimes have become 'a focused and intensified arena of public justification' (Abbot and Snidal, 2000: 125) and the terms of policy-making have become largely *legal.* As the legal competence is the basis of all formal policy-making, the participants come to acknowledge the status and importance of these legal norms and rules simply by participating in discourses about them over extended periods of time.

Further, the *regime ultimately defines what legal regime norms must mean in terms of application,* and thus also what non-compliance means. Although state actors may have been important in this process, it is the regime that pronounces on what the 'correct' interpretation is.

From these considerations we can conclude that the legal character of regimes is important in ways other than of potential threats and sanctions, and contributes to strengthening the role of regime actors such as experts and bureaucrats in secretariats. Further, to the extent that intangible power resources become more important in international politics, we can assume that regimes have more of an impact.

This amounts to a stress on the importance of *persuasion* as a tool for furthering 'national interests' in international politics. While the regime actors may have the upper hand in managing the process of persuasion – as indicated above – states must at least participate if they are to be influential. Thus, there appears to be a logical connection between the types of power relevant to a particular decision-making situation and the impact of the regime in which decision-making is embedded. As stated before, *the more intangible power resources are involved, the more regime impact we can expect. This implies that the human rights regime can be expected to wield much independent impact through its regime-specific policy tools.*

This hypothesis is implicitly suggested by the discussion in Chayes and Chayes (1995), and is also present in the literature on international regimes. For instance, in the literature on the EU there has been a focus on the powers of the Commission, especially with regard to the importance of agenda-setting and expert-based networks, but little explicit theorising about what kind of political power is important in such a setting. Some studies in IR have turned their attention to the role of knowledge, such as the studies of 'epistemic communities' and the 'power of knowledge' (Haas, P. 1992; Haas, E. 1990).

There is a general suggestion in the literature on internationalisation that intangible power enables small states to be influential, and that they are also the building material for international regimes, which thrive on policy-making based on scientific input, expert-based solutions and input from international 'epistemic communities'. However, as of yet it is unclear whether the substance of policy is the independent variable, of simply an intervening one. What seems clear, though, is that more and more international policy-making involves intangible power resources rather than tangible ones in the sense that persuasion takes place in a discourse based on knowledge and justification.

This general fact may enhance the role of regimes, but also that of national government. Regimes typically possess both knowledge in the issue area as well as the formal right to interpret legal norms. Governments may build up actor capacity in terms of 'ideational power' despite being small. This does not suggest that geopolitical size or economic might is irrelevant, but that other sources of power are also important under certain circumstances.

This adds to the hypothesis about regime impact: *they may be expected to be important beyond arenas of new calculi.* They may also be providers of input to the policy process in terms of expert knowledge and setters and timers of the agenda, and channel this substantial policy input into the various phases of the decision-making process at optimal times for themselves. This list of potential regime impacts, however, requires attention to two aspects: the influencing institutions (norms, rules, practices, other regime-specific resources) as political resources that enable regime actors as well as state executives. *Therefore we need to specify under which conditions regimes can be expected to have independent impacts on states, and not only look at how state actors may utilise regime resources.*

Actors and loci of policy-making

So far we have talked about regime impact and the general role of international institutions and organisations. However, we need to specify who the actors in these regimes are. Neo-realism and neo-liberalism both see states as the main actors: in neo-realism states are the only actors, whereas in neo-liberalism states are the predominant actors, but as we have seen, non-state actors may also have important roles. They are, however, not seen as being of equal stature to states.

In the *interaction* between states and international institutions, both neo-realism and neo-liberalism posit states as the only relevant actors. Indeed, all important interaction is seen to take place through states.

The main departure from the two models outlined above in terms of actors is that there are other actors as well, not only states: media, norm entrepreneurs such as NGOs, and IOs themselves.

National actors – government representatives or civil servants – act within an embedded structure at home as well as in the regime. Formally they will have a mandate of some kind – promote a 'national interest' – and the changes they make to this in the course of policy-making will have to be justified in terms of the latter. When they act domestically, they have to persuade their colleagues that new positions make sense. The interesting question here is how and for what reasons positions change – are network participants motivated by a national interest or is this only a façade? Are they rather sharers of collegial and professional views of a problem, developing loyalty to the regime's view of the policy issue? Are interests instrumental and exogenous to the regime policy process, as neo-realism and neo-liberalism assume, or are positions formed much by the regime activity itself? These are some of the main empirical questions of this study and which concern the issue of regime impact in the literature.

Finally, *regime impact will probably vary between states*. Tonra (1997) found this to be the case, and it seems a rather commonplace assumption. Risse-Kappen ties together a focus on domestic structure, consisting of political institutions, societal structure and political culture (1995: 20). Regime effects can be assumed to vary with domestic structure in the issue area but also 'state autonomy and governmental control over policies are affected by the degree of the state's embeddedness in international structures of governance' (p. 29). The importance of domestic structure is underlined in a large literature on 'second-image reversed' causality, as well as on the literature centred around 'bringing the state back in' (see Moravcsik, 1993 and Risse-Kappen, 1995, for surveys). But as Risse-Kappen remarks, 'the interaction between international norms and institutions, on the one hand, and domestic politics, on the other, is not yet fully understood; work in this area has just begun' (1995: 31). As stated, this study is primarily concerned with the 'impactor', viz. the IO which impacts on various states, not with the 'receiving' end, the state itself.

The impact of values

Traditionally, theories of international politics operate with the assumption that states pursue national interests. These interests are material – security-based and/or economic. Realism and neo-realism both postulate that security interests are the real drivers of national action, and these interests are largely given by the geopolitical structure of the state. In neo-liberalism we find the same emphasis on material interests, although here these are primarily economic. It is unclear whether sheer power enhancement counts as a national interest as neo-realism seems to imply, but it must be assumed that the search for power and wealth sums up the traditional view of what national interests are all about.

There is little reason to doubt that these motivations are major ones in politics, but the universe of international affairs is rapidly expanding beyond this. Today there are a host of issues that require expert knowledge and which are clearly international in scope, such that solutions cannot be had according to national territories. It makes little sense to even speak about national interests in these cases. There are national positions on every issue that is dealt with internationally, but they are not given or indeed easy to deduce.

Thus, *the contents of national interests need not be material* – summed up in security and wealth. Increasingly they concern non-material issues, such as value questions of various kinds – the environment, human rights, etc. States will form national positions on these issues, and they will add to the set-up of traditional national interests.

In the many UN conferences in the last decade it is these value questions that have been at the fore. On the theories of neo-realism and neo-liberalism one should expect states to take little interest in these. But this has not been the case: they have been key actors and these states' positions have varied very much, and there have been severe clashes between them. Some states have promoted the environment; others have been wary. Some have fought vigorously for issues like abortion, called re-reproductive rights in UN parlance, while other states have been equally adamant in their opposition. At the conference on population and development in Cairo in 1994 there were more conflicts than in most international conferences; and the same was true in Beijing at the UN's Fourth World Conference on Women the year after.

This indicates that the national positions at these conferences were just as deeply held as traditional national interests concerning security-based and economic interests. Indeed, it seems only logical that value-based positions are strongly held because they are based on internalised convictions. Thus, what we henceforth call 'value-based interests' are also national interests, in addition to security-based and economic interests. They are rising to prominence at a time when international issues increasingly concern human rights.

Interest formation: instrumental and normative logics

Another feature of the traditional theories of interest formation is the assumption of instrumentalism. The caricature of this is Count Metternich's comment when his counterpart in negotiations, the Russian ambassador, died. 'I wonder what he meant by that', the count is reputed to have said.

Clearly much, if not most, political activity is instrumental: values are promoted because it looks good and human rights are often much less important than economic interests. The Western lack of nerve in being critical of China is an example of this: the punishment is loss of trade. But prima facie there is no reason why value-based interests are not really motivated by those values, thus, that they are promoted on a normative logic and not on an instrumental logic.

March and Olsen have pioneered work along these lines in their work on the logics of appropriateness and instrumentalism (1989). They underline that instrumental self-interest does not always motivate political action. The context of action may 'dictate' another response, according to what is considered appropriate in that specific context, but this is another kind of instrumentality: the adaptation to expected behaviour as a way to further one's own interests. March and Olsen, however, are not making this point. Rather they stress that instrumental interests-based political behaviour is only one type of political logic.

Thus, an interest need not be material, it can be value-based; and an interest need not be motivated instrumentally, it can be motivated by the norms themselves.

Thus, the argument is that national interests are based on material as well as non-material causes, and that value-based interests are becoming more important. Such interests are assumed to be rationally pursued, i.e. that the stakeholder pursues his or her interest in a manner which maximises the interest. Rationality means the ability to wield power wisely in the pursuit of a given end, viz. the interest in question. It is just as rational to pursue value-based interests as it is to pursue material interests. Human rights NGOs may be, and must be, expert tacticians, strategists and negotiators, in their pursuit of such interests, which both Finnemore (1996) and Risse et al. (1999) underline.

How are interests formed? This is a key issue in the field. Neo-realism holds that interests are largely given, by geopolitics and size of the state. Neo-liberalism holds that interests are formed at the domestic level, in a struggle between various stakeholders such as interest groups, rival political factions and business actors. However, interests may also be formed at the international level, in an interaction between domestic and international processes.

Thus far there is little knowledge of the impact that the international level has on domestic interest formation. The regime literature is preoccupied with the impact of regimes, and such impact is thought to go beyond a mere arena function. In the neo-liberal view, state interests are formed at the domestic level and presented in an international negotiation. The national position may be changed in the course of this negotiation, if the incentive structure makes it logical to do so. The *arena* function of the regime is that of presenting a new calculus in the interaction between various actors, which sometimes suggests a renewed definition of the national interest. Thus, interests change in international decision-making, but this change has mostly been attributed to new calculi.

However, if interests are not always instrumental, but move on a normative logic, we may expect learning, discussion and persuasion to be key movers for interest change. Here the regime and its actors, such as experts, secretariat, etc., may play independent roles in interest formation. National positions or interests may on this view also be formed by the international level. Here we may assume that scientific learning and epistemic communities play a role; likewise that international secretariats do the same. The UN conferences in the 1990s have only produced soft law documents, but the effect of this norm creation and norm diffusion onto the national level is probably a major one. Further, when organisations in the 'UN family' start to operationalise such norms, they take on real political effects.

The concept of value-based interests

The concept of interest in neo-realism as well as neo-liberalism is relatively unproblematic: states pursue 'national' interests that are largely given by economic and structural parameters.

However, the 'concept of the "national interest" . . . proves elusive' (Kratochwil, 1982: 1). Despite the fact that the concept has no substantive content, it continues to be used as one of the main bases in both neo-realist and neo-liberal models of IR. Whereas the older version of interests in Europe referred to a common understanding of *legitimate* interests within say, a balance of power system, contemporary versions refer only to self-interests. Kratochwil's discussion concludes that 'the discourse on interests had a discernible logic and the arguments it sustained had to satisfy certain criteria, which turned out to those of a weakened form of the public interest discourse' (ibid.: 25). He argues that in the modern neo-liberal as well as neo-realist version of interest, there is no such discussion. If political actors merely seek to maximise power, just as economic actors seek to maximise income, then it makes no sense to speak of '*national*' interests. He is indeed right in pointing to the weakness in political scientists' treatment of the key concept of interest. Usually assumed to be about self-interest, there is little discussion of how self-interest related to the nation-state or to politics as such.

We stated that interests were assumed to be formed at the domestic level in both these theories. The contents of national interests differed, however: in neo-realism security concerns that arise from geopolitical location come first – survival of the state remains the long-term goal. Economic interests are also determined by structural aspects. In neoliberalism the picture is much more undetermined, but actors are seen to struggle among themselves to achieve their own interest. But in none of these theories does one assume that interests are imposed or proposed from the international level. Even Putnam's sophisticated theory of two-level bargaining (1998) assumes that interests are generated at home, although he relaxes this assumption somewhat in some places. However, if one allows for the influence on national interest formation from abroad, then regimes may be the more important.

The assumption of domestically generated national interests is a logical one, given the set-up of the international system of formally sovereign states. There has to be an identifiable national position for any state officials entering into international negotiations. However, the fallacy here is to think that the existence of such a position means that it was generated *within* the state. If international politics is increasingly interdependent, and territorial borders mean less, then we can assume that national attachments mean less for the real definition of interests and that there is no clear demarcation between the national and the international in this respect. Actors at the domestic level act also internationally, and move back and forth in both contexts. There is no reason why we should assume that the 'national' interest is fixed and static once the actor moves to the international level. Thus, the determination of interests at the domestic level – an explicit assumption made in neo-realist as well as neo-liberal theory – has to be questioned. The *locus* of interest definition is no longer obvious.

Further, what if interest generation and change do not follow this cost/benefit calculus? If positions are influenced *substantially* by norms, institutions, and the process of persuasion and justification that may be important in policy-making, especially at the regime level, as Chayes and Chayes argue? We are here *not* suggesting that interests are *either* self-interested calculations *or* constituted by norms and institutions, but that they are not always the former. In other words, neo-liberal interest theory needs to be supplemented by a theory that allows for the study of other motivations and influences on interest formation and change.

March and Olsen (1989) suggest that norms do not only act as justifications for instrumental interests, but that they themselves influence and explain action. In the words of Katzenstein, 'obligatory action contrasts with consequential action. Behaviour is shaped not only by goals, alternatives, and rules of maximization or satisfying central to rationalist models of politics. Behaviour is shaped also by roles and norms that define standards of appropriateness' (1993b: 28).

Norms may influence actors and their identity, as argue March and Olsen, as well as the interests that they define. One may conceive of this approach as one that directly challenges both the ontology and the epistemology of the neo-liberal model. On such a view, human beings sometimes act on instrumental interests according to a cost–benefit logic, and sometimes act on a logic of appropriateness.

Here we seek to find out whether norms and institutions have an important bearing on the definition and/or change of interests at the IR level, thereby implicitly invalidating an interest approach that focuses exclusively on instrumental interests. In this we seek to develop the suggestion made for example by Krasner and Keohane above, which constitutes the main challenge for regime theory today: viz. to show in which ways regimes matter. It is implicitly suggested here that this ambition is irreconcilable with a theory of interests which posits interest formation at the domestic level and instrumental interests are the only relevant ones. Even if international regimes are conceptualised to matter beyond being mere arenas, it is hard to see how this is possible with the assumptions that are made about interests.

Interests are, by definition, intimately connected with instrumentality. An interest is something that has been defined within the context of how to reach it, entailing a strategic consideration. But interest pursuit is a *mode* of human behaviour; and does not determine the *contents* of the interest in question. This is where there is much confusion in the contemporary IR literature. On the one hand, one polemicises against a narrow definition of the contents of state interests – that they are either security-related, as in neo-realism, and/or economic, as in neo-liberalism. On the other, one postulates constructivism as an alternative, arguing that interests are learnt through the changes in the identity of the actors themselves, thus presumably privileging the impact of norms and values.

Here there is a false bifurcation. First, there clearly are security and economic interests on the part of every state, and these interests are largely given, especially the security interests. Geopolitics does matter: in the case of Norway, we would go so far as to say that geopolitics largely determines the relationship with both the USA and Russia. Second, economic state interests are also often given, and have to be pursued by a given state. Again, in the Norwegian case, the sale of petroleum and fish are the key sources of national income, and the promotion of these interests takes up a large part of Norwegian foreign policy. There is not much room, if any, for changes in these interests, and they both can and should be analysed within a neo-realist analytical framework.

Second, the *mode* of interest pursuit is confused with the *contents* of interests and the way in which they are formed. As stated, the concept of an interest assumes a certain instrumentality and rationality: the moment I have defined something as my interest, I also think about how to reach my goal of pursuing this interest. But this instrumentality does not say anything about the contents of this interest: it need not be economic or security-related at all. It can be value-based. For instance, when I, representing the Norwegian government, pursued women's rights or environmental causes, these were clearly interests that were hammered out at home, often in cooperation with, and under pressure from, interest groups, but they were not security-related or economic.

There are thus other interests in addition to these, and these other interests we propose to call 'value-based'. They are typically found in areas such as environment, gender, human rights, etc. Moreover, value-based interests are becoming more and more salient in world politics. The entire decade of UN conferences in the 1990s onwards, with themes such as population, development, women, environment, small arms and light weapons trade, child soldiers, housing and so forth, were about values and norms. All these themes engaged governments in serious conflicts and differing opinions, and the interests held by those who for example promote abortion as opposed to those states that do not, were clearly defined, arrived at in compromises with interest groups, and were pursued strategically, engaging the government representatives in question just as much – if not more – than do economic and security interests.

In sum, value-based interests are pursued with vigilance and determination, often with clever strategies of public diplomacy, and are certainly no less strongly held than security and economic interests.

Goldstein and Keohane (1993) come closest to this view of interests in their analytical framework for 'ideas and foreign policy change'. In their introduction to the various case studies they note that ideas do not constitute interests, but that they can inspire and form the basis for interest formation. As Weber correctly stated, 'Not ideas, but material and ideal interests, directly govern men's conduct' (Weber, 1968). Values or ideas have to be specified as interests in order to be influential in politics, but there is no prima facie reason why ideas and values should be less important than security- or economic-based interests. What we see today is that the remit of foreign policy includes more and more 'value questions'. It is thus to be expected that states have to develop interests in these fields, especially in response to international agenda-setting.

This brings us back to the question of the formation of value-based interests. We maintain that whereas security interests and to some extent, economic interests, are largely given by geopolitics and by natural resources, value-based interests are very different. The impetus to play a role and to profile one's government in these kinds of questions can be driven by domestic interest groups, for instance in areas such as gender or the environment, but can also be the deliberate choice of the government. The many UN conferences in the last decade have provided a major arena for such profiling of states, and almost all Western states have seen it as very important to have an active role in this public diplomacy. Also those states that have not shown an interest in proactive public diplomacy have been forced to develop national positions – interests – in this area. Only some Asian and African states have remained rather passive in this area, judging by the UN conference venues.

Interest formation for value-based interests can thus start at home, with the government's own strategic programme and/or the active work of domestic interest groups. It can, however, also start at the international level, through transnational advocacy coalitions (which are often connected to the state's domestic politics), or through IOs. Risse et al. (1999) argue that human rights norms impact only where there are vocal transnational advocacy networks, and that this is a condition for learning and internalisation of norms. But so far there have been no studies of how IOs impact on states in the human rights area. This study purports to do this, by analysing how the European human rights regime impacts on new democracies in Europe. The hypothesis here is that the regime in question, well defined, impacts differently depending on the regime powers each embedding IO commands, and also that the IO itself has an independent impact on these states.

The issue that the constructivists are preoccupied with, enters here: are norms and values influential in only an instrumental way, or are they so important that they change the identity of state actors, and in this way internalising new norms in a persistent manner?

Hypotheses and research design

The literature on the impact of human rights is still relatively small, and Risse's work is among the few that have generated hypotheses about *the conditions under which* such impact occurs and *how* it occurs. Finnemore and Sikkink's study (1998) of three cases of normative impact shows how governments gradually adopted the first Geneva Convention, but it fails to demonstrate whether this adoption came about for instrumental or persuasive reasons. Her argument is that an identity change occurs in actors, which in turn leads to an interest change. This is, as stated above, the core constructivist argument. However, empirical evidence of this kind of causal link is scant if non-existent, and in studies that claim such an identity change, there is little discussion of how such a change can be studied empirically (see e.g. Risse et al., 1999; Finnemore and Sikkink, 1998).

Most norm adaptation can also be explained in instrumental terms, as advantageous to the actor in question, for reasons of internal or external pressure, or both. One may venture to say that only in-depth, anonymous interviews could reveal the real motivations of actors. Prima facie there is, however, little reason to believe that actors are 'free' to change identity and follow their own convictions in matters of national positions. In my own foreign policy experience I found that almost all foreign policy was instrumentally motivated, constrained by geopolitical national interests, by economic ones and by national and/or national advocacy networks, etc. Even value questions were highly contested by major states, and traditional pressures from big powers – the USA, the EU and so forth, were brought to bear. The difference between value and other issues was that they involved more public diplomacy and non-state actors than in security and economic policy. Thus, at the outset it is not the constructivist hypothesis that seems warranted, but rather the instrumental one.

The *first hypothesis* is therefore that

> H1: Value-based interests are adopted by states for instrumental reasons, as responses to international pressures in the form of shaming and conditionality.

Risse also agrees that instrumental logic is behind the initial adoption of human rights norms in states that want to become members of Western-type organisations. He postulates that there is a 'spiral model' at work here, whereby initial adoption takes place for instrumental reasons and that persuasion happens – perhaps – later when there are vocal domestic groups that drive the issues. This may very well be – the literature on 'norm cascades' and the domestic internalisation of new norms strongly indicates that the importance of transnational advocacy networks are also key here (Matláry, 2001). However, much of this norm adoption may also be instrumental, for fear of criticism or marginalisation. Noelle-Neumann's empirical study of when opposition to a norm is silenced shows that fear of shaming explains this to a large extent: once a norm has become so acccepted that it is no longer tolerated in public opinion to oppose it, opposition is effectively silenced (1993). This means that power and not persuasion is also at work at this stage of value's impact.

What is meant here by instrumentality? The word connotes lack of internalisation and inner, real, persuasion. For instance, one embraces democracy because others expect one to do so, and because there are pressures to do so, often with punishment as the result of non-compliance. To comply is thus to one's advantage.

As proposed earlier, there are two reasons for compliance: *'shaming'* and *conditionality*. Chayes and Chayes (1995) as well as Koh (1997) found that legal regimes are complied with for reasons of 'shaming; one's international reputation suffers. This reason may at first seem to be a persuasive one, consistent with the claims of constructivism that not instrumental interests, but new identities emerge from learning and interaction. Over time this may indeed be so, although it is hard, if not almost impossible to prove empirically.[1] However, the 'shaming' reason is entirely consistent with instrumentality: as a state's reputation grows in importance for its credit ratings, investment rating, its access to aid and membership in international organisations, it is clear that it needs to pay careful attention to this factor. 'Shaming' and conditionality, which is the direct use of sticks and carrots, are both reasons for compliance which are instrumental.

The 'spiral' model is so far the most interesting and comprehensive theory about norm impact. The hypothesis is that the initial adaptation is carried out for instrumental reasons, as a result of external pressures. However, as new norms become the subject of debate, another logic enters, that of justification and argument. Here, argues Risse, instrumentality gives way to socialisation: 'Over time people come to believe what they say, particularly if they say it publicly' (Risse et al., 1999: 15). However, this remains a conjecture. Risse concedes that the empirical evidence in his book is not conclusive on this point:

> it is hard(er) to identify empirically the extent to which movement along the socialization path of our 'spiral' model can be accounted for by referring to instrumental interests and strategic bargaining among actors . . . as compared with argumentative rationality and processes of persuasion (ibid.: 250).

Of the cases investigated, he and his team found that all the states had reached the stage of instrumental adaptation and that argumentative rationality occurred, as Risse terms it, after this; but that does not means that persuasion occurs. This is a key point for the argument about socialisation. One might think that justification and argumentation according to human rights norms imply that socialisation takes place, but this is not easily proved. In fact, arguments according to legal and normative logic are typical of international regimes and international negotiations, yet this does not mean that the actors in this exercise leave their national interests behind. Risse seems altogether too optimistic about this importance of the discursive process, claiming that 'people become convinced and persuaded to change their instrumental interests, or to see their interests in new ways, following the principled ideas' (ibid.: 14). By the very process of engagement in discussion, actors are presumed to change interests: 'They become entangled in arguments and the logic of argumentative rationality slowly takes over' (ibid.: 16).

He also places 'shaming' in this category of socialisation, arguing that shaming, by creating 'in-groups' and 'out-groups', 'implies a process of persuasion, since it convinces leaders that their behaviour is inconsistent with an identity to which they aspire' (ibid.: 15). Again, here we take issue with the assumption of persuasion and interest change: actors rather see that their incentive structure has changed, and adapt accordingly.

As stated, we think one can only determine whether socialisation has taken place by in-depth and frank interviews with these actors themselves, and even then this issue may not be easy to determine: actors may want to say that they have learnt and internalised human rights norms because it sounds good and 'politically correct'. Noelle-Neumann in her book with the telling title *The Spiral of Silence* (1993) has analysed how opposition to new norms and norm change is effectively silenced once the norm has acquired enough domestic support to make it very unpleasant to have a divergent view. This means that instrumentality is much more important than persuasion, and that norms may change even in the absence of persuasion and socialisation. They may simply be adopted and accepted for instrumental reasons, also during the domestic public debate phase.

The *second hypothesis* of this study is that *international organisations have an independent impact on states*. This is dependent on the policy powers of the IO itself, and on the type of regime that is embedded in the latter. A legal regime may have its own court, or it may not. The court may be supranational, or not. A politically binding regime may be embedded in an IO with strong policy powers, such as the EU, or in one with weak powers, such as the COE. The regime itself determines which policy powers of the embedding IO are activated: if the human rights regime engages for example EU trade policy, there are strong tools that empower the regime. Thus, the human rights regime as outlined in this study, while consisting of the same elements, is variously embedded in the three IOs under study and therefore has differing impacts.

> H2: The stronger the policy powers of the embedding IOs, the more independent impact will result from the regime.

This is naturally an obvious statement, but we should recall how the debate about the 'arena vs. actor' function in regimes is a key one in the regime literature (Underdal, 1992). There is still scant empirical evidence of regimes as actors.

In this study we trace, first, how the human rights regime is embedded in each IO, specifying which *regime* properties it has (*legal/non-legal; specific/general*) and then which regime policy powers the embedding IOs has. As Goldstein et al. (2000) so well analyse, a regime may by itself contain strengths that make it more or less likely to be complied with. In addition, the embedding organisation disposes of policy powers that are specific to the IO in question, and which may be used to put power behind the regime. The extent to which the IO can do this depends on the centrality of the regime in question: for instance, the human rights regime in the EU was until recently hardly of much importance, but after 1993 the elements of this regime have become integrated in all trade and association agreements in the form of political conditionality. Thus, the EU today places considerable policy power behind this regime.

Another vital part of the delineation of IO policy powers is to determine what direct influence member states have on the IO in question. This analysis naturally tells us about the relative importance of states and IOs, which is necessary in order to assess the relative importance of the IO itself.

We shall study the impact of IOs, in contrast to both states and transnational NGOs. The role of the states will be discussed implicitly in the analysis of the IO's regime impact, for we have to delineate the ways in which the IO itself has powers. As regards the other set of actors, the NGOs, we seek to complement Risse's study which argues that it is the NGOs that play the leading role. We are not able to contrast the relative importance of these sets of actors here, but there is no prima facie reason why the NGOs should play the main role. After all, there are few if no NGOs in the Balkans, the Caucasus and in the former CIS states, and these groups do not play any significant role in Central Europe. Their role in impacting on human rights may therefore be greatly overestimated.

We should rather assume that it is first of all other states that are the most important actors in wielding power in this area, by putting pressure on the 'receiving' states. In the case of Milosevic's arrest, it was direct and public US pressure – with the 'price tag' of USD 100 million – that led to the arrest. The date limit for the arrest was set at 31 March, and the former dictator arrested some hours later.

Then we should assume that IOs, backed by member states, wield influence, and lastly, we should assume that transnational advocacy networks are important. The latter actors are probably more important inside a given state, in the process of formation of domestic opinion, than in the initial phase of norm impact from the international level.

The outline of the empirical part of this study is as follows. In Chapter 3 we presented the contents of the human rights regime of Europe. This regime is variously embedded in the three IOs we are studying; the COE, the EU and the OSCE. The regime itself is internally consistent and very well developed. It consists of the core values of human rights, democracy and rule of law. When delineating the regime, it is important to assess whether it is a 'strong' or a 'weak' regime. If it is a legal regime, we must ask whether it is equipped with enforcement tools, such as a court with enough jurisdiction to allow enforcement. Abbott et al. (2000) provide a useful typology for doing this. They ask whether the legal regime is strong in terms of *obligation* (what kind of language do we see in the regime?), whether it is *precise,* i.e. defining very clearly what the regime rules are; and finally, whether power is *delegated* to the regime so that it can enforce regime rules. The legal–political relationship can also be termed 'hard law–soft law'. The more legalised a regime is, the harder it is. Pure political agreements, such as the OSCE rules, are in the category 'soft law' . Abbott and Snidal (2000) have done useful work along these lines. Here we will ask first what the regime properties are: how was the regime formed, how internally consistent is it; why is it most developed on Europe? What is the content of the regime; how are its norms related to each other in terms of human rights, rule of law, and democracy?

In Chapter 5 we ask how the regime is embedded in the COE and how its strength can be measured. Here the regime is embedded in a court system with direct effect in the COE. In Chapter 6 we ask how the regime is embedded in the OSCE and what its impact is; and in Chapter 7 we do the same for the EU. These three chapters then discuss what the particular strengths of each IO are in respect of how they are embedded. Here we look at the policy and legal tools of the organisation, but also at the extent to which states constrain regime actors. How much power rests in the regime itself? How much is accounted for by member states? If we find that member states are unable to fully control the regime, we have important findings for the question of autonomous regime impact.

The chapters then go on to document and assess actual regime impacts in new member states or candidate member states. These include Central Europe, the Balkans and CIS states.

In Chapter 8 we discuss the role of values in hard power intervention.

Part II

The Impact of the Human Rights Regime

5
The Impact of the Council of Europe

In this part of the book we look at the actual impact that the human rights regime has on states that are new to the world of democracy, rule of law, and human rights. Europe after the Cold War offers a historically unique laboratory for testing theories of international politics. After 50 years of communist rule, all of a sudden states with some, but not much, democratic experience became *de jure* democracies. Most of these states had experienced the Second World War just prior to the communist takeover, for example Poland, Hungary and the former Czechoslovakia. These states were truly European in terms of culture, education and values, but their development had been 'frozen' by Soviet dominance and the imposition of communism. This was also true for the Baltic states.

Further to the east and south, we have states that are far from being as European and developed as the Central European ones. The former Soviet republics, such as the Ukraine, Belarus, Moldova and the states of the Caucasus, are now on their way into European organisations and networks. These states have no democratic tradition at all, and are suddenly expected to perform as independent states and to conform to the standards of the European human rights regime. All of these states are OSCE members, and there are OSCE missions or an OSCE presence in all of them. In Belarus, the OSCE mission is the only Western presence in the entire state. The ambassadors of Western states were withdrawn in 1997 when they were thrown out of their premises by the whimsical dictator Lukashenko.

To the south in Europe we have the Balkans, now renamed 'South-East Europe' in political parlance in order to avoid the rather stigmatised expression 'Balkans'. The Balkans proper include Albania, FYROM,[1] Bosnia, FRY[2] and Croatia, although the latter country has always resisted being included in this group. Then we have Bulgaria and Romania, not Balkan states, but situated in south-eastern Europe.

The states of South-East Europe are partly candidates for the EU, some of them being in the process of preparing for membership. Bulgaria and Romania are in the group of applicant countries which are in a formal process towards this end. Croatia and Serbia have developed close ties with the EU after the democratic elections in both countries, and the EU's sanctions against Serbia have been lifted. The Balkan states are all members of the OSCE, and Serbia which was suspended from 1992, was readmitted in 2000, as a reward for the democratic development earlier that year. In terms of the COE, all the Central European states are members and were admitted early in the 1990s, while the Ukraine, Moldova and Croatia were admitted some years later. Bosnia is still a candidate for membership, while Armenia and Azerbaijan were admitted in December 2000.

As is evident, there is considerable activity on the part of the IOs in this study towards these states. The OSCE has had most of them as members all the time, only with the exception of the suspension of FRY in 1992. The COE has chosen to admit as many new states as possible, given the requirement of some progress towards democracy and rule of law. The EU has the most stringent admissions practice, but EU membership entails much more than membership in the other two organisations. Also, the impact of the EU is in general much larger, given the wide spectre of reforms and programmes in the association process. This probably 'spills over' in the specific domain of the human rights regime.

In the following three chapters we analyse the impact of the human rights regime as it is embedded in the COE, then the OSCE and the EU. Each chapter follows the same structure: first, we look at the *general* impact of the IO in foreign policy, on its powers and policy tools. Here it is clear that the EU ranks first as the most important IO, then comes the OSCE and lastly the COE, but that does not imply that it is the same 'ranking' for *regime-specific* impact. This specific impact, which is the object of this analysis, depends on a number of factors: on the embeddedness of the regime – that is, on the general IO strength, but also on the tools of the regime itself, such as rule specificity, legal vs. political status, monitoring and implementing mechanisms and so on.

The states under scrutiny for each IO do vary because there is no 'natural' population of states that 'fit' with all the IOs together. We have chosen, as far as possible, similar cases where two or more of these IOs have attempted to impact on a given state. There are two groups of states: the Central European states, the Visegrad countries, fall in the 'sophisticated' category where shaming is hypothesised to have an impact; the second group of states are in the Balkans, the former USSR, in particular the Caucasus, and in these states we expect incentives and punishment to play a key role in explaining human rights compliance.

The time frame of the influence of each IO also varies: first in time after 1990 the OSCE made its impact felt, and all the states in question automatically became OSCE members once the USSR disintegrated. Then the COE came on stage from 1990, accepting new states as members very quickly. The EU was the last in terms of membership negotiations, but had some programmes in the Visegrad states prior to this stage. The IO impact therefore falls in stages.

For the COE, we look at the Ukraine, where the COE has conducted fact-finding missions and repeatedly demanded compliance with commitments undertaken; then we also look at the COE's role towards Chechnya/Russia, as both the COE secretary-general and the commissioner for human rights have taken specific measures here. We further analyse the role of the COE in the Balkans, in Albania and in Bosnia. Finally, we look at the COE's more general role in terms of the court, and here Turkey stands out.

Turning to the impact of the OSCE in Chapter 7, we have selected some cases which are partly overlapping with the COE cases: Chechnya/Russia is one, then in the Balkans, Bosnia and Albania; and further Kosovo/Serbia. In addition we have some interesting new material on Azerbaijan which the OSCE's way of introducing human rights, but where the COE was also involved. This concerned the parliamentary elections in 2000. We also look at the impact of the high commissioner for national minorities, especially in the Baltic states.

To study the EU's impact in the human rights area in Chapter 8, we have chosen to look at two groups of states: one is the regime-specific impact on the candidate countries in the Visegrad group; the other is the impact of possible accession, and its effect on states like Croatia and Turkey, both a long way from membership, but extremely eager to attain this goal. The other class of states are those that cannot be considered for membership, but where the EU has a very active role in the regime area: the Balkan states of Serbia and Bosnia, to single out the most important of these. Although the EU is far from being the most important actor in the field in the Balkans, it has a considerable role that is often overlooked.

Thus, the cases of this study are not directly comparable, and could never be, as the three IOs have chosen different states and have different mandates in those states. The 'outer' ring of the OSCE included all the states at the end of the Cold War – the CIS states were successor members from the Soviet Union. As members already, these states did not have to 'perform' in order to be inside a Western organisation.

The 'second' ring is the COE. Also here new states were admitted before they were democratic in any meaningful sense of the word, but they had strings attached when they entered, and it was not automatically easy to do so. Bosnia is still in the antechamber to membership because there is no real multi-party system in place and there are too many local 'warlords' who in reality rule. The EU is much more selective in its membership, and spends a lot of money and energy on preparing members. The 'inner' circle is thus much smaller than the other two.

In terms of time, we see that the three IOs differ as to *when* there was an impact on their part. The OSCE was present from the very beginning of the post-Cold War period, the COE made its presence felt gradually, but it was also part of the foreign policy of the Visegrad states from the start of the 1990s, and during the decade admitted several of the other states. The EU has not yet admitted any of these states, but has extensive cooperation across both political and economic areas with several of them. There is thus an impact from several IOs in the same state simultaneously.

However, this influence does not take the same form or engage the same political processes. The COE meets twice a year at ministerial level, twice a year at parliamentary level in Strasbourg, and monitors compliance in selected human rights fields. The state in question sends its own reports. It is rare that the COE sends a fact-finding mission or establishes a presence in the state itself. When a case is in the court, it is argued by the lawyers assigned to it there. Thus, the COE does not act directly in and on the state unless there is an exceptional situation, but works slowly to make changes in the rule of law institutions in a given state. As a rule, it is only when there is a very grave breach of human rights that the COE acts in other ways, using public diplomacy and travelling to the state itself.

The OSCE, however, has a presence in the states discussed here, and often has a mandate that confers powers to intervene directly in the state's government and to use public diplomacy very actively. The OSCE makes for a very visible presence, but the state itself has the power to change the mandate. But as long as an OSCE mission is in place, it is usually very well known and visible in the state, and is perceived as the representative of the international community.

The EU's impact is visible in the states close to membership: in the assigned personnel under the 'twinning' agreement[3] who work, as expatriates, in the ministries and local government of the state in question. Also, the EU Commission's embassy in each state will play a leading role in terms of foreign presence, in addition to the US embassy and the embassy of the presidency of the EU. The Commission is, however, the key player vis-à-vis the applicant state, and as such, very important as a 'listening post' which reports back to Brussels.

Thus, it is possible to discern *who* influences *what* in these states to a great extent. The states who are on the 'receiving end', as it were, are all *demandeurs,* those who demand something; it is they who are the dependants in this case. They want membership in the EU, they want investments and therefore a good international reputation, they want aid money, and they want security by being included in Western organisations. There is at the ouset a *clear power asymmetry* between these states and the IOs in this study, and this allows us to infer that they will comply with IO demands.

We discussed the question of compliance at length in Chapter 4, arguing that the reason for compliance is basically *instrumental.* IO pressures include: the fear of shaming because it damages the chances of both membership and foreign investment; the realisation that the human rights regime is the only ideological alternative in the world today, and that investments will only come when rule of law is real. There may of course be learning in the form of internalisation and socialisation taking place, but this is in any case very hard to show empirically. It can only be done through in-depth interviews with actors. But the interesting fact is that instrumental adoption of the human rights regime is logical because all the reasons mentioned above pull in the same direction, viz. towards not only 'talking the talk' of human rights, but also of complying by implementing them. As we shall see below, in some of the cases they have barely learnt to 'talk the talk', and do not know that non-implementation will be exposed. Two such cases are the Ukraine and Azerbaijan. In other cases, such as Croatia, they have learnt that implementation simply has to happen after a given time period – a kind of 'period of grace' tolerated by IOs. And finally, in Central Europe, they are hard at work on implementation because they have realised that there will be no EU membership without it.

The Council of Europe as a foreign policy actor: tools and powers

The Council of Europe (COE) was founded after the Second World War by 12 states eager to ensure that democracy would reign on the continent. It has indeed been a major achievement – not caused by the existence of the COE, but by many other factors as well – that war between European states is unthinkable today. Admission to the COE is seen as a *major qualifier* for a new state.

As mentioned, the OSCE constitutes the 'outer ring' of the European organisations, having membership from Vancouver to Vladivostock, as it is commonly put. The OSCE is not a strictly European organisation with its US and Canadian members, but its main membership is nonetheless European.

The COE is the 'second ring' of membership for new states. In the period after the fall of the Berlin wall there has been an extensive expansion of the membership, including the Baltic states, the Balkan states (except FRY), the Central European states, Russia, as well as Ukraine, Moldova, and in late 2000, Armenia and Azerbaijan. Thus, the borders of Europe are effectively defined in a wide circle, but each state admitted to one of the IOs must agree to become a respecter of human rights, democracy and the rule of law.

The core tasks of the COE are made up of the human rights regime proper, the ECHR, and its supranational court of human rights. This regime-specific tool is without doubt the most important part of the IO in terms of compliance control. But the Council of Ministers and the Parliamentary Assembly (PA) also play important roles in monitoring and imposing human rights compliance, in a new and more proactive way after 1998. Finally, there are bodies attached to the COE, such as the so-called Venice Commission, which is charged with education for constitution-making and the rule of law. This commission, made up of legal experts, does major work on helping new member states develop their legal and judicial institutions.[4] The many new treaties that the COE has developed over its more than 50 years of existence, more than 170 of them, also place major new obligations on it. Many of these have monitoring mechanisms in the form of committees of experts who work on state reports on implementation submitted to them, but the specific treaties often deal with areas outside of the human rights regime proper.

The COE's secretariat has about 1600 staff, and as such is bigger than the OSCE with its mere 250 permanent staff at HQ in Vienna, but much smaller than the EU Commission with about 13 000 officials. The core mandate of the COE is the human rights regime, which is our concern here, but also includes social cohesion and culture. The Second Summit in the COE's history, in Budapest in 1997, agreed that it should consolidate its work on the core mandate. During the years there have been too many new tasks added on to this core, and the COE needed to show a clearer profile.

Outside of the core tasks are projects on children and school curricula, culture and social affairs, and the fight against corruption. These themes are, of course, related to the rule of law and democracy, but are not key ones in this. For instance, GRECO, the group of states against corruption, is a new actor inside the COE charged with monitoring two conventions in this field. Many other such groupings and committees could be mentioned here, but the point is to illustrate that the COE consists of a *vast network of legal and quasi-legal bodies that work on monitoring and compliance of specific conventions.*

The COE as a general foreign policy actor in Europe is not very high profile. One would not look to the COE first if asked to name IOs with such a mandate. For many years the COE was a comfortable club of like-minded democracies, which played a major role only occasionally in post-war Europe: when Greece withdrew before it was suspended after the coup in 1967; or when the Central European state Hungary was the first to enter the COE after the Cold War.

But in the latest decade, from 1990 onwards, much has happened. New members have been admitted long before they were ready in terms of being democracies with rule of law in place, and the COE has undertaken a major effort to teach them how to install these institutions. The COE has also become much more proactive, something both needed and desirable. In my conversations with both the outgoing secretary-general of the COE, Daniel Tarschys, who left in 1999, and the incoming, Walter Schwimmer, they both stressed the need for the COE to become more visible on the European scene and in the field, as well as becoming more adept at using compliance mechanisms other than 'shaming'. They now deal with states where there is no democratic tradition, and must use much more clear-cut means in order to succeed.[5] The COE has thus undergone a *major change* in the latter part of the 1990s in terms of strategic thinking and the development of new policy tools and a new policy style; whereas it used to be a community of rather like-minded jurists who would settle things in discreet and well-mannered fashion in Strasbourg, one now has to add to this tradition a much more proactive and political profile in order to deal effectively with new member states and their commitments. This is an exciting and risky time for the COE: will it succeed in this endeavour, or will its work largely be superseded by the EU's new task expansion? There is clear overlap between the work of the three IOs in this study, and it would be naïve to assume that they do not compete for political space and attention.

Regime-specific tools of the COE

The COE has several tools at its disposal for the promotion of the norms of the human rights regime. First, the ECHR is the most advanced legal machinery in the world for the promotion of human rights: the European Court of Human Rights in Strasbourg issues rulings that have a *direct effect* in the member states, and *individual citizens have a right of petition* in all the states that have ratified the ECHR, regardless of what their state may think of their case. This is in fact a supranational juridification of human rights that is equalled only in the newly created but not yet operative International Criminal Court (ICC), with the difference that the ICC will only be able to hear cases when national procedures have been exhausted. The European Court may also be compared with the ad hoc tribunals for Yugoslavia and Rwanda, but still with the difference that with the court, each and every citizen can bring a case before it. In this sense it is the most supranational of all institutions in the state system today, although the EU Court in Luxembourg, the ECJ, also judges with direct effect in the member states, and individuals and firms can bring cases before it.

Impressive as the European Court and the ECHR are, the COE has in very recent years also acquired new political tools for ensuring compliance with its norms. After 1990, it has doubled its membership, accepting in rapid succession virtually all the Central European states, the Baltic states, the Balkan states and some CIS states as well as Russia. This so-called 'therapeutic admission' was not undisputed, and it meant that the COE has had to become operative as a democracy-building organisation, somewhat akin to OSCE.

In addition to courses, in-kind aid, and workshops in the new member states, the COE developed two sophisticated monitoring mechanisms after 1997; one *public* procedure in the Assembly, and a *secret* procedure in the Committee of Ministers. The actual workings of these tools are largely unexplored in both the scholarly as well as the popular literature. But this does not mean that this work is unimportant. There is, however, little analysis in general of the COE by political scientists as such.

The expansion of the COE: therapeutic admissions and new tasks

In the period 1990–2000 the COE expanded its membership by almost doubling it, including almost all the new states in Europe and beyond. These admissions were not uncontroversial, and were dubbed 'therapeutic admissions', pointing to the fact that these states were far from being democracies with rule of law and respecters of human rights. Huber refers to the debate surrounding whether or not to include them, pointing out that it was not new in the COE's history to admit states that were in the very process of becoming democratic, such as readmitting Greece in 1974, admitting Portugal in 1976 and Spain in 1977. The analysis within the COE has been that membership has contributed to democratisation, and the very same analysis has laid the foundation for the inclusion, in very rapid succession, of states in Central Europe, the Balkans and beyond (Huber, 1999: 7).

Hungary was the first Central European state to join in 1990. Like all new states in the COE, it first acceded to the European Cultural Convention. This convention, based on the assumption of a common European cultural heritage, serves as the 'antechamber' of membership. Hungary's leadership was well in tune with the democratic principles of the COE, whereas in most of the other states in the region there was still authoritarian leadership. Almost all the COE's conventions were open to non-member states, but none of these states had acceded to any of them. By the mid-1980s, relations with Hungary were well developed, but they were poor with these other states.

In the COE, members are admitted by the Council of Ministers, but only after the opinion of the PA has been elicited. Thus, in the COE, the PA has real power. It investigates applicant states by making detailed reports by its various committees, sends missions, and initiates interparliamentary contacts. The committees that report are the Political Affairs Committee, the Human Rights and Legal Affairs Committee, and the Committee on Relations with Non-Member Countries. The inquiries can take several years, where committee members work closely with the applicant state, and where there are several types of COE programme in democracy-building to aid the prospective member state. In this process these committees play roles akin to that of the Commission in the EU, albeit on a much smaller scale.

After Hungary's successful application, Poland was next in line. Here opinions were more divided. Eventually Poland was admitted, but with *specific conditionality* for the first time: for instance, elections would be held in the spring of 1991, and they would be observed by the COE.

All the later entrants have gone through the same procedure: first accession to the European Cultural Convention, then a period of assessment and entry, which means acceptance of the ECHR and the specific conditions applicable to each state. Some states have been knocking on the door for several years, such as Bosnia, which has special guest status in the COE's ministerial meetings, and naturally uses these occasions for lobbying.[6] The interesting factor here is that admission is obviously seen as being of key importance to a state's reputation and standing.

The admission in late 2000 of Armenia and Azerbaijan raised fundamental questions about the borders of Europe. These two states cannot be said to be either democracies or European, but the decision of the COE shows that it intends to include states rather than keep them out. This also means that there is a precedent for defining Europe far to the east and south: Turkey has been a COE member for a long time, and is now a formal candidate country for EU membership. The Caucasus is, however, a 'powder keg' on a par with the Balkans, but this has led to the COE becoming engaged there rather than distancing itself. This new membership in the august and traditional political body in Strasbourg implies a radical change to the COE's procedures; in order to be effective, it simply has to develop new ways of working. This development was well under way in 2001.

What is the *general* impact of the COE as a foreign policy actor? This is a question that is hard to answer. Until recently it was unseen in European public diplomacy, working in legal ways, silently ensuring compliance through the cumbersome procedures of a large number of international treaties. But after the Cold War the COE has chosen to admit new members that completely lack the democratic tradition of Western Europe, and has followed suit by developing new tools. It is still too early to assess how the COE will succeed in what amounts to a new role for itself. There has been no lack of soul-searching in the COE itself. As mentioned, both the former secretary-general Tarschys as well as his successor Schwimmer have repeatedly stressed the need for renewal of the COE.

Thus, the COE has not been very visible in the European foreign policy debate, but this may change. As we shall see below, a more proactive role has been attempted in the case of Chechnya.

However, the conclusion on the general foreign policy impact of the COE is that it is quite modest. The tools 'with bite' are primarily the legal ones, especially that of the court. One may perhaps more adequately say that that the legal impact of the COE is considerable, but the political impact is small. This is only natural, as the only foreign action that receives much attention is the public diplomacy of travel to a 'hot spot' and diplomatic statements immediately afterwards, referring to an event. Slow, detailed work of a legal kind does not easily receive such attention. However, it is a fact that the judgements of the court have received much more attention at national level during the last few years, and this is consistent with the increased interest in human rights. There are also more proactive policy tools used by the COE that mark a more visible political profile in human rights. These are discussed below.

The court still remains the key actor of the COE system.

The impact of the European Court of Human Rights

The ECHR and its court are the key instruments of the COE. The court has one judge from each member state, all in all 43 judges, and a large apparatus in its new building in Strasbourg. However, with the entrance of new members, the case load has increased: there is now a backlog of more than 11 000 cases. Most of them will never make it to the full court treatment, but they will need to be reviewed before they can be rejected. There is a major increase in cases from the new member states, especially from Poland and Hungary,[7] and this means that 'waves' of cases can be expected from these states once they become familiar with the possibility of individual petition. The president of the court, Luzius Wildhaber, stressed the need for more funding, saying that it is impossible to work on the backlog with its present size. The court got additional funding for 2001, but it was not enough. The danger exists that the backlog will present such big problems of court capacity that its normal work will be delayed, and it will lose legitimacy for this reason.

The financial problem is generic to the COE as such, and is a graver problem now than before because the mandate of the COE is being 'taken over' by the EU in the field of human rights. As long as the EU does not have a treaty-based human rights regime in the form of a convention, the COE still has the only human rights court in Europe, but the moment the charter of the EU is incorporated – possibly in 2004, at the next IGC – the danger exists that it will duplicate the role of the COE. Also, the OSCE's main field of work, on-site missions and democracy programmes, is being imitated to some extent by the COE – or should one say 'complemented'? The danger persists, however, that the COE is moving into the OSCE area of action where there is also the danger of duplication. It is clear that the COE does not have the institutional set-up that field operations require.

The court needs more resources in order to fulfil its mandate, especially under the new conditions of so many members without any democratic and judicial tradition. The president of the court is quite clear about this need, but realistically one cannot see funding easily forthcoming, with much member state attention focused on the EU, also with prospective entrants.

The court has been reformed in recent years. As of 1998, it no longer has a human rights commission which reviews cases before they are admitted to the court. Now there is only one court which both views initial submissions of cases and which judges (protocol 11 to the ECHR, 1998). The intention is that only the judges shall be responsible for the entire legal process.

The court has one judge from each member state, and with the admission of so many new states, the caseload has increased dramatically. The cases registered with the court number, as mentioned, about 11 000, whereas the number of cases that are admitted are 6–8 per cent of that. After the reform of the court it is the judges themselves who decide on admissibility.

Also, the right to individual petition has been improved. It used to be necessary for the state where the plaintiff lived to recognise the competence of the court. Now, however, individuals can bring the case directly to it (Drzemczewski, 1999b). The independent functioning of the court has thus been strengthened. This is, needless to say, a major improvement in terms of the human rights logic. The court is now *entirely independent of the state logic* in the right of individual petition.

There has also been an increase in the budget for hearing witnesses 'on location' in states like Turkey, Russia and the Ukraine. More and more often the judges have to go on interview missions in the states themselves, a more costly and cumbersome procedure, but also one that promises more effective impact. The knowledge in the member states that the court's representatives may come on such a visit makes it more visible and present in national politics. It is not a faraway institution in Strasbourg, but part of the calculus of national politics.

The court process, both of screening of cases and of rendering judgements, thus takes time, effort and money. This is what it is mandated to be: an impartial court that is able to render ultimate judgements in complex cases involving nationals from all European states and even beyond. But given the problems of execution, what is the rate of implementation?

In the history of the court we find the surprising fact that its rulings have all been implemented by the member states apart from one case against Turkey; the so-called Loizidou case.[8] It concerns a woman whose house in North Cyprus cannot be used due to the Turkish occupation. The court judged that Mrs Loizidou be paid damages by the Turkish state in a judgement in 1998, but Turkey responded that this case, and the many others on the same basis that are pending, will only be settled after a political settlement of the Cyprus issue has been reached.

Both the COE and member states have protested against this unique case of non-compliance with the court's rulings in very strong language: 'deploring that Turkey has not yet complied';[9] 'strongly urged Turkey to review its position'. It is seen as absolutely unacceptable that a state can place political conditionality in a human rights case such as this, thereby making it into a political question instead of a legal one.

The high rate of implementation in Western Europe, which has been the remit of the court until recently, can be explained by the similarity in legal and political tradititions in these states, but also by the high degree of legitimacy that the court and the convention enjoy. One does not contest the judgements of a court that one has erected and accepted, and it is generally seen as highly unacceptable to do so when a judgement goes against one's own state. That is certainly not the time to contest them if one wants to be seen as a responsible and legitimate actor in the international system. It has thus become the custom that Western governments simply note the judgements rendered in their disfavour, and take the necessary measures to comply.

It will be interesting to see if the new member states are able to follow this norm. In Western democracy, there is a very strong norm not to mix politics and the law, and politicians therefore never enter into discussion about the substance of a judgement, but accept it as valid for them.[10]

The human rights monitoring machinery and its impact

The new states in the COE, however, present a new challenge: they have to be *taught* what the rule of law means and how to develop it in practice. The COE has therefore realised that it is not enough to render judgements on these states, and expect that their house will be put in order. There has had to be developed, as Checkel also notes, a set of 'carrots' as well as 'sticks' (Checkel, 2000a). The COE, like the OSCE and the EU, employs conditionality as well as teaching and persuasion. In 1998 two new human rights monitoring mechanisms were adopted: one public one, where 'shaming' plays a key role; and one discreet procedure, where persuasion and learning play the main role.

The COE, 'in so far as monitoring is concerned, has to become more pro-active', states the head of the monitoring unit of the COE (Drzemczewski, 1999a: 4). This has resulted in the adoption of additional and specific criteria for admission of new member states with fragile democracies, but also monitoring mechanisms, both in the PA as well as in the Council of Ministers.

When a new member is admitted, that state must sign and ratify the ECHR rapidly, which means that one accepts the individual right of petition to the court. Thus, the legal mechanisms are accepted immediately. However, it has also been viewed as necessary to have a compliance monitoring mechanism, which also creates pressures on the state in question.

Twice a year the Council chooses a theme within human rights, democracy and rule of law on which to monitor and test member states. The themes examined in the 1996/97 were freedom of expression and democratic institutions, including elections. In 1998 the themes were the judicial process and local government.

The procedure is that all member states report on their laws and practices in these fields. The council consults other evidence and information, such as the OSCE, the EU, etc., while making its own assessments. These are returned to the member states, which in turn comment on them. The entire text is circulated to all member states, but it is not published. In session the Council of Ministers discuss improvements with the states that are criticised, and make conclusions which are to be followed up (see COE documents: 'Monitoring of Compliance . . . 1999; 'Compliance with . . . , 1999; Drzemczewski, 1999a).

The Council of Ministers may then issue an opinion or recommendation – which naturally is public; it may send a communication to the PA in order for them to act publicly; or it may act to suspend the state in question from the COE. There is one case of such suspension in the history of the council, viz. Greece in 1969, an action spearheaded by the Nordic states. Greece had, however, acted in anticipation of this, and withdrew from the COE before this date. It was later readmitted.

In the PA there is a *public* monitoring procedure. The PA wields real power in the admission of new states because its opinion must be sought before the council invites new members. Also, in the monitoring procedure, the PA may be more influential than the Council of Ministers simply because its criticism is public. When the issue is suspension of a member state, the PA must also be consulted, and according to the COE itself, this provides the PA 'with considerable political weight' (Drzemczewski, 1999a: 7).

There are also consultations between the two bodies, and the secretary-general has a right of initiative. He can solicit information from any member state on a human rights situation, despatch delegations, and make recommendations. This has been done with much more frequency over the last few years. Secretary-general Walter Schwimmer takes a proactive approach to his job. He seeks to be more visible by undertaking trips, using his right of initiative, and by coordinating the tools of the COE.[11] Recognising that 'given the nature and the scale of the human rights problems that have arisen in the wake of the enlargement process, the traditional treaty-based approach is no longer sufficient in all cases'. [12]

The high commissioner for human rights

In 1999 a new institution was added to the COE 'toolbox', viz. a high commissioner for human rights. The commissioner does not have legal mandate, but will supplement the court and council. The first commissioner is, however, a lawyer – Spanish law professor Alvaro Gil-Robles – but underlines that his office is non-legal in approach and agenda.

I conducted several meetings with him right after taking office, when he was in the process of fleshing out his mandate. He stressed the need to be proactive and visible, desiring to travel to the 'hot spots' of human rights abuse, and to play a role in public diplomacy. He wants to set the agenda by rapid reaction and on-site visits. *Inter alia* through his long-standing friendship with Russian foreign minister Ivanov he was able to make a visit to the Russian-dominated areas of Chechnya in late 1999.[13]

The office of high commissioner for human rights is meant to complement the court, with its legal competence, and the council and the

PA with their political monitoring mechanisms. The high commissioner will not himself engage in individual cases, but will make on-the-spot visits to highlight problems, and act as a liaison between states and the council secretariat. The high commissioner enjoys a major freedom of initiative, according to his very general mandate.[14] The first visit made by the first commissioner was to Moscow, on the subject of Chechnya. This visit attracted major press attention, an important tool in applying pressure. The commissioner intends to use similar tools in the future.

The fact that the COE has erected an office of high commissioner for human rights is itself indicative of the perceived need to be more visible and proactive in this policy field. The legal part of the COE's mandate, the ECHR and its court, will of necessity have to work slowly and without much press attention. The tools for ensuing compliance are therefore limited, although the norm of 'auto-compliance' that we have seen at work in Western Europe has been important in the COE's history so far. However, the Western states are committed to the norm 'pacta sunt servanda'. In line with the findings of both Chayes and Chayes (1995) and Koh (1997), these states do comply because it is the done thing. In other words, it is not necessary to be able to force them to comply. The combined 'sticks' of possible shaming for non-compliance and a resultant loss of reputation with the so-called 'shadow of the future' mean that these states know that compliance is in their own self-interest.

But when new states without this knowledge and democratic tradition enter the council, we see the need for additional policy tools. The UN has its high commissioner for human rights, Mary Robinson; the OSCE has its high commissioner for national minorities, Max van der Stoehl; and both organisations have several special envoys and special representatives for 'rough' areas and 'rogue' states. The EU has also developed this type of institution in terms of special representatives – all three organisations have, as one example, special representatives for the Balkans. The COE has followed this policy trend in naming it own human rights commissioner, in order to add the tools of public diplomacy to its toolbox. The legal tools are long term, while the commissioner's work is to be able to react rapidly and publicly to a human rights situation.

The conclusion regarding the *general* impact of the COE in foreign policy must be that it is smaller than that of both the EU and the OSCE. It consists of the important impact of the court in human rights, but also of the impact of many other conventions and programmes – lesser known and less visible. Then we should add the direct political impact of the new, proactive attempts at public diplomacy: the travels, on-site visits and fieldwork of the secretary-general, the human rights commissioner, the Venice Commission, and the fact-finding missions of the Council of Ministers as well as the PA.

All these efforts have an impact, but the COE is new at using them. The real powers behind them are the role of the court, which by necessity must remain separate from the political work of the council, as well as the ability to warn and possibly suspend member states from both the Council of Ministers and the PA. As we shall see below, it is the *cases where there has been major press and public attention* that the COE and the PA leadership have been able to exert some influence. This supports our thesis about the importance of public diplomacy and 'shaming' for compliance in the states that are outside of the traditional Western group.

When we confine the COE to the human rights regime as such, we find that it is still in this sphere that the most important tools and powers reside. Like the OSCE and unlike the EU, the COE is basically a human rights organisation. We would exclude the work on social cohesion, culture and standard-setting in many of the 170 additional conventions under the COE as relevant here. The most important tools remain *regime-specific*: the court, the monitoring mechanisms of the PA and Council of Ministers, and the human rights commissioner. There is no extra leverage added to the regime by the COE's *general* powers, as is the case with the EU. Both the COE and the OSCE remain primarily devoted to the *core tasks of the regime of human rights*, and it is therefore the regime-specific tools that are the important ones.

Below we present some cases which give evidence of the *specific* impact of the COE in the human rights area.

Turkey

Turkey has received a number of unfavourable judgements on serious human rights violations in the court, about 15. Many of these concern the security police's treatment of the PKK, the Kurdish party. In this connection the COE's Council of Ministers has urged Turkey, though a resolution, to improve its human rights apparatus. The judgements against Turkey are serious ones: breaches have been found of the ECHR's art. 2 on the right to life, the prohibition of torture and degrading treatment in art. 3, and the right to respect for private and family life in art. 8. Also, investigation into the Kurds has revealed breaches of the rule-of-law articles of the convention, especially concerning arrest, torture and imprisonment without court rulings and access to legal defence (arts. 6 and 13). In 1999 the court judged in an additional 13 cases regarding the Kurds – mostly on complaints from individuals who had been sentenced in Turkey for speaking for the rights of the Kurds. There is thus overwhelming evidence that the Turkish state is far from the Western standard on these issues, but this has not led to much soul-searching in the Turkish political elite. But in other cases, the Turkish government has complied.

Thus, Turkey has been found to break many of the most important human rights concerning the rule of law, and the contestation of these judgements by the Turkish government has led to renewed attempts by the COE to ensure full implementation. The COE's Council of Ministers issued a resolution in which the Turkish defence of its own human rights record was included, but where more measures were called for. Here the COE states that Turkey must take further measures in complying with the judgements of the court.

It is a serious matter for a member state to have a resolution like this against it, but this kind of criticism seems to mean less to Turkey than to a Western European state. This is a *significant finding regarding the function of shaming:* the latter means less, it seems, the further one is from this Western tradition. As we shall see regarding Russia in the case of Chechnya, there is a response to criticism that echoes old-fashioned state sovereignty and non-intervention. The same can be said for Turkey. The mentioning of minority rights and cultural rights for the Kurds immediately leads to *contestation that such rights exist as international human rights*, a response that one would hardly find in Western Europe. Here one would typically discuss the *contents* of such rights, where the contestation is seen as a valid one, not the *existence* of such rights. Here one would also do everything possible to avoid being shamed through a public resolution, and rather agree to some kind of compliance measure in order to avoid this.

Turkey now stands out, with states like the Ukraine, Russia and the Balkans, as a difficult and recalcitrant state in the area of human rights – not a nice reputation for a prospective EU member.

The Ocalan case in 1999 contributed to consolidating this impression. The PA was going to observe the trial, but had great difficulties in being invited to perform this role that it was entitled to. The problems presented for foreign observers – practical ones about accommodation, entrance, visas, etc. – who were legally mandated to observe the trial was probably a counterproductive move for the Turks in terms of the reputation of Turkey in the human rights field. The death penalty for

Ocalan, although never to be carried out, is also a break with the COE's condemnation of the latter, and was followed by a negative press statement by the COE's leadership. Protocol 6 to the ECHR forbids the use of the death penalty, and the COE has been adamant in making signature of this conditional for membership. It is also this protocol which is the major reference point among international human rights instruments, and is invoked as the key instrument against the death penalty.

In Turkey the COE has also used *learning* as a policy tool, and has tried out some on-site programmes, such as police reform training, partly financed by Norway. Here the aim is to retrain the Turkish police in the human rights area. This programme, which lasted from 1997 to 2000, showed large deficiencies in the Turkish police in this respect, but also a willingness to learn.[15]

In sum, shaming has not worked well in the Turkish case, and there is little possibility of using conditionality. Turkey is 'beyond' the class of Western states where reputation means much, and must be put under pressure in order to effect reforms in human rights practice. So far pressure has also failed, but there is a little evidence that it is starting to work when launched by the EU which has outlined a detailed reform programme. There are some signs that the Turks are responding to this conditionality.[16]

The Ukraine

There was dissatisfaction with Ukraine in the COE after some time as a member, because of its sluggish reform rate in human rights. It had been a guest observer at the COE from 1992 to 1995, and was admitted as a full member in 1996. As Checkel concludes, there was a good compliance record until then: the government passed a law on minorities that allowed Russians to obtain citizenship, and ethnic tensions were eased (Checkel, 2000a). The COE's on-site learning and persuasive efforts made an important contribution – many workshops and seminars with Ukrainian officials were held during those years. 'Interviews reveal that incentives offered by the COE and careful, strategic calculations by Ukrainian elites were factors [explaining compliance], for membership in the Council would legitimate both Ukraine's return to Europe and its independence from Russia' (Checkel, 2000a: 17).

However, *after membership was conferred, the compliance record weakened.* Upon entering, the government undertook to comply with both the ECHR and specific conditions, such as abolishing the death penalty by the year 1998. This did not happen. For instance, the death penalty is still being used despite the signing of protocol no. 6 to the ECHR which abolishes it, and the parliamentary system of government is much like a Potemkin village: the president wields disproportionate powers. The major demonstrations that took place in February 2001 seemed destined to succeed in toppling president Kutschma, but failed.

There were further problems in the situation of the Crimean Tatars, something which also engaged the OSCE, and in general, slack or non-existent implementation. Here the longevity of the old Soviet system is an explanatory factor, but it must be noted that once the 'prize' of membership had been won, the pressure was eased in the sense that there was no immediate incentive for compliance. It was no longer at the top of the foreign policy agenda.

On the death-penalty case, the COE used a two-track approach, also described by Checkel: shaming and public criticism, but also dialogue and persuasion, teaching how to comply. There was an escalation of public pressure on the Ukraine through hearings and meetings in the PA, as well as a high-level visit by the secretary-general. The report from the COE visit, which included the secretary-general and the chairman of the committee of ministers, put extensive pressure on the Ukraine. Unless urgent measures were taken to fulfil the breaches of commitment, said the COE, that is, within three months, the Ukrainian delegation to the PA would see its rights suspended.[17] While using threats, the COE also offered help through programmes on democratic development in new member states. The threat of suspension led to full mobilisation from the Ukrainian side, and measures were taken just to be able to avoid this consequence. However, the extent to which these promises really led to changes, is uncertain. The COE's election observers to the presidential election in 1999 concluded that the incumbent, Leonid Kutschma, had a major advantage in press and media coverage. Thus, human rights and democracy problems persist in the Ukraine, as became very evident in 2001.

The final conclusion is not yet to be drawn in the Ukrainian case. The local elites claim that the death penalty has so much support that it is 'suicide' to abolish it, while the COE maintains that this has to happen. Probably the process of persuasion and public pressure must be maintained in combination, but it is clear that the only major compliance took place when there was an incentive to comply, viz. COE membership. Afterwards there was much less interest in compliance. This strengthens the thesis of instrumental reasons for compliance.

Also in this case shaming in Ukraine itself had no effect: it simply did not matter to the Ukrainian government at home that it is criticised. This is naturally also due to the lack of a free press and a mechanism of recall of political power. As long as physical power is the only variable necessary for the president when quelling opposition, one cannot expect that reputation will matter to him and his government.

The Balkans

The COE has also taken a proactive role in democracy-building in the Balkans. In Bosnia, the ECHR has become the national law of the land – it has in fact become fully incorporated into Bosnian national constitutional law. This is an important element of the impact.

In addition, there is a court to implement this law, called the Human Rights Chamber. It is entitled to pass judgements like the court in Strasbourg, and it is the COE which has named most of the judges to this chamber. In addition, the COE has erected the constitutional court of the country, naming three of its nine judges. The COE has its own representation in Bosnia, and has more than 60 democratisation projects there. The COE also has its own offices in Albania and Montenegro, and has many projects on the rule of law and democratisation.

The COE role in these states is mainly one of *teacher*: it has complemented the OSCE in implementing the civilian aspects of the Dayton agreement, offering its special expertise in rule of law. But admission to the COE is also practised differently. Croatia has been admitted, but not Bosnia.

Chechnya

In the case of Chechnya, the COE has been active, proposing a presence in the province as well as sending various missions to the location. The COE's Committee for the Prevention of Torture has visited, as well as the COE high commissioner of human rights, Alvaro Gil-Robles. The secretary-general used his own powers of inquiry for the first time with regard to a state party, Russia, and made a visit to Moscow to ask to set up an office in Chechnya, something which was denied. The PA also made a visit, and threatened to suspend Russia from the COE because of the disproportionate use of force against the population in Grozny.

Russia's voting rights were suspended from the PA on account of the disproportionate use of violence towards the civilian population in 1999, and were only restored in 2001. Here we see a major attempt to 'shame' Russia which attracted international headlines. The Russians were very displeased with this, and continued to use very harsh political language when speaking about the opponents in Chechnya. They are 'bandits' to be fought at all cost, and this battle is an internal

Russian affair. However, later in 2001 there were TV interviews with Russian generals on the ground who were willing to talk about possible human rights abuses by Russian soldiers without outright rejection of this language, something unheard of only a year earlier.[18] Suspension of the Russian voting rights in the Council of Ministers has not been carried out, despite threats to this effect.

The COE has been able to play a visible role regarding Chechnya, more so than both the EU and the OSCE. The OSCE's mission to Grozny was withdrawn and moved to Moscow in late 1999 due to the security situation, only to return in March 2001. The EU has not been engaged very much in this case, but the COE seems to have picked it out as a 'test case'of its new public diplomacy. The human rights commissioner, Gil-Robles, managed to establish cooperation between the OSCE, the COE and the Russian human rights commissioner Kalmanov, whose office was set up as a response to the public pressure from these two organisations, especially the work of Gil-Robles and his close connection with foreign minister Ivanov. [19] The Russian office has few resources and knows little about how to undertake human rights monitoring in the field, and the OSCE/COE cooperation has helped it with both training and software. This case is elaborated further in the next chapter on the OSCE.

The Chechnya case is one of COE engagement, and one where new tools have been used. The reason why engagement and some results have been possible, is again a combination of discreet work and public pressure. Despite a few changes in rhetorical behaviour – of making some signs of 'talking the talk' of human rights – the Russians have responded to criticism about their war in Chechnya with old-fashioned views of sovereignty: non-intervention; 'this is our combat with bandits, and we need no assistance here at all'. The OSCE chairman Vollebæk insisted on visiting the region himself in December 1999, but was almost totally rejected. Thus, the type of intervention that the OSCE mandates was completely ignored by the Russians. In view of the extreme difficulty of the case it is remarkable that the COE has managed to put effective public pressure on Russia, to the extent of Putin mandating a human rights monitoring office in his staff. The impact of this office is discussed in the next chapter.

Conclusion: the impact of the human rights regime of the COE

The impact of the COE in recent years has increased, with new policy tools and more proactive activity. However, the most important part of the COE's impact still rests with the court. It is clear both that the court's impact has become more visible and attended to in recent years, and also that the new policy tools, such as the high commissioner on human rights and the more field-oriented work of the COE have made the latter more versatile and activist. But the COE may in some ways duplicate the work of the OSCE in the field, while the EU, as we shall see, adopts a human rights charter akin to the COE.

The main *regime-specific* tool of the COE is the ECHR with its supranational court. Other activities are auxiliary to this, and largely derive from it. It is this convention that is the basis for all the later conventions, although they remain separate from it. It is also the convention that marks the major emphasis on rule of law as the key part of the human rights regime in the COE.

It is obvious that much of the council's work must remain low-key, in training and education, combined with some pressure and some measure of shaming. However, the tools for public diplomacy in this sense are not yet well developed. The COE is therefore best equipped to deal with stable, like-minded democracies where 'pacta sunt servanda' is a well-established norm. This was the case with the membership until the beginning of the 1990s. The new type of member state after this date – which now make up almost 50 per cent of the membership – requires more than the legal approach in order to install the human rights regime. One side of this is *teaching*: simply how to establish an independent court system or a multi-party system; another is to have a tougher side to the tools, viz. means of exerting pressure and punishing non-compliance. Such tools are rare in the COE, but, as stated, a start has been made to develop them over the last few years.

Shaming, we argued, will probably only work in states that are close to European public debate and tradition, and whose populations follow the international press. One state of long-term COE membership where this tool had little or no effect is Turkey. The human rights debate in Turkey is also marked by old-fashioned state sovereignty, contesting the validity of interference and also the very existence of certain human rights, such as cultural and minority rights. Turkey, and Russia with its similar response regarding Chechnya, stand out as the only European states[20] with an 'old-fashioned' state sovereignty response in the European human rights discourse. The fact that the court's judgements are implemented elsewhere in Europe testify to the fact that the rest of the membership obey the central norms that govern liberal democracy in the European tradition.

Those new members which form the 'second ring' of states, the states of the former USSR and the Balkans, need the new tools of 'sticks' and 'carrots' in order to comply. The imposing of the human rights regime means that the IO must also *help* the state in question in order to see results. Shaming in the public policy sense has little or no effect on such states.

The cases examined here are not sufficient to prove that these hypotheses hold. They indicate that the hypotheses are right, but they do no more than that. There is a major reason for this: the 'newness' of the new type of state in the COE makes for few cases of non-compliance to examine as of yet. Also, the new tools of the COE are so new that there are few instances where they have been used. The high commissioner for human rights was only established in 1999, and the new monitoring tools of the COE and the PA were established in 1998.

In conclusion, the COE promises to develop these tools which it deems necessary to effectively impact on the new member states, but it is also a question of member state willingness to finance this work. For the time being, the COE experiences great difficulty in financing its court and other institutions, such as the high commissioner. The ordinary budget only covers the permanent institutions, and the high commissioner, as one major example, is not covered by it. His office has to be financed by voluntary contributions by states. This is also the case with much of the fieldwork of the COE, for instance the police training programme in Turkey. Such a financial basis is clearly not satisfactory, and it makes member states able to sanction the work of the COE as they wish. The court cannot be manipulated by member states, but it can be slowly 'strangulated' by the lack of funds to cope with the large backlog of cases. Unless new funds are forthcoming, the court will be in danger of being criticised for lack of effectiveness – the cause of which will at least partially be lack of resources from the COE member states.

The larger issue of competition vs. complementarity between the COE, and the EU and the OSCE means that the overall future role of the COE is uncertain. This is not a question of any radical change in the COE's mandate, but one of funding and member state priorities, which may marginalise the COE among the European IOs.

6
The Impact of the OSCE

The OSCE as a foreign policy actor: tools and powers

The Organisation for Security and Cooperation in Europe (OSCE) was originally the CSCE, the C denoting 'conference', not 'organisation'. The CSCE was, as this name indicates, a process rather than an organisation. It was only in 1992 that the name changed, and the degree of institutionalisation changed from an ad hoc process to organisation.

The OSCE is a security organisation, exclusively employing soft power tools. But in Bosnia, as the implementing agency of the Dayton peace accord, the OSCE has major 'hard' powers. It can accept or reject elections, suspend politicians, determine the rules of free and fair elections, etc. These powers it uses constantly: a look at the OSCE website will reveal an extremely active use of public diplomacy, 'shaming' parties and politicians that break Dayton rules, while also imposing such sanctions in Bosnia itself. The actions of the OSCE in all the field missions are available in real time to the entire international community through its internet site and its free press subscription service.[1]

Both Bosnia and Kosovo are de facto international protectorates where the IOs wield major powers. It is therefore not quite correct to say that the OSCE always disposes only of soft power, although it remains true that it basically relies on such tools: advice, assistance, learning and persuasion.

By 2000 the OSCE had become a comprehensive security organisation with a wide array of instruments at its disposal, but as of yet, little systematic, scholarly attention has been paid to the impact of the OSCE, apart from important articles like Flynn and Farrell (1999), Bothe et al. (1997), Ghebali (1996) and Hopmann (2001). It has been widely assumed that the OSCE lacks power because of its consensual decision-making style and its lack of hard power tools. This chapter seeks to show that there has been considerable impact of OSCE activities, in a variety of ways.

East–West meeting point

The CFSE started in 1973 as a process of rapprochement between East and West, at the suggestion of the then Soviet Union. It was only in 1992 that the name changed, and the degree of institutionalisation changed from ad hoc process to organisation.

The famous Helsinki process of the 1970s was a unique meeting place between East and West during the Cold War, where human rights were discussed under the less conspicuous name of the 'human dimension'. As stated in Chapter 3, the discussion about human rights continued despite political confrontation, in itself a major achievement. The Helsinki Final Act laid down principles about security and human rights in a path-breaking manner considering the date, 1975: the Cold War was still a reality (Maresca, 1987; Bloed, 1990, 1993; Buergenthal, 1990).

The OSCE is a security organisation, with military types of tasks as well as non-military ones. Its security concept is comprehensive and its tools are non-military, although some of its missions are backed by a military presence, such as in Bosnia and Kosovo. As mentioned, the OSCE is an extremely understudied organization in the academic literature and has in general been seen as rather insignificant. But, as Flynn and Farrell argue,

> the CSCE mechanisms have proven to be the real workhorses of the international community in its attempts to control sub-state conflict in post-cold war Europe . . . in reality CSCE mechanisms have been involved in managing far more potential sub-state conflicts than either of the other [NATO and EU] organizations (1999: 507).

As we shall see, human rights norms play an important part in conflict resolution (Matláry, 2000).

As laid out in Chapter 3, the Helsinki Final Act pioneered the political agreement on human rights norms despite the Cold War. But the form of government and its ideology were not discussed – they were still an 'internal' matter. Only in 1990, after the demise of the Cold War, did it become possible to discuss the political requirements for the implementation of human rights. The Copenhagen Conference on the Human Dimension in 1990 marks a watershed in the sense that one now could agree that only democracy and the rule of law could ensure human rights realisation (Buergenthal, 1990). This marks a major change in the formation of the human rights regime in Europe: it was from then on an integrated whole with democracy and the rule of law as intrinsic companions of human rights (Matláry, 2001). Buergenthal called this nothing less than a 'democratic revolution' (Buergenthal, 1990).

As discussed, it is in the OSCE documents that we see the *explicit* linkage between democracy, rule of law and human rights for the first time, in the Charter of Paris in 1990. But these values – human rights, democracy and the rule of law – are of course implicitly embedded in different declarations and conventions. The UN's human rights *acquis* is authoritative, especially the Declaration of Human Rights and the two Human Rights Conventions of 1966. Later, as well as regional documents, all correspond to, and are inspired by, the former. But in the OSCE documents we see an elaboration of the practical aspects of human rights implementation: what does it mean, in policy terms, to implement freedom of religion? What does it mean to implement freedom of the press? No other human rights document is this precise in telling law- and policy-makers what to do. As we shall see below, there are specific requirements laid down for acceptable implementation of freedom of religion.

Further, the linkage between human rights and democracy-cum-rule of law means that it is possible to make this kind of specification. For example, freedom of the press entails that power is dispersed and that there is a separation of powers; while freedom of religion means that there is respect for the apolitical character of churches and space for public as well as private worship.

Thus one may say that the greatness of the OSCE's approach lies in its *practical* character: this human right entails that you do this and this, very concretely; and that your democratic and legal institutions really function. There is no room for ambiguous statements that lend themselves to various types of interpretation. The fact that the OSCE had to write texts for new and learning democracies meant that these texts must be a 'vade mecum' for the practitioner. The OSCE documents are thus very advanced as instructions to policy-makers, something which in our view makes them extremely attractive as policy tools since they cannot easily be manipulated.

But what about the powers of the OSCE? Can it impose its normative basis? Can it induce states to follow the latter? Or must it simply rely on the goodwill of member states?

The OSCE tools of norm implementation

The OSCE has at its command several types of policy tools, of which some are traditional, diplomatic ones, whereas others are missions of short or long duration in a host country. In addition, there are tools of early warning and conflict prevention, of post-conflict management and democracy-building as well as public 'shaming' in review conferences on human rights.

The OSCE sends missions to states with democratic and human rights problems. The first long-duration mission was to Sandjak, Voivodina and Kosovo in 1992. By 2001 there were about 20 missions, and these were often large. The mission in Bosnia counts around 290 people, who are experts in democratisation, such as elections, as well as in military affairs such as weapons collection and demobilisation. The OSCE mission in Bosnia is in charge of the civil implementation of the Dayton peace agreement, and has conducted party registration, election monitoring, press development and so on. The Office of the High Representative (OHR) is Bosnia's highest authority until democracy is installed, and the OSCE mission has been responsible for all aspects of democracy-building. This is very practical work that requires expert insight into how to create a multi-party system and the rule of law, but also into the practical consequences of human rights as such.

In the case of the Dayton agreement, the head of the OSCE mission has real powers of sanction. The long-term leader of this mission, ambassador Robert Barry, has for many years been the most important decision-maker in Bosnia next to the OHR (the high representative of the Western powers) and the commander of the SFOR forces. Dayton allows the international community to cancel elections not properly held, to remove elected politicians if they do not cooperate on democracy-building, to close presses that spread nationalist and xenophobic propaganda, etc. In short, the OSCE in Bosnia is part of the direction of an international protectorate. This also applies to the governance of Kosovo.

There are other missions that have been equally large, such as the mission in Croatia with a mandate to monitor and sanction transgressions of press freedom, abuse of presidential powers and impartiality of judges, to mention a few elements. The OSCE leader can act against transgressions of democratic government, but also has to keep up a working cooperation with the host government because ultimately it is this government which decides to keep a mission by renewing its mandate.

The largest OSCE mission to date has been the Kosovo Verification Mission (KVM) which counted 2000 personnel. It was deployed in Kosovo after protracted negotiations with President Milosevic, and started its work in December 1999, but had to be withdrawn amid escalating violence on 17 March 2000. Shortly thereafter, on 24 March, NATO started its attack on Kosovo and Serbia. There were many voices that maintained that the KVM could do nothing as it was unarmed, and increasingly the object of attack. This physical danger was indeed the reason why the Norwegian chairmanship withdrew the mission, as it had by this time become clear that there were major troop movements from Serbia into Kosovo and also incidents aimed at the Kosovars as well as attacks on KVM observers.

But the KVM had managed to document the extent and escalation of human rights violations. The infamous Rajack massacre in January 2000 in which 49 villagers were found executed was brought to the world's attention by the KVM leader, ambassador William Walker. Other abuses were also documented by the KVM. But it is always clear that an OSCE mission will not stay if its work is being made impossible by the host state and its members are taking undue personal risks. Such also were the reasons for the eventual withdrawal of the mission in Chechnya, the Assistance and Monitoring Group (AMG) in 2000. The security situation for the group was by that time so precarious that its members could not perform their functions, but had to stay in headquarters all the time for fear of kidnapping and ambush.

Further, the missions are sometimes contested by the host government. Some governments try to restrict the mandate and to make the mission a hostage to its own political goals. This was the case with the Croat governments under Tudjman, where there were several attempts to manipulate the mission and to oust it. But international pressure, also from the EU whose weight was the most important to Croatia, kept the mission in place. Similar situations occurred in some of the Baltic states, where the OSCE was seen as intrusive on minority issues.

The contested character of the missions is also an indicator of their importance. On the one hand it gives international legitimacy to have an independent 'eye and ear' in a state; on the other it is unpleasant to have monitoring inside one's own state. For instance, Latvia maintained that it was so 'Western' that it did not need a mission, and that such a mission was stigmatising; however, pressure from the EU and other IOs made it retain its mission.

Regime-specific tools

The human rights issues also form the core of the OSCE's comprehensive security concept: there is no stable peace without democracy, rule of law and respect for human rights.

But there are also specific instruments for the implementation of the human rights regime. They include the ODIHR (Office of Democratic Institutions and Human Rights) in Warsaw, the HCNM (high commissioner for national minorities) located in The Hague, as well as democratisation work that is intrinsic to the mandates of the mission. One such mission, the so-called Advisory and Monitoring Group in Belarus, has a mandate exclusively concerned with implementing the human rights regime (Timmermann, 1998) and is in fact the only international presence in that state after the withdrawal of Western ambassadors in 1997.

As seen above, the Helsinki Act provisions were later developed by a so-called Follow-up Meeting in Vienna which lasted for three years, between 1986 and 1989. Here Western governments proposed a *mechanism to monitor compliance* with these norms, called the 'human dimension mechanism'. This consisted of a Conference on the Human Dimension (CHD) which was to be held in order for the Eastern states to catch up in their own democratic development. The approach was to gradually enable these states to achieve Western standards. Three such conferences were held, in Paris in 1989, Copenhagen in 1990 and in Moscow in 1991. Here various tools were adopted: in Vienna, a *four-stage procedure for mandatory inter-state dialogue on human rights*; in Copenhagen, a document which defined human rights in more detail than the Helsinki Act, especially in the field of *minority rights;* and in Moscow there was further elaboration on the Vienna mechanism by making it possible to create *independent fact-finding missions*, even without the consent of the state in question (Bloed, 1993). In the view of an expert, 'The Moscow mechanism constituted significant progress, allowing for the first time third-party supervision, fact-finding, and mediation' (Daftary, 1998: 252).

However, these mechanisms are rarely used, in order to try to help the development rather than to sanction countries that strive to become democratic. But their very existence functions as a disciplinary force. The fact that a fact-finding mission may be sent to a state even without its consent means that there is an ultimate threat in store.

The high commissioner for national minorities

Another creation of the OSCE is the high commissioner for national minorities (HCNM). A very large part of the human rights issues that are typical in OSCE member states relate to questions of minorities, and the idea that ethnic minorities have rights to language and culture, including their own religion, is often very contested. The work of high commissioner Max van der Stoehl is close to legendary in current diplomacy. The former Dutch foreign minister has travelled to all conflict areas where national minority rights are stake, and has solved a number of potentially violent conflicts in a peaceful manner (Zellner, 2001). Especially noteworthy is his work in the Baltic states on Russian minority rights, but also his work in the Balkans and in East-Central Europe (Flynn and Farrell, 1999).

He can travel to any OSCE country and consult with the actors he finds relevant on any potential or present conflict, and he reports to OSCE meetings and institutions. In extreme cases he can issue a 'solemn warning', a tool used once in Macedonia in 1999 to warn the international community about the dangerous tension between the Albanians and the Macedonians, who are Slavs. This early warning was very warranted, as violent insurrection instigated by the Albanian guerrillas of Kosovo led to heavy fighting in and around Tetovo in March 2001.

To mention another example, van der Stoehl's work has been and is very important for religious freedom, as it often consists in explaining what this right means and suggesting how to implement it. The idea of pluri-religious states is quite foreign in Central Asia for example, and in the Balkans the very intermixing of politics and religion makes it very hard to rediscover what religion without instrumental interests really means. Here the roving diplomacy of the high commissioner, using only soft power tools, has been very important. However, its importance is difficult to measure because the conflicts that have been averted by prevention measures have not surfaced (Zellner, 2001). But one can at least say that the high commissioner's work is very highly regarded in every OSCE state, that he has automatic access to all persons of influence, and that the fact that he reports back to the OSCE's central institutions means that all will be known that is problematic in a given state.

The Office For Democratic Institutions and Human Rights

At the Paris summit in 1990 there was an institutionalisation of the human rights norms. An Office for Free Elections (OFE) was established in Warsaw, then later renamed the ODIHR. There was furthermore a change in the consensus procedure for decision-making in 1992, allowing for *consensus-minus-one* in order for the OSCE to be able to take measures against states in cases of 'clear, gross, and uncorrected violations of OSCE commitments' (Bloed, 1993: 832). This procedure was used against FRY when President Milosevic refused to let OSCE observers enter Kosovo and persisted in violations of all human rights commitments in that province. The FRY was suspended from the OSCE, and the OSCE mission of long duration in Kosovo, Sandjak and Voivodina had to leave.

The ODIHR's mandate was strengthened at the Prague meeting, making it the key human rights and democracy tool of the OSCE. Each year there is a review and implementation meeting of all the OSCE member states under the auspices of ODIHR, lasting for two to three weeks. Here states are criticised or praised, and major discussion of implementation failure takes place. It is significant that NGOs are also allowed as full participants in these meetings, and the tone can often be very sharp between certain states not used to democratic criticism, and NGOs like Human Rights Watch or the Helsinki committee. The only NGO from a Central Asian state which criticised its own government at the review conference in 1997 had the experience of its chairman being severely beaten up outside the hotel. Suspicion fell on the secret services of the home government, although in all fairness one cannot pass judgement.[2] This example is useful because it illustrates the novelty of Western institutions to many new OSCE states: what these institutions mean, and what human rights entail, must be taught rather than imposed. After all, it took many centuries to agree on and implement the human rights of freedom of religion in Europe.

The ODIHR's tasks are threefold: promotion of free and fair elections, democracy-building through the promotion of civil society and democratic institutions, and monitoring and implementation. The most well known of these activities is undoubtedly election supervision and monitoring. The office is directly responsible for election processes in most new democracies in the OSCE area. This is also security policy: an election thought to be manipulated can easily lead to armed conflict, as in Albania in 1997.

But the ODIHR is usually involved at an earlier stage, helping governments arrange free and fair elections – how to make an election law, how to make a voter registry, to mention two frequent tasks. To illustrate the range of activities in this field, in 1998 the ODIHR helped create a voter registry in Albania, provided advice on election systems, media regulation and voter registration in Montenegro, and helped make an election law in Armenia. There was further a major undertaking in Central Asia with a programme to train and advise election officials from all the five republics which face parliamentary or presidential elections in the 1999–2001 period. In one year alone – 1997 – there was election monitoring in Croatia (twice), Bulgaria, Albania, Bosnia and Hercegovina, Serbia, Republika Srpska and Montenegro.[3] Election monitoring takes place with observers seconded from member states of the OSCE as well as with other IOs such as the European Parliament and the COE.

In the field of democracy development, the ODIHR is also very active. In 1997 for example, there were memoranda of understanding (MOU) signed with the Central Asians republics on assistance to develop their democracies, as well as several projects in the Caucasus. In the long-term mission in Croatia and Bosnia, to mention two major missions, the democratisation element is absolutely essential. In order to avoid so-called 'forum shopping',[4] there have been joint delegations sent to these various areas, consisting of representatives of the EU, the COE and the OSCE. 'A joint mission also sends the message to countries in need of assistance that the international community has mutually reinforcing standards and common goals in the fields of human rights and democratisation' (Flynn and Farrell, 1999: 388).

The general foreign policy impact of the OSCE

The OSCE has had an evolving normative development as well as an evolving tool kit. Further, the human rights regime acts as an 'umbrella' over all of this organisation's foreign policy. Security is intrinsically bound up with human rights, democracy and the rule of law; indeed, these norms are the very basis for the security policy of the OSCE. It is therefore not easy to delimit 'foreign policy' and 'the human rights regime' of the OSCE. In the examples below we will see how the 'human rights logic' is the basis for all OSCE tools, and it therefore makes little sense to speak of any general impact of the OSCE in separation from these norms. True, the CFE treaty (Conventional Forces in Europe) is deposited with the OSCE, and this treaty is not directly related to the normative basis, but this is a minor exception to the rule that the OSCE's security policy identity is intimately related to its human rights regime.

Security is seen as possible only when stable domestic institutions prevail. This is what we have referred to earlier, in Chapter 1, as the concept of 'human security'. This refers to the right of the individual to physical security of person, and typically embraces themes like conflict prevention and resolution, democratisation and protection of minority rights, as well as physical security measures such as police sector reform, de-mining, demobilisation and weapons destruction, child soldiers and measures against small arms and light weapons proliferation (Lodgaard, 2000). The concept of human security, as a complement to traditional state security, is in the process of becoming established on the international agenda.[5] The OSCE is, however, the pre-eminent human security organisation, without it having been planned as such. The core of the OSCE's 'marriage of human rights and security policy' is as follows.

The normative agreement is that only democracy can secure human rights, and that the OSCE states are collectively responsible for ensuring such a democratic development. This introduces a major normative change in favour of intervention: it changes the norm of state sovereignty and non-intervention to becoming subordinate to the human rights logic. This is of enormous importance for security and foreign policy in general, as Flynn and Farrell also note: 'With the recognition of some linkage between the "quality" of a state and its internal political institutions, the norm of non-intervention was given a much more restricted content' (1999: 526).

State security, with its norm of non-intervention and state sovereignty, had been the reigning paradigm for security policy, where territorial defence was the key task. But most modern 'wars' occur inside states, in so-called 'weak' or 'failed' states, and this paradigm does not apply there. The causes of such conflicts are invariably the lack of stable institutions, such as a government that can provide the human security citizens have the right to, as well as their other human rights. The causal link between democracy, rule of law and human rights, and the general security of the population and stability, is at the core of the OSCE. The recognition that stable peace requires a functioning democracy has led to the development of tools that are aimed at security as well as democratisation, based on 'soft power' intervention. The UNSC has developed such 'human security' interventionism in the 1990s, as will be discussed in Chapter 8, but it has had to use the state security logic as its basis and justification. The only mandate for intervention that the UNSC has, is when there exists a 'threat to international peace and security',[6] and this naturally means a security threat that transgresses borders.

As we shall see, the UNSC has fit entirely domestic situations into this definition, thereby stretching it. *But in the OSCE, unlike in the UNSC, there is the acceptance of intervention based on the human rights logic alone,* in order to rectify or ameliorate a *security* situation. Security policy in the OSCE thus has a basis in the human rights logic in a formal sense, but this type of intervention is limited to the use of 'soft power'. It is clear that the OSCE does not command any sort of 'hard power'. For instance, when the Russians denied access for an OSCE team to investigate Chechnya, and the OSCE had to accept it.

But again, 'soft power' tools can be powerful, although they clearly will not do in tough cases like the one mentioned above. Examples of these OSCE tools are the rights of the HCNM to request a visit to a place with ethnic tensions within a fortnight, thus making it imperative for the state in question to invite him and let him talk to all parties he wishes; the right of the OSCE chairman to dispatch a special representative to any state; the right of the OSCE to mandate 'directed conciliation' of a conflict also against the wishes of the state in question: and the ability to send a fact-finding mission[7] to a trouble spot without the consent of the state in question.

The latter two tools depend on the so-called 'consensus-minus-one' procedure which was adopted by the OSCE in 1992. That spring the FRY was excluded by this procedure because of massive human rights violations – the only suspension in the organisation's history – but the OSCE missions in Kosovo, Sandjak, and later, Voivodina lasted for some time beyond this. These missions were termed 'missions of long duration' and superseded the Moscow mechanism because it was too cumbersome. These missions, led by the Norwegian ambassador Bøgh, continued into 1993, when Belgrade refused further cooperation.

Thus, although the right to intervene exists, transgressing traditional state sovereignty and non-intervention, the physical force of intervening naturally does not exist on the part of the OSCE. If a state is suspended, as in the case of the FRY, there is no source of internal OSCE pressure to be launched. The state is no longer bound by all the OSCE obligations. In this light it is all the more remarkable that Milosevic did allow both the 'missions of long-term duration' and the KVM into the FRY. This indicates that even dictators see the need for international acceptance and they know the use of having an international presence on the ground – to some extent, at least.

The *general* political impact of the OSCE is thus as a *security* policy actor – conflict prevention, conflict management and containment, conflict resolution and post-conflict assistance – but the basis for this work is the human rights logic and the human rights regime. The logic is that of 'constructive intervention', as Flynn and Farrell (1999) term it, because the enabling basis for intervention is human rights and a universalisation of democracy and rule of law. As we have seen in Chapter 3, the OSCE documents for the first time lay down that human rights can only be realised with democracy and the rule of law, and the follow-up meetings, especially Moscow in 1990 and Prague in 1992, add policy tools for intervention on this basis. Thus, we have the normative basis, then the tools to implement these norms; and the third logical link: from human rights to security policy. This third link is given in the nature of modern armed conflicts: ethnic tensions, failed states, weapons-based conflict resolution, anarchy, etc. The 'cure' for all these causes of armed conflict is in the human rights regime.

The reason why we stress the importance of the new norm of 'intervention for democracy' is that it is establishing itself in various ways. Through the use of soft power tools in the three organisations of this study, but also in the justification for hard power intervention. There can be no doubt that we find the most explicit linkage between the human rights regime, soft power tools of intervention, and security policy in the OSCE. This is why this organisation is so important here: it is in 'forefront' of an international trend.

Below we present some cases of OSCE impact in this field, choosing to illustrate its impact in three ways: through the example of the impact of a *single human right,* in this case freedom of religion or belief; through the example of the impact on *specific states* though the OSCE missions there, and through the example of the *HCNM* and the *ODHIR.* These impacts are all based on the cross-cutting human rights regime of the organisation.

Evolving norm development and impact: the example of freedom of religion

The OSCE does not have a single mandate, like the COE and the EU. It has a core set of principles whose implementation it monitors, the 'human dimension' or the human rights regime, as we call it in this study. In addition, it is a security organisation in the 'soft' security sense, and has various mandates in the missions. There is thus not one central 'power base' for the OSCE, but generic tools that it may use in a combination of mission mandate, human rights documents, and deployment of its tools like the HCNM. In order to illustrate the general impact of the OSCE, we therefore pick one central human right as an example, viz. *religious freedom*, to see how it is actually implemented and how the OSCE works in this sphere.

As discussed in Chapter 3, the OSCE norms of human rights are well developed and comprehensive. They encompass all the internationally agreed human rights, but are distinct in their clear link between human rights and democracy and the rule of law. This link can also be found in the major human rights conventions and declarations in the form of political rights to vote, freedom of assembly, right to form parties, freedom of the press and so on. But here the link between democracy and human rights is less explicit. In the OSCE documents, there is an elaboration of the necessity of rule of law and multi-party democracy for the realisation of human rights, and there is also the prescription of practical politics of what must be done to achieve this.

As stated, the OSCE has embraced all fundamental freedoms and human rights as they are developed in the central human rights instruments. In the Helsinki Final Act, principle VII of the 'Decalogue', it is declared that member states will also respect freedom of religion or belief (Helsinki Final Document, cited in Bloed, 1990).

After Helsinki, the negotiations about the 'human dimension' continued in the so-called Madrid conference, which lasted for three years. There was in this conference, according to a prominent negotiator and expert in international law, Thomas Buergenthal, an atmosphere of heavily conflictual and almost stalemated ideological contest between East and West. However, the most surprising and positive result came in the field of religious freedom where this right was defined in *precise and practical* terms: 'The most significant achievement was in the area of freedom of religion' (Buergenthal, 1990: 346).

In the Concluding Document of Madrid from 1983 this freedom is elaborated on. It means, *inter alia*, that member states will

> recognise, respect and furthermore agree to take the action necessary to ensure the freedom of the individual to profess and practise, alone or in community with others, religion or belief, acting in accordance with the dictates of his own conscience. . . . They will favourably consider applications by religious communities of believers practising or prepared to practise their faith within the constitutional framework of their states, to be granted the status provided for in their respective countries for religious faiths, institutions, and organizations (Concluding Document of the Madrid Follow-up Meeting, 1983).

Here it is clearly stated that churches and religious communities are to be recognised by host states, and that public worship is allowed. These specifications of what freedom of religion means in practice naturally makes it more difficult to evade the obligation to implement this right. This method of defining what a human rights means in practical–political terms was, according to Buergenthal, pioneered at the Madrid conference, and 'it has been employed with ever greater frequency and sophistication in subsequent OSCE documents and has become the hallmark of the OSCE norms-setting practise' (1990: 347).

The right to freedom of religion was further elaborated in 1989, in the Concluding Document of Vienna. Here it is laid down that states will take effective measures to eliminate discrimination of individuals and communities on grounds of religion, that they will ensure equality between believers and unbelievers, and that they will 'foster a climate of tolerance between believers of different communities as well as between believers and non-believers', and further, that they will grant religious communities legal status and facilitate their work.

The implementation of freedom of religion will naturally depend on how well the OSCE manages to aid and monitor the implementation of human rights as a whole. This particular human right is part of a whole, and arguably did not play a prominent role in the OSCE until the Norwegian chairmanship in 1999, whose Christian-Democratic government put it on top of the agenda. In addition, there are problems in implementing freedom of religion in states that have been atheist for a long time, such as the CIS states, and in states where nationalism and religion are mixed in an unholy alliance, as in the Balkans. Thus, at the outset one may assume that the record on promoting freedom of religion is not too impressive in the OSCE.

Summing up, we see that freedom of religion in the OSCE has been well defined in an implementable way. The concrete measures to be taken by states are laid out in detail in the Vienna Concluding Document. They include the substance of the art. 18 definition of religious freedom in the UDHR, and derives policy implications from this.

Regime impact of a human right: freedom of religion

As stated, the OSCE has developed several monitoring mechanisms, such as an inter-state complaints procedure called the Vienna mechanism which states may use against non-compliance in other states; the Moscow mechanism whereby the OSCE can send missions of experts and *rapporteurs* to investigate a breach of commitments even against the will of the state in question; ad hoc missions; and the review conferences (Bloed, 1993).

Each year the OSCE states meet to review their implementation of human rights, the so-called humanitarian dimension. The method of work is to let both states and NGOs make plenary statements where they offer praise and criticism, sometimes naming the states in question. When not named explicitly, everyone knows which state is meant. The equal participation of states and NGOs is unique for international conferences. However, this is a useful manner in which to present constructive criticism, as states may be reluctant to name other states in such an endeavour.

If we look at the OSCE record from the review conferences, we find that *non-implementation of religious freedom has been a persistent feature.* For example, at the review conference in 1999 there there was strong criticism of several Western states for their strict definition of sects. The USA, one of the states most concerned with religious freedom, voiced heavy criticism of Belgium, France and Austria for labelling new religious groups with the pejorative term 'sects' and for establishing 'anti-sect' agencies tasked with the monitoring of such new groups. In the case of France, these groups were not even allowed the right of response, but were simply defined as 'sects' or 'cults', according to the US statement.[8] The issue of what is a sect and what is a religious or belief community is surely a contentious issue, not to be discussed further here. What is of interest in this context, however, is the fact that Western states also criticise each other in an open and frank manner in this forum.

At this conference there was major criticism by several delegations of the new member states of Central Asia, Uzbekistan, Kyrgyzstan and Kazakhstan. The charge here was that Christians are persecuted and sometimes imprisoned, that missionary activity is forbidden or restricted, and that new religious communities are not granted legal status. Both the USA and the EU mantained that in Uzbekistan there were more than 200 people were imprisoned on account of their faith, arrests were arbitrary and abuse pervasive. In this state Muslims are also harassed and arrested. The government used terrorism charges as pretexts for this, it was stated.

Further, Azerbaijan was criticised for persecution of Baptist missionaries, one of whom, a Norwegian national, was arrested and held in captivity for a long time. Many of these missonaries were subsequently expelled, clearly a breach of religious freedom.

Greece and Turkey also received criticism on account of ill treatment of religious minorities; the former for maintaining laws that are used against religious minorities despite several rulings against this in the European Court of Human Rights, and the latter for forbidding the wearing of religious insignia in public places, such as headscarves, and for restrictions in public manifestations of religious faith.

There was also persistent criticism of Russia's law on religion from 1997, which privileges the Orthodox Church by creating categories of religious communities with different levels of legal status. This law, vague in wording and unclear in interpretation, has led to much discrimination of non-Orthodox churches, such as making demands that they be in Russia 15 years before they can obtain legal status. The Western criticism of Russia in this respect has been unified.[9]

Finally some other states were criticised for impending legislation that would lead to discrimination, and their parliaments were urged to repeal laws not in conformity with international standards. These states included Bulgaria, Hungary, Romania and the Ukraine.

It is difficult to assess the *impact* of this type of criticism. The public 'shaming' effect is dependent on how many members of the press were present at that particular meeting, on how the criticism of a state is reflected in its national public debate, and on how much the state's reputation suffers in the international diplomatic and political community. To date the OSCE meetings have had very little press attention, unfortunately, one may add, as public attention is an important trigger for change. There have also been few NGOs from the new OSCE member states in the Balkans and in the CIS. The concept of the NGO is one that has to be developed in these states, and that takes time. In order to help this process along, the OSCE has funded participation for NGOs from such states.

But if the public shaming effect from the review conferences is as yet not very large, there is an *internal* OSCE effect. The human dimension issues are followed up in the missions, and they take note of the criticism that is voiced in the review. The various missions pursue comprehensive security policies, which means democracy and human rights along with political stabilisation. The actual strategies for each case naturally varies with the problems at hand. The review conference acts as a *stock-taking of all human rights problems, and its conclusions are well disseminated afterwards*, both in the OSCE central secretariat as well as in the states where the missions are. Thus, the review conferences provide a 'diagnostic' for the member states.

What probably could be better integrated, is the follow-up in the missions. During the Norwegian chairmanship we tried to 'mainstream' consideration of religious freedom into the missions, as well as obligating them to consult local religious leaders on how they could help in conflict resolution.

But implementing freedom of religion is not easy. Some examples in Bosnia illustrate this. In Bosnia there is a major problem since the three ethnic groups largely follow religious affiliation. One is hard pressed to find a state where the non-fulfilment of religious freedom has been more pronounced. The suggestion to rebuild Catholic churches and mosques in Republika Srpska is still seen as a provocation, and when a Catholic outdoor mass was held in Derventa in 1998, there was an attack by the local Serbs on Croats that came by bus to the celebration. Only SFOR intervention saved the worshippers, including the cardinal of Sarajevo.

Other examples of complete religious intolerance can easily be identified in other parts of Bosnia. For example in Mostar, which used to be a sophisticated example of religious coexistence and tolerance, there is now a 'war' between Catholics and Muslims: the electric clockwork of the Catholic churches sounds at maximum volume whenever the legion of new mosques, financed by Middle East states, turn on their electric muezzin equally loudly. The sound blasts out in the narrow valley of Mostar, in a competition to silence each other. The Catholic bishop and the imam alike refuse to cooperate with the international community and its representative. When I was in Mostar in 1999, the OSCE mission leader there, an American Catholic, was frustrated that his bishop simply refused to meet him. The Croat nationalist cause has clearly also become the cause of the local Catholic church.

These few examples, which could be multiplied throughout the Balkans – Serbs misusing the Orthodox Church for nationalist politics; Croats misusing the Catholic Church for the same purpose; Kosovars burning Orthodox churches; Bosnians attacking churches in 'their' areas – all this has happened and continues to happen. The OSCE has to have an integrated approach to this kind of abuse, which is a violation of many human rights at the same time.

Initiatives by the Norwegian chairmanship

During the Norwegian chairmanship we decided to highlight the importance of freedom of religion in two ways. One, as a basic human right, indeed, as one of the most important ones; and two, as a basis for conflict resolution, on the logic that instrumentalised religion often plays a major role in creating and maintaining conflict, and that it can therefore contribute to resolving it.

We decided to arrange two major OSCE conferences on these topics. First, we arranged a so-called 'supplementary meeting' on freedom of religion in Vienna in March 1999. This conference gathered experts and representatives from almost all OSCE member states as well as around 70 NGOs. As mentioned before, in many OSCE meetings NGOs have equal rights of participation with states. Second, we arranged a high-level round table in Oslo later in the year in which the recommendations from the Vienna conference were discussed by church leaders and politicians.

In the Vienna meeting there were three topics: religious dialogue and conflict prevention, religious pluralism and limitations on freedom of religion, and a report on the ODIHR advisory panel on freedom of religion and proposals for future work for the panel. Our aim with this exercise was to arrive at concrete recommendations for the OSCE to improve its work in these areas as well as to make member states much more aware of the importance of the obligations they had undertaken as members of the OSCE.

The Vienna meeting resulted in several proposals for the inclusion of religious leaders in conflict resolution and for using field missions in this work, for more emphasis on the need to accept, help and tolerate missionary activity in new states where there is no tradition in this regard, and finally in the strengthening of the ODIHR advisory panel on freedom of religion.

Thus, the Norwegian OSCE chairmanship put major emphasis on strengthening the human dimension, including religious freedom. This was a regime-specific tool: the chairman, Foreign Minister Knut Vollebæk, alone decided on this agenda-setting, and took an active interest in how one could use religious dialogue and religious leaders in the work for peace. He undertook to make the OSCE work more actively on what religious freedom really entails, as well as for the organisation to use religious dialogue in its conflict resolution work. This latter aspect of reconciliation had not been developed before within the OSCE. In the words of Vollebæk,

> in the work on the human dimension we have also stressed the connection between culture, religion, and conflict resolution – if religious leaders cannot agree on a peace message, what chance do

> peace conferences then stand? Culture and religion has become the symbol of conflict in many places, but true religion and culture is in fact the very opposite. They are therefore both important tools in conflict resolution. As chairman we have taken several steps to increase the consciousness of this within the OSCE and in particular in the missions.'[10]

What were these concrete initiatives? First, the Norwegian chairmanship reactivated the OSCE expert panel on religious freedom, led by Rudiger Knoll. This panel was given funding of NOK250 000 to make a list of priorities and to initiate some projects. The chairmanship further arranged a special conference on religious freedom in Vienna in March 1999, as mentioned above. This conference gathered more than 150 experts from all member states as well as the major NGOs in the field, and led to a set of recommendations and conclusions about further work in the field.

Later in the year the chairman arranged a high-level conference, at political level, in Oslo on religious freedom and how to use religion in conflict resolution. Here representatives of the major conflicting parties in Kosovo also attended, along with actors like the Communita di Sant' Egidio.

During the chairmanship one also decided that all missions should, as a routine task, consult religious leaders in their host countries on how they could contribute to peace building, thus aiming at integrating the monitoring and fostering of religious freedom in the missions themselves.

Freedom of religion in the OSCE documents has been defined in very precise terms to guide policy-makers in new democracies where this right is largely an unknown. While the specification of what implementation in this regard means is very clearly stated, it is hard to measure the impact of the OSCE in this regard. There are persistent problems in the OSCE area in this field, such as the law on religion in Russia, the lack of Central Asian understanding of what this right entails, the conflicts where religion is instrumentalised in the Balkans, and the need to agree further on what freedom of religion also means in Western states (see the disagreement on this at the 1999 review conference).

The Norwegian chairmanship sought to highlight the importance of religion in several ways: both as a source of conflict when instrumentalised and as an avenue for conflict resolution, and as a primary human right which the OSCE has defined in very clear terms. One moved the issue of religion to the forefront of the OSCE agenda during the chairmanship year through expert-level and political-level conferences, and also sought to streamline the follow-up on the conclusions from these conferences into the standard operating procedures of the missions.

Regime impact through missions: Bosnia and Albania

The OSCE's impact in Bosnia is an ongoing saga. In this large mission – about 270 personnel – the OSCE has a mandate that gives it hard powers in the sense of command power. It is the implementing agency for the civilian part of the Dayton agreement, while SFOR is the military implementor. This means that the OSCE is mandated to develop democracy and rule of law, human rights and fundamental freedoms, in all of Bosnia. The head of mission, the US ambassador Robert Barry, has been in the job for several years, and is well respected as reasonable and firm. I worked closely with the mission during the period 1997–2000, observing its work and partaking in it as the representative of the chairman-in-office in 1999.

There are no academic studies of the OSCE's impact in Bosnia, although many studies carried out by policy and NGO groups are sceptical about the progress. 'Is Dayton Failing?', is the title of a study by the International Crisis Group.[11] The task is enormous, and the easiest part is the military one. There is little violence in Bosnia, and full military control by SFOR. But the task of creating incentives for going from weapons-based to law-based power is a formidable one.

The OSCE has the power to determine how and when elections are to be held, whether to accept or reject election results and parties as well as candidates, whether a party platform is in conformity with OSCE norms, and whether policies carried out by Bosnian politicians are acceptable according to those same norms. Bosnia is being equipped with Western-designed political and legal institutions, and the OSCE uses its powers extensively. Ambassador Barry has cracked down on nationalist politicians and parties several times, especially in the Republika Srpska. A pragmatic line has been taken in cooperating with Serb politicians, also with those who probably were under sealed indictments for war crimes. For example, I had good cooperation with Biljana Plavsic when she was president in Srpska. She worked constructively with the international community, but gave herself up to the ICTY in The Hague in January 2001. She had no hard power protection at that stage.[12]

The OSCE's impact in Bosnia is that of teacher and controller. The policy line is to use the 'carrot' for all those who want to cooperate along Dayton lines, and use the 'stick' only when necessary. With the slow onset of minorities returning from 1999 onwards, there is a greater chance of ethnically mixed communities in the future. So the OSCE, like the rest of the international presence in Bosnia, is systematically using economic conditionality: the areas that allow for minorities to return, get money. With more than 1 million displaced persons inside the two parts of the Bosnian confederation, there will be no political consolidation before this issue has been settled in the sense that people have a choice of returning to their homes.

Within the span of five years the OSCE mission has managed to install multi-party systems in both parts of the confederation, as well as rule-of-law institutions. There is a multi-party system, albeit one with a plethora of parties, as well as a free press where attempts at nationalist and xenophobic articles result in shutdowns of the paper in question. Elections to the rotating presidency (between the three ethnic groups) and to the parliaments have been held, as well as to municipal assemblies. There is, however, no doubt that some of the old hard-liners still hold power, and that the economy is largely corrupt. This also holds for the court system. However, five years is a short time in which to install a democratic culture in a place where weapons have provided the only reliable source of security for centuries.

The OSCE uses both persuasion and teaching, as well as shaming and sanctions, in its work in Bosnia. The shaming is also broadcast internationally, in an excellent web-page[13] which has daily press briefings and press statements.

In Albania there is a more 'normal' OSCE mandate which is negotiated with the government. The mission, around 25 people, has a general mandate to advise and monitor the development of democracy and rule of law. The mission has been very well received and is extensively used as a resource group by the government.[14] During the crisis of the pyramid games and attempted *coup d'état* in 1997, the OSCE mission played a key role in restoring political order. But to date the real territorial power of the Albanian government extends only to the immediate area around Tirana, and the infrastructure of the country is largely lacking, from roads, electricity and sewage systems to basic legislation such as property registries.

The OSCE mission in Tirana continues to be the main international observer and adviser. For instance, prior to national elections in the summer of 2001, ODHIR director Stoudman visited in order to put pressure on the local election commission. He held a press conference in which he detailed the demands on the commission and the government,[15] thus making it quite explicit what were the 'benchmarks' to be achieved, and the conditions for OSCE election monitoring. This is again a combination of advice and assistance on one hand, and 'shaming' on the other. International pressure is alerted and kept up, while the local government gets help in meeting the targets set. In the words of Stoudman himself, 'we introduce some degree of public shaming, and then help the government in question on how to get out of the situation with a good result. If compliance is not forthcoming, however, we use more public shaming.'[16]

Regime impact through the HCNM: the Baltic states

The conflicts that erupt, are reported. The conflicts that are prevented, go unnoticed. This is the reality of conflict prevention, and a reason why it is difficult to achieve. The OSCE's work is not seen very much, but that may in fact indicate success. It is only seen when it is conflictual; when there are some violent tensions, but not when things go well. This reality of international affairs is especially important for the HCNM, whose success is the *lack* of conflict. His mandate is 'early warning' and early conflict prevention.

Max van der Stoehl's work is low-key. He prefers to work with national minority questions behind the scenes, opting not to use public diplomacy. The strongest tool in his tool kit, the issuing of a so-called 'solemn warning', has only been used once in the history of his office.[17] In his own words, he thinks the low-key approach is more useful.[18]

This, however, does not mean that such an approach is toothless. The power behind the HCNM's office lies in his ability to demand access to any group or person within any state, and to take an issue to the public forum if it turns out to be impossible to resolve. There is thus considerable pressure on the parties to reach a solution through the good offices of the HCNM.

The most spectacular success of van der Stoehl's silent diplomacy has been in the Baltic states. Here he has prevented major conflicts from erupting. Minority rights have a strong formal–legal protection in the COE's 'Framework Convention for Protection of National Minorities',[19] and the OSCE often refers to this text as the most important one. However, the OSCE documents also contain major emphasis on this important area of human rights.

The HCNM and the OSCE missions mediated in the tense situation in the Baltic states in the early 1990s. Here it was not enough to put pressure on these states from the EU and NATO, and the 'carrot' of eventual EU membership was not enough. There was a need for constant presence and monitoring on the ground, as the issue of citizenship rights for the Russian minority, especially in Estonia, represented a major conflict in the population. Here there was an urgent need for peaceful conflict resolution. 'in no other post-Cold War situation have the vital interests of Russia and the West come so close to directly conflicting with each other' (Flynn and Farrell, 1999: 508).

Van der Stoehl and the missions were actively engaged in teaching the Baltic governments how to deal with the minority issue, including the implications of non-compliance. The Russians, on their side, wanted to use the mission in Estonia as a clearing-house for Russian interests, while the local population naturally resisted this. The OSCE managed to avoid becoming politicised in this, and steered a difficult course between great power interests and making the Baltic states understand that compliance with minority rights standards was in their own interest. This issue is still a very contentious one in the Baltic states, ten years after the HCNM worked on it. This indicates how difficult it was at that time.

Also in other states the work of the HCNM has been instrumental to prevent conflict. He has worked with governments and minority groups in Slovakia and Romania, but his method, based on the premise that the governments in question understand the importance of minority issues, is not useful in areas where this condition does not obtain, such as in the Balkans. The need for hard power control and potential use seems a crucial precondition for compliance in such places. Only where the parties understand that a peaceful solution is needed, can the HCNM work successfully.

Regime impact through the ODHIR: Chechnya and Azerbaijan

The outbreak of the second civil war in Chechnya in 1999 has led to much international attention, also from NGOs, but to little impact on the Russian war efforts. Representatives from various IOs criticised the disproportionate use of force in the republic, and the lack of humanitarian assistance to the population.

The war in Chechnya has been inaccessible to international observers and humanitarian organisations, to such an extent that the thousands of refugees and displaced persons have been without the most basic kind of assistance. The international community, in this case the UN, the EU, the COE and the OSCE, have tried, largely in vain, to access the area and ensure adequate humanitarian aid. The record on this has been dismal. The Russians have responded with traditional notions of sovereignty and non-intervention: that this is an internal matter, that they are fighting bandits and terrorists, that there is no need for any international help, mediation or humanitarian assistance. When OSCE chairman Vollebæk insisted that he wanted to visit Chechnya in December 1999, the Russian response was a very blunt 'no'. Only after much insistence was he allowed to visit some of the areas under Russian control near Grozny and in Ingushetia.

Likewise, the aid given by the UNHCR and various national organisations was all to be channelled through Moscow and Russian aid agencies, thus in effect making it impossible for foreigners to be in Chechnya. It is also true that the security situation regarding kidnappings is precarious, thus making it impossible for foreigners to be in the region even in peacetime.[20] As stated, the OSCE mission in Grozny had to be withdrawn to Moscow during 1999 because of the security situation: its members could not go out, and could hardly trust their bodyguards.

The international criticism of the Russian offensive in Chechnya emphasised that it used disproportionate levels of force and that it did not allow humanitarian assistance and transparency. The norms in question are both covered by the Geneva conventions. But most foreign criticism fell on stony ground.

To date only a *small impact* can be evidenced, viz. the erection of a human rights office directly under President Putin. Staffed by the new human rights commissioner, Kalamantov, and about 35 human rights monitors who are supposed to out in the field, this office is the first of its kind in Russia. The work of the COE human rights commissioner Gil-Robles was probably the triggering factor, but sustained international criticism was a major explanation why this office was erected.

Once set up, it quickly became clear that the monitors lacked training and knowledge in this area. The ODHIR chairman Stoudman and the COE's Gil-Robles therefore offered training courses in human rights monitoring in Warsaw and Strasbourg, and the OSCE also offered the entire software concept for monitoring developed for the human rights reports from Kosovo. In this unique 900-page report,[21] used by the ICTY as evidence against war crimes and crimes against humanity in Kosovo, the KVM, evacuated to Skopje on 17 March 1999, some few days before the bombing began, continued its work by systematically interviewing refugees who left Kosovo. The questions and material were classified in very detailed fashion, by geographic place of origin, about the human rights transgressions that took place in each place, including names of persons massacred, places of massacres and burials, etc. The wealth of information needed to be processed in proper ways that allowed for retrieval and cross-indexing, and the software developed specifically for this were offered to the Russian human rights office. Computer experts from the ODHIR went to Moscow to install the programs and teach staff how to use them.

This example of the impact in human rights may seem miniscule, but it is a fact that Kalamantov's human rights office is the first ever in Russia, and that all the training in the actual human rights monitoring has been undertaken by the OSCE and the COE. By 2001 the Russian human rights office had published two reports on the conditions in Chechnya.

Despite all political difficulties, it is seen that learning here may have an effect. In February 2001 there was a well-publicised army exercise in Russia, the purpose of which was to train officers and soldiers in the application of the Geneva conventions. The reason for this, said the commander of the Russian army, was that the Chechen experience had showed that there was much amiss in this field.[22]

Turning to the case of Azerbaijan, we find a good illustration of how the ODHIR combines aid and 'shaming' in achieving results. For the election to the Azeri parliament in December 2000, the COE and ODHIR sent about 220 observers. They were to observe the actual polling and counting in polling stations in and around Baku. The Azeri government welcomed the observers, as any election held in states where there is doubt about the viability of the process, is observed by international observers, usually from the OSCE, COE and EU when in Europe, or from the UN and other regional organisations elsewhere.

A government will almost invariably want observers to come, lest their election is deemed fraudulent. It is also part of political conditionality that observers be let in. The few cases where the OSCE has refused to observe an election include the parliamentary elections under Milosevic in 1999 and elections in Belarus. These cases were deemed to be a direct legitimation of a fraudulent regime. But in cases where fraud probably will be attempted, but where the elections may be 'free and fair' if observed properly, the OSCE and other international observers normally decide to come.

One such case is Azerbaijan. But when the election observers came on surprise visits in the polling stations after midnight on election day, they discovered enormous attempts at fraud. One estimate is that as much as 80 per cent of the election was fraudulent: there were fake election protocols that the observers confiscated, and legion cases of ballot stuffing. Also, the OSCE observers were physically thrown out of the polling stations in some places, and were threatened. They also witnessed that the ruling party of President Heidar Alijev, Musavat, called in the police to arrest political opponents present in the polling stations, and this happened before the eyes of the international observers. The director of the ODHIR, ambassador Gerard Stoudman, was himself present and witnessed this incredibly blatant attempt at fraud.[23]

The existence of such an open fraud made it easy to detect, and the OSCE confiscated all the evidence and demanded an instant meeting with President Alijev. He seemed surprised, but naturally could not have been ignorant of the situation. He asked them what to do to rectify the situation as 'Azeri membership in the COE was conditional upon a straight election'. In fact, Armenia and Azerbaijan were both going to be admitted to the COE after the Azeri elections, a fact that one would think extremely important for the elections to run smoothly!

This case shows that there are states where the elite has not even learnt to 'talk the talk' of human rights properly, even less take the minimal, necessary steps to let action follow rhetoric, even in a case where the incentive structure is so clear. It seems almost incredible that such fraud and such treatment of COE and OSCE observers were possible when the election was the 'test case' for COE membership.

In the meeting with President Alijev, the OSCE demanded new elections in all the cases of fraud, and a public annulment and recognition of fraud by the national election commission. Then, as always, what happened would be made public, and press releases sent out. The press release the day after the election warrants quotation:

> The elections were marred by numerous instances of serious irregularities, in particular a completely flawed counting process. Observers reported ballot stuffing, manipulated turnout results, premarked ballots, and production of either false protocols or no protocols at all. Additionally, party proxies frequently suffered intimidation, harassment and sometimes even arrest whilst carrying out their legitimate activities. Unauthorised local officials often controlled the process and sought to influence voters. In several instances, international observers were denied access to polling sta-

> tions and were frequently expelled from election commission premises.[24]

President Alijev agreed to the conditions set by the OSCE and scheduled new elections. The election commission was presented with the overwhelming hard evidence of fraud that the international observers had collected, and had nothing to say in their defence, but cancelled the elections in these precincts through a public statement.[25]

This case is interesting for two reasons: one, it shows the OSCE's *combination of persuasion and shaming* as complementary tools. This is also a combination which is found in the COE (Checkel, 2000a) and in the EU, and which makes it very hard to disentangle the effects of instrumental variables vis-à-vis learning and socialisation. In this case, shaming was probably a necessary condition for any internalisation of the democracy norm to take place, and we have no indication that it has been internalised at all.

What the OSCE did was to offer further assistance on the set-up of an acceptable election, which does not mean that even if their advice is followed, it has resulted in any real acceptance of the democracy norm. It may simply mean that the regime is smart enough to realise that their non-compliance is a problem for them. This realisation hardly requires much learning.

Two, this case illustrates the 'edge' between the states that have already realised this, and those that have not. All the Central and East European states were eager to join the COE and now try to meet EU criteria. They are acutely aware of *their need to be seen as compliant*, and will do their utmost not to receive criticism from the international community. But when we move to the Balkans and to the Caucasus and beyond, we find that the leadership in those states have often not even started to 'talk the talk' of the human rights regime. When the chairman of the OSCE visited the five Central Asian states in 1999, there were cases of religious persecution and severe repression going on in some of them while he was visiting, and a clear rejection of intervention when he tried to put this on the agenda. In this part of the world they are still far from the influence of Western media and Western shaming. In the Caucasus they are closer to Western integration, seeking it actively, and thus in need of approval. But President Alijev's lack of control of the situation with regard to fraud on the eve of his country's admission to the COE tells us that there is still a lot to be learnt about public diplomacy and the effects of shaming in Baku.

In the region beyond Central Europe there are other cases of non-compliance which stand out: the Ukraine's refusal to abolish the death penalty despite its legal obligation to do so, to mention one.

In conclusion, these two 'hard' cases show that there is a certain impact of the human rights regime even here. In both these cases, although the states are OSCE members, they claim non-intervention and traditional state sovereignty. But this is a fluid picture where shaming usually has an effect. In Russia the repeated visits by the COE representatives and the suspension of Russian voting rights in the COE's parliamentary assembly were taken note of. The Russian army exercise was partly a response to this explicit event. Russia has now regained its voting rights in the PA.

Role of states vs. IO powers

How much impact is wielded by the OSCE itself – secretariat, special representatives, missions, the HCNM, the chairman-in-office? How much is dictated by the member states, especially by the strongest ones?

With the hindsight of having worked as deputy to the Norwegian chairman-in-office for a year, my first conclusion is that major member states are important. Decisions or initiatives by the chairman are always taken in consultation with these states, and often such states make demands on the chairman. There is no doubt that the chairman's power depends on being sensitive to the interests of major member states, but by skilful consideration of such interests and by building alliances, he or she may create the basis for strong political initatives and consequent agenda-setting.

Above all, the chairman sets the OSCE's agenda to a large extent. During the Norwegian chairmanship, there was an emphasis on themes like religious freedom, the Roma-Sinti, gender issues and trafficking, to mention the most important.[26] The chairmanship launched conferences at both expert and political level on these issues, and thus created the basis for political measures. The missions were alerted to these issues in particular, being instructed to take action on them. One result was the successful rescue of 17 kidnapped women from the Ukraine by the mission in FYROM. These women were destined for brothels in the West, Montenegro, Albania and FYROM serving as main transit routes.[27]

The impact of the chairman's agenda-setting can be seen in the review conference on the human dimension in 2000, where many projects in the areas chosen by the Norwegian chairmanship were reported on. For example, in the area of religious freedom, there were recommendations for immediate recognition of faith communities as legal entities, for the prompt return of confiscated property to such communities, and for a new conference devoted to the right of religious communities to be registered.[28] These are old problems in the OSCE, but since there are so many different areas of concern within the human dimension, it is essential that issues are kept on the agenda in order for them to receive political attention. One can follow the issues from the Norwegian chairmanship the year after, thus at least finding that the agenda-setting has remained.

There is also major power vested in the independent work of the missions and the HCNM. The member states cannot change mission mandates or interfere with the HCNM. In recent years new and similar offices have been erected, such as the Special Representative for the Freedom of the Media, an ombudsman for media freedom who speaks up against abuse on his own initiative; and an Office for Economic and Social Development. The OSCE's member states thus cannot control the day-to-day running of the organisation, which is set by existing mandates and routines. However, when it comes to an issue where major political interests are involved, such as setting up the KVM, it is clear that the USA, the major European states and the Russians had to be closely consulted.

Conclusion: the impact of the OSCE's human rights regime

The impact of the OSCE is usually seen in slow, detailed processes, not in quick changes. Great power interests often make it impossible for the OSCE to have an impact at all. Russia's refusal to grant full freedom of religion is one such example: despite adherence to the OSCE principles, Russia has passed a law on religious communities which denies both the right to conduct missionary activity and the right to be registered on a par with the Orthodox Church. Likewise, Russia denies the OSCE the right to visit Chechnya, and responds to criticism about its use of force in the region with a simple call for old-fashioned 'non-intervention'. One could also mention the US's continued frequent use of the death penalty despite the OSCE norm to abolish it. Indeed, it can be said that the OSCE is not an instrument for intervention in its major member states, none of which have missions in them.

The OSCE's impact is primarily in the new and weak democracies in Central Asia, the Caucasus, in some of the former Soviet republics, and in the Balkans. During 1999 and 2000 the OSCE missions were established, under various mandates and in various forms, in both Central Asia and south Caucasus. In places like Minsk and Grozny[29] the only international presence has been the missions. It is obvious that in these places one starts from the very beginning in teaching about democracy, human rights and the rule of law. The OSCE impact here is unique – there is simply no impact of any other IO.

Another important variable is the fact that the missions are present, on the ground. This makes for very powerful monitoring. One relies on local staff as well as expatriates, and this allows information to be gathered by people on the inside of the society. This method is also echoed by the EU in its monitoring missions in the Balkans, the ECMM. Relying on local informants and trust, the reports from the ECMM have been the very best sources of information about what really is happening in local society. It turns out that reports from afar are often inaccurate, especially when they are 'doctored' to make the IO in question seem efficient and productive. Thus, as regards monitoring and assessment, the OSCE is much more able than the COE and the EU in determining what the problems on the ground are, and thus to prescribe a cure. The reporting to the COE is often based on states' own reports, which naturally suffers from the 'doctoring' problem. It is only by missions in the field that accurate information can be acquired.

7
The Impact of the EU

The EU as a foreign policy actor: tools and powers

The EU has gone from being an economic community to a political union, at least in name, but also rapidly in real terms. It has steadily, in small steps, consolidated its foreign policy, often codifying practice that has evolved. The ambition to forge a political community and a union means that the EU seeks to develop policy in all relevant areas. This has also resulted in work on human rights, democracy and the rule of law, as well as on security and defence policy.

The sheer political and economic weight of the EU clearly makes it the most important actor of the three IOs in this study. The EU's laws are binding on member states, and the European Court of Justice (ECJ) in Luxembourg has increasingly 'constitutionalised' the treaties through its rulings (Graver, 2000; Weiler, 1999; Alter, 2000; Fossum, 2000). Most policy areas have been gradually more or less integrated, some through supranational legal transfer of sovereignty, such as commercial or agricultural policy, others through small steps, such as foreign policy. Human rights became an EU policy area as late as 1986, when it was mentioned in the Single European Act (SEA), and only became an operative part of foreign policy in the 1990s.

In this chapter we first analyse the *general* tools and powers of the EU in the foreign policy field to see what kind of an actor it is in this field, assessing secondly the *general* impact it has. Then we look at how the human rights regime is embedded in the EU, and investigate whether there are *regime-specific* tools that pertain to this regime. Finally, we analyse the impact of the human rights regime on third states, in particular in the enlargement process.

From the EPC to the CFSP

With the creation of the European Community, trade and commercial policy was made into a supranational policy area. Member states handed over their national sovereignty in this area to the EC. Thus, before the creation of the so-called European Political Coordination (EPC), an informal cooperation between EC foreign ministers, the EC developed a unitary actor presence in the economic area internationally, an area more often than not classified as 'foreign economic policy' or even as 'foreign policy'. This development was facilitated by the growing interdependence of foreign and trade policy throughout the 1970s:

> The EC has developed its own foreign policy personality in the international system . . . its foreign policy activity spans a wide swath of bilateral, multilateral, summit, and regional diplomacy. It sends and receives diplomatic representatives and missions to and from a majority of the world's states. It is a signatory to many international covenants and participates in over forty international conferences and organizations as a full member or as an observer (Ginsberg, 1989: 42).

The EPC started in 1970 as an intergovernmental forum for the coordination of the 'high politics' of the member states. It was the result of a long tradition of more integrationist attempts at building political union which proved impossible to agree on: the 1954 European Defence Community (EDC), the 1954 European Political Community, and the so-called Fouchet Plans from 1961–62 aimed at creating a common foreign policy. The EPC, however, was possible to launch because it entailed no legal base in the treaties, no budget or secretariat, and had no official ties to the EC. At The Hague summit in 1969 EC foreign ministers were charged with reporting on how to achieve foreign policy cooperation, based on a French proposal. At the same time the French accepted British entry into the EU.

The ensuing document, called the Luxembourg report, proposed consultation on all major foreign policy decisions in an extra-EC framework, biannual meetings among foreign ministers, and the creation of a Committee of Political Directors (the Political Committee) consisting of high-level representatives of member states. The EPC was further developed in a series of summit reports drafted by central European politicians. In 1972 the EC summit in Paris furthered the EPC's contact with the EC. The Commission was now to be consulted on matters relating to EC competences, and the summit stated that the

EC must develop a role for itself on the world stage, as the 'European voice'. It also requested a second report from foreign ministers on how to develop the EPC, which resulted in the so-called Copenhagen Report in 1973. Here the EC's political identity was underscored, and the need for common action as one actor. The structure of the EPC was refined: so-called political correspondents were to be named in each foreign ministry, they were to consult, study and work together, embassies in foreign states were to consult with each other on a regular and routine basis, the EPC and the EC were to work towards political unification and the same goals (Ginsberg, 1989: 49).

Here we see a *gradual deepening* of the EPC's EC dimension. Now the work towards coordination of national positions in IOs and conferences got seriously under way. At the 1974 EC summit the European Council was established, also implying that foreign policy goals were to be discussed in this new forum. Here both the Commission and foreign ministers were present. At this summit it was decided that EC and EPC meetings were to be held in the same place, meaning further informal coordination and networking.

In 1981 what was called the London Report further developed the relationship between the EPC and the EC, by prescribing joint consultations between EC members in international negotiations, underscoring the need for common positions and consultations before national foreign policy was made, and by emphasising the aim to achieve joint *actions* by EPC states, not only joint *declarations*.

In 1986 the time had come to include the EPC in the treaty framework. The proposal to do this had been launched several years before. This was the result of a gradual 'maturing' of national views and of extended discussion of the ideas that eventually came to be adopted in the codification in the treaty. This historical record supports the view that sees the intergovernmental conferences as codifications of 'practice' (Pierson, 1996). The SEA's inclusion of the EPC built on the ideas that had been floated and discussed in the EPC and in the EC for many years. Petersen concludes that 'the SEA amounted mostly to a codification of existing practices and understandings' (1993: 14).

The SEA art. I links the EC and the EPC in one objective, viz. the aim of European unity. The scope of foreign policy was extended, although not to military security. The member states were obliged to consult each other and to take 'full account' of other states' positions as well as to seek common positions. Common principles and positions were to constitute a 'point of reference' for national foreign policy. The apparatus with meetings of political directors continued, and the

Commission was to be fully 'involved' in EPC meetings. The European Parliament (EP) was to be informed, but neither the roles of the Commission nor of the EP in relation to the EPC were further defined. A secretariat manned by national officials was set up in Brussels.

The Common Foreign and Security Policy (CFSP)

The CFSP, the name given to the EPC when incorporated into the TEU, was the result of reactions to the momentous changes in Europe in 1989–90 as well as the internal workings of the EPC.

CFSP was the name given to the extension of the EPC in the TEU in 1992. The adoption of EMU by Germany was made in return for promises of the creation of political union. The decision to hold intergovernmental conferences (IGCs) on EMU and political union was made at the same time, in an agreement between France and Germany. The unification of Germany meant that France saw the need for tying Germany into a more integrated foreign policy framework. Commission President Delors called for the inclusion of security policy in the EC. Also the EP acted, drawing up a Report (Martin I) which called for the integration of the EPC into the EC. This was seconded by a Belgian proposal for a 'truly joint foreign policy'. Also the Italian government supported such a move. In a joint statement by France and Germany on 19 April 1990, a 'common foreign and security policy' was called for. The IGC on political union began in December 1990.

The EP, in its so-called Martin II Report, proposed a 'communitarianism' of the EPC, that the Commission should share in the external representation of the common foreign policy, and that the EP should have a role in decision-making. Security issues should be included in the agenda.

The Commission, for its part, proposed that security policy in the EC should entail a security guarantee akin to NATO's para. 5, in other words, a mutual security clause. It also proposed a shared right of initiative for itself and a share in the preparation of proposals, and the introduction of QMV in foreign policy.

At the IGC, both Belgium and Greece supported a strong common and integrated foreign policy, while Denmark opposed any supranationality in this issue area (Laursen and Vanhoonacker, 1992). But the larger states were in favour of a common foreign policy: Italy published a memorandum advocating the inclusion of the West European Union (WEU) into the EC, including a mutual security guarantee, and far-reaching military coordination. This proposal was also supported by Spain.

There followed a joint Franco-German proposal which was a compromise between the German insistence on 'communitarianism' and the French wish to retain intergovernmentalism. Then there were calls for the inclusion of the WEU in the EC, the gradual development of a joint defence policy, but a retention of unanimous decision-making.

In the negotiations there was a stress on the need for consultation with the EP, a specific role for the Commission, and an opening for QMV in foreign policy. On the inclusion of security policy there was much more vagueness, probably because of British opposition.

The CFSP evolution as EU foreign policy

During the 1990s a consensus was formed on *scope* – it should encompass defence – but there was nonetheless opposition to this from Ireland and Denmark. The major issue of defining 'defence' was left to the next IGC.

As regards the *depth* of commitment, there was a difference between states' interests. In the TEU's art. J.2 we find the areas of cooperation where 'common positions' may be had, but in J.3 we have areas of 'joint action'. More areas will gradually be transferred to this category but they must be in areas where the member states have 'essential interests in common'.

The *decision-making* mode is a hybrid one: the CFSP remained outside the Community framework, but within its institutional structure. The General Council is the policy-maker, not the meeting of foreign ministers. Meetings are prepared by COREPER, replacing the Political Committee. Further, the European Council shall lay down the guidelines for the CFSP (art. J.8) and decide which issues will be the subject of joint action.

The Commission is to be 'fully associated' with the CFSP, with some right of initiative and external representation (art. J.8.3). But the Presidency will have the daily management – as part of the troika – and also be the official external representative. The EP is to be informed and its views are to be taken into consideration.

There was still no majority decision-making as a main rule, but the possibility exists. Some states favoured it as a general rule, such as Italy and Belgium, whereas France and Germany wanted a middle position where implementation decisions were to be taken by QMV. The result was art. J.4.2 which states that the council can decide unanimously to decide something by QMV – akin to provisions regarding some aspects of environmental policy. This was a compromise which introduced the QMV principle into the CFSP.

The IGC that resulted in the TEU concentrated on Economic and Monetary Union (EMU) and left the issue of political union to be negotiated at the next IGC. At Maastricht the CFSP was created, based on the modest text on the EPC in the SEA. There were significant changes, as discussed above. The agenda for the the new IGC was about further development of this area.

The so-called reflection group, made up of the personal representatives of the member states, presented their report in December 1995 (Reflection Group's report, 1995). One of the three main aims of the IGC-96 should be to give the 'Union greater capacity for external action' (III). The problem was the discrepancy between the economic power and the external economic action of the EU and its weak political action capacity, and 'the time has come to provide this common policy (CFSP) with the means to function more effectively' (VIII). A major example of inefficiency was the inaction in the former Yugoslavia; 'it is a truth universally acknowledged that the EC has failed in former Yugoslavia', as Simon Nuttal expressed it (Nuttal, 1994).

Concretely it is suggested that a unit of analysis and planning be established and that decision-making procedures are improved in ways that allow for flexibility. There was, within the group, dissension on whether QMV should be extended to the CFSP. There was also no agreement on whether to create an office of a 'foreign minister', called 'Mr CFSP'. There was major agreement on the need for coordination between the Foreign Economic Policy (FEP) and the Commission's role in this, and the CFSP and the council.

Defence and security policy required development from the text written into the TEU, but not elaborated beyond this. Here there were major disagreements between states. Some wanted the WEU to become integrated in the treaty; others baulked at this idea. The IGC should take steps to develop 'the European identity, including in the security and defence policy field' (IX). Here there is apparently wide disagreement on the relationship between the EU and the WEU.

The results of the IGC were that 'Mr CFSP' and his strategic planning unit were incorporated into the treaty as the secretariat of the council, and that this secretariat was given the task of developing policy that had in principle been adopted by the European Council in the form of strategies. The dynamic and skilled leadership of Javier Solana has led a major presence of the EU in everything from peace negotiations in the Middle East to the situation in Kosovo. It is clear that the EU is making more and more of an impact in all foreign policy fields, save defence in a traditional sense. But at the UN and in most other international fora the EU speaks with one voice and is the major Western actor besides the USA, and in third country agreements political elements are inserted along with trade. It is this very potent political conditionality we will examine next. This is also the area where we find a major impact from the human rights regime.

In conclusion, the *foreign policy of the EU has developed from a coordination between member states to becoming more of a united actor capacity,* although it is still possible for states to opt out of particular policy actions. However, the EU is perceived as and expected to be *one actor* with a response from the world around it, and advocates itself as such.

The use *of soft power tools is typical* of the EU, although it has ambitions to develop the defence part of its foreign policy. However, so far the CFSP is carried out by public diplomacy and classical, bilateral diplomacy. The EU speaks with one voice in most international conferences, and issues statements on current events. It also presents démarches on worrisome situations in national capitals, and conducts traditional foreign policy talks, like a nation-state 'writ large'.

As we shall see below, some of the soft power tools are becoming intertwined with hard power economic tools.

EU foreign policy embedded in other policy areas

The CFSP is, legally speaking, unrelated to the external economic policy. However, in political practice this is not so. There has been an evolution of a foreign economic policy on the part of the EU that includes distinct elements of 'pure' foreign policy, such as economic sanctions, and the 'mixed' agreements with Central Europe where economic elements are mixed with conditionality clauses for human rights and democracy.

The Commission, charged with making trade and commercial policy, has consistently tried to enhance its role in foreign policy by using its competence in foreign economic policy to include new foreign policy areas under this label. This has been done in two ways: one, by using the legal competences expansively; two, by defining new policy as within the remit of foreign economic policy.

We assume here that the Commission is interested in task expansion and institution-building in order to enhance its role. This is well documented in many studies of the Commission's role in various issues areas. These studies indicate that the Commission uses both internal opportunities, such as basing new policy on existing competences, as well as external 'windows' of opportunity where the EU is called upon to respond. In the case of foreign policy, we see a mixture of these methods. There is extensive legal competence in the area of common commercial policy (CCP), and the Commission has used this expansively, to gradually define developmental policy and economic sanctions as part of its policy remit under this competence. This has only been possible because of the intermingling of political and economic elements in the 1980s – *vide* the situation in Central Europe after the Cold War. Here security and economics are now tightly linked, whereas this was impossible during the Cold War. This provided ample opportunities for agenda-setting, linkages and the design of foreign policy based on existing competences, as will be seen below. Another example of such task expansion is the so-called Barcelona process, whereby the EU is developing a comprehensive policy towards the Maghreb region, fusing political with economic elements (Barbe, 1998).

The 'task' expansion in the EU has taken place primarily through the redefinition of new policy within the remit of the competition policy or the single market. Sometimes a 'window of opportunity' has presented itself that the Commission has been able to utilise. Yet in the case of the CFSP, the Commission's direct influence has been smaller, albeit growing throughout the 1990s.

We thus first search for evidence that the Commission has followed the usual 'task expansionist' strategy in foreign policy other than the CFSP, and then look at how this is linked to the CFSP.

The issue of 'competence' is an intensely conflictual one. John Usher, a lawyer, states that

> Competence is . . . a crucial issue. . . . As an independent political animal, the Commission is keen to extend its power and play a politically strategic role . . . this means a constant quest to identify potential for new areas of competence. In tactical terms it means the Commission will seek legal justification for the selection of treaty bases requiring QMV (1994: 149).

Turning to the issue area of external economic relations, there is an increasing difficulty of separating the political and the economic aspects of foreign policy-making. It is a commonplace that economic aspects have taken over much of the traditional role of foreign policy, and this trend 'aids' the Commission in establishing an influence also in the CFSP area.

The external role of the EU has increased steadily despite the fact that the first treaties – ECSC and Euratom – contained no provision for this, but nonetheless the Commission's function was a pivotal one.

> Many of the problems faced by the Commission in the pursuit of external relations are effectively 'boundary problems' because it is impossible to say what is 'economic' and what is 'political' in foreign policy, and likewise, where foreign policy begins and domestic policy ends. Also, where is the boundary between security, defence and foreign policy in Europe in the post-Cold War era? This is indeed a time in which the Commission can utilise its defining ability as agenda-setter (ibid.).

This bears directly on the question of 'competence'. Wherein lies Commission competence in external affairs? DGI, responsible for foreign economic policy, was split into DGIA and DGIB, responsible for foreign policy and external delegations, after the TEU. These DGs were merged into RELEX in 1999 including four DGs: Enlargement, Development, and the former DGIA and B. The international and European trends have drawn the Commission into more of the mainstream of foreign policy.

Long before the EU had any foreign policy competence, the EEC treaty granted the Commission competence in the area of CCP in articles 113–114 and 228 EEC. The Commission has exclusive competence here, although, as Smith notes, 'it is increasingly unclear how the boundaries around the CCP can be drawn or maintained'(1994: 251). In the EEC treaty the main articles are 110–116, which have remained unchanged in later treaty revisions.

The CCP is the corollary of the customs union which established a 'border' between the EU and the outside world, necessitating external coordination and representation. The Commission's competence was understood to be exclusive, but has remained contested, and in trade policy there is today a 'mixity' in terms of competence, where the member states and the Commission negotiate together, at the WTO, for example. Also, trade agreements with third countries must be signed by both member states and by the Commission, another feature of 'mixity' or 'mixed competence'.

Art. 113 is a key one in establishing both the exclusive competence of the Commission and the use of QMV in the CCP. In art. 229 the Commission's negotiating role in international trade organisations is established. Governments who want to take unilateral courses of actions must ask permission from the Commission. As for art. 113,

> the strength of the grant of competence, allied to a certain vagueness about the range of commercial policy areas in which it was to be exercised, has proven a major boon to the Commission as an international actor. But it has also led to tensions with the Council of Ministers and individual member states' (Smith, 1994: 252).

Further, the Commission can base its action on the so-called 'implied powers', which are recognised in art. 228. Here the rule is that where the Commission has an internal, 'domestic', competence, it automatically also has an external competence. This is also an area of great tension and uncertainty. This principle is based on a ruling from the ECJ (Case 22/70, Commission vs. Council (1971) ECR 263) on the European Road Transport Agreement. The ECJ ruled that the Commission has implied powers to conclude treaties with third countries. This in fact meant that 'where common rules affecting internal policies were laid down, the Member States no longer had the right to conclude treaties with non-member states' (Smith, 1994: 252). Here a conflict has arisen between member states and the Commission as to whether 'internal policy' is restricted only to areas where there is legal competence in the treaties or also to policy in the form of declarations, resolutions and recommendations, i.e. non-binding policy, which extends to areas like education, culture, etc. States that conclude bilateral agreements that could prejudge internal EU policy can be taken to the ECJ under art. 228. Smith concludes that 'the room for debate about the Commission's rights and obligations in this area is thus considerable' (1994: 253).

Further, EEC art. 238 is the basis for EC's treaty-making power with third states and IOs. This article has been used for developing the Lomé conventions (the EC's development policy), the EEA agreement, agreements with the Mediterranean states, as well as the 'Europe' agreements with Central Europe. In both the areas of association and enlargement there is no exclusive Commission competence, and these agreements are usually referred to as 'mixed agreements' or 'mixity'.

'Mixed agreements' occur when 'the subject matter of an international agreement falls partly within a member state and partly within Community competence' (Smith, 1994: 252). Both the EC and the states sign agreements with third countries in those cases. ECJ rulings have confirmed the validity of such mixed competence. Smith continues: 'The important point here is not so much the apparent ambiguity in areas of mixed competence as the revealing nature of potential sources of tension over boundary disputes between the Commission and the member states. Community competence is not a static concept' (1994: 254).

In trade and commercial policy, the Commission has developed a complex set of policy instruments. Among these are anti-dumping measures. DGI, later RELEX, has been built up, but other DGs also have now an 'external 'side.

The cases of 'mixity' are based on art. 113: here the Commission gets a mandate from Council, acting on QMV, the Commission then negotiates with the third country or in an international conference, and the agreement is ratified by QMV. During the negotiations, member states keep watch through the '113 Committee', also aptly called the 'Le Comité des belles-mères'. The Commission monitors and can institute anti-dumping measures, and art. 113 can also be used to institute economic embargoes and other economic sanctions, a tool that is expressly a foreign policy one.

Other EU policy areas with external implications are the common agricultural policy (CAP), with its ability for setting import duties on produce, the common fisheries policy, air transport policy the environment, development policy, and so forth.

Bilateral treaties can be conducted regarding economic cooperation between member states and third countries, but here also there are disputes. 'It is clear that the role of the Commission is determined not merely by the formal treaty provisions but also by the nature of the issues at stake and the attitudes of other EU institutions' (Smith, 1994: 257). The process of policy formation is thus political as well as legal and technical. 'The political/administrative mix highlights the problems of the establishment of boundaries around policy domains' (ibid.).

External representation at conferences is a problem – often with threefold representation, the Commission, the Presidency and member states. Here cases are decided ad hoc each time, and

> the Commission's strategy in this area is to seek to extend its own competence where possible. It does this by building precedents, for example where preambles in its own text reflect previous Council declarations in non-related areas, or by using implied competence in one area as a precedent for acquiring competence in a new area (Smith, 1994: 258).

The Commission is at the helm of all international trade negotiations, which today is 'the highest of high politics', argues Smith (1994: 259), and there is also 'an intimate linkage between external relations, "foreign policy", and security policy in the changing conditions in the 1990s' (ibid.). The Commission acts as a 'linking pin' between many policy styles and areas, and has its own logic of operating. Smith concludes that 'external relations is subject to this trend as are other areas, but one crucial difference is the intersection of external relations with almost every other area of Commission concern' (ibid.).

In the WTO, UN and OECD, the Commission is the speaker and negotiates, but the member states are individual members.

The Commission's 'task expansion'

The Commission has thus been able to *'use' its legal competences to expand on the remit of foreign policy*. This has been possible because of the evolving foreign policy agenda in Europe. First, there are the general factors of an increasing intertwining of what formerly used to be separated as domestic and foreign policy. In the case of the EU, there is no clear demarcation here. As we saw above, it is a matter of defining at any point in time what falls under the 'domestic' and the 'foreign' headings. Most policy areas in the traditional 'domestic' portfolio within the state now have a 'foreign' dimension – commonly referred to as the internationalisation of foreign policy. This development is also evidenced in the Commission's various DGs, as discussed above. Moreover, foreign policy – traditional 'high politics' such as defence – is today increasingly about foreign economic policy, as we have touched on. Thus, to separate out the elements that belong to the Commission's competence and those of the CFSP is a question of defining what is what in each case; something which is an intensely *political* activity.

Below we focus on the empirical evidence for the Commission's 'task expansion' in foreign policy with regard to making 'inroads' into the remit of the CFSP. As recounted above, the Commission was granted a formal role of participation in the CFSP in the TEU, and this role was extended in the Amsterdam Treaty to include rights of initiative as well as being the coordinator ensuring consistency between external economic policy and the CFSP.

The Commission has 'gradually established itself as a key participant' in the meetings of the G-7 as well as in the World Economic Summits. The role assigned to it as the coordinator of the G-24 group of the OECD in its policy development towards Central Europe is a case in point, and this is discussed in more detail below.

But in developmental aid too, there has been a steady development of an EU aid policy, based on the competence of the CCP. However, here there is also a 'mixed' competence. The Lomé conventions (of which there are four) are based on art. 238 EEC, and administered jointly by DGI and DGVIII (Development). This policy is based on national allocations and is being negotiated with member states, but the Commission is the 'linking pin' organisation here and has built up considerable legitimacy for its role in this, also becoming a major coordinator of foreign emergency aid.

The case of Central Europe

The Commission has used its position well in building a role for itself in the case of Central Europe. Friis documents this in detail, concluding that the Commission used the exceptional 'window of opportunity' given to it very well. First, it was given the role of coordinating the policy of assistance to the East by the G-24, consisting of OECD states as well as all EU states. There was no 'competition' for this role, as there seemed to be no state or other IO that could assume it (Friis, 1996). The EC had a long history of trade agreements with the CMEA (see van Ham, 1995), and as the major changes set in, there was a parallel development in the Commission to develop a common policy in this area. It was the Commission and small states like Belgium which initiated this, as they were fearful that the big states would dominate the scene in this regard (Friis, 1996: 115). However, this policy-making was slow and uneventful, and Friis records that the central role assigned to the Commission at the OECD meeting in July 1989 was not the result of its own lobbying, but rather because no other state or IO was ready to assume it (Friis, 1996: 116).

The Commission has a central role in both the establishment and the monitoring of association and cooperation agreements, also of a regional nature. These agreements integrate political and economic issues and thus keep the question of Commission competence on the agenda.

The Commission took charge of all the political aspects of the agreements: 'Even the discussions . . . on the tricky political issue of conditionality . . . were conducted by the Commission' (Nuttal, 1994: 294). This role, remarks Nuttal, himself instrumental in this development,[1] was one 'which would have raised eyebrows at the time of the SEA . . . it would have been deemed rank heresy a decade before that' (p. 294).

His conclusion is that 'the Commission has over the years developed a powerful set of management procedures for its core external relations business, and . . . the boundaries of its activity had expanded considerably even before the transformations of the 1990s' (p. 271). This method was used in integrating the human rights regime in enlargement programmes, as we shall see below. The economic policy instruments were thus used for foreign policy reasons. Below we will see in more detail how political conditionality has been used progressively throughout the 1990s.

The general impact of EU foreign policy

The EU carries much more general weight than the other two IOs in this study, which have a limited mandate and far fewer policy tools. Patten mentions the political weight of the EU as a major reason for its impact. Not only the 15 members, but also all the associated and like-minded states usually align themselves with a common position. This makes for a powerful actor in the sense of representing all of Europe. This unitary actor speaks as one not only bilaterally, but also in UN conferences, in the UN general assembly, in the Human Rights Commission in Geneva and in the Third Committee in New York.

As analysed above, the EU has grown from being a trade and economic organisation to becoming – or rather, aspiring to become – a political union with a fully fledged foreign policy. The development of a security and defence policy, albeit still rudimentary, is a major step in this direction. It is important to be able to muster hard power in extreme cases, of which there have been two in the last ten years in Europe: Bosnia and Kosovo. Both these cases showed that the EU had far too little weight and ability to coordinate itself.

The human rights regime is new in the EU, but is also an important part of having a foreign policy. Both security and defence as well as human rights are key areas of a fully fledged foreign policy: the former provides hard power for the extreme cases as well as credibility in extreme situations; the latter provides the more lofty and noble goals of a modern foreign policy.

The impact of this new human rights regime in the EU has so far not been much studied, but some cases are presented below. First, however, we outline the *general* impact of the EU in the foreign policy area.

There is currently little theoretical coherence to the development of analytical approaches to the study of how the EU changes the state. Here we wish to consider the empirical findings on the role of the Commission and the European Court of Justice (ECJ) to make the case that these non-state, regime actors play an important role as political actors. The conclusion from much EU research in the post-1985 period is that although intergovernmentalism – explicitly or implicitly – has remained the theoretical approach, many of the empirical findings have shown that EU actors and regimes have important impacts. The two main actors to consider are the Commission and the European Court of Justice (ECJ), and in this case, sometimes the European Parliament (EP).

The role of the Commission

The formal powers of the Commission are laid out in the Rome Treaty: it is the *guardian* of the treaties – it can intervene in cases of non-compliance, for example with competition legislation, and indeed has increasingly done this in the post-1985 period. It has the the *exclusive right – and obligation – to initiate and formulate policy* within the terms of the treaty, and importantly, in order to 'further integration'. Finally, it is the executive branch of the council and obliged to *implement* its policies. Here much is left to the member states themselves. The issue of implementation is relatively understudied in the literature on the states–EU relationship, but is a very important one in assessing the importance of the Commission.

'The Commission can exercise a good deal of discretion that it can use to expand the scope of integration', notes Lodge (1989: 40). The exclusive right of policy initiation is therefore in this analysis of substantial interest. This includes the goal setting and 'operationalisation' of policy – the key role of the Commission's leader. The right to develop policy goals with a general European interest as the only limitation allows for a strong potential leadership role for the president of the Commission. But policy initiation can occur at many levels below the president, and does. Ludlow reports that 'the function of *animateur* permeates the whole structure and ethos of the institution' (Ludlow, 1991: 97). He notes that the Commission was formed with the *Commissariat du plan* as the model – the point was to produce policy ideas on a large scale. Once a vision has been agreed upon, there is a great opportunity of formulating issue-specific policy under this aegis that still conforms to it, but which is highly technical and specific, involving experts in the many working groups and fora.

The point here is that when the Commission provides a general goal to which member states agree, then this goal is the reference point and legitimation for the development of issue-specific policy, which also can be interpreted quite freely. This means that issue-specific policy-makers in the various DGs may be very important actors. Whenever there is conflict with interest groups, the Commission invokes the general mandate of this goal as a legitimation for issue-specific policy. This is a very powerful tool because the policy style in the Commission is, as stated earlier, one that is *not* based on interest argumentation but on legal–technical arguments.

Summing up, the Commission has important formal roles but it depends on the cooperation of both the states and other Community institutions. It is not a major force in implementing policy or supervising the treaty obligations within the member states, and is in many ways small, often ill-coordinated, and unable to monitor the competition policy in the member states because it lacks the resources. This would also be politically controversial. The role of leadership and member state legitimacy appear to be major factors in explaining when the Commission's policy-initiating role is activated. The formal roles of the Commission also enable it to play important informal roles.

The importance of the Commission's many roles may be seen better if we distinguish between arena and actor roles. An actor influences the output of policy in an independent way, as a standard understanding of the concept goes (Underdal, 1992). The criteria for defining someone to be an actor must as a minimum include that there exists an ability to act at the outset – some degree of autonomy, some independent resources and so on. But arenas may also be politically important. Underdal argues that they may be important for different reasons, but not necessarily in less ways than actors (1992).

The Commission's *arena* roles include its agenda-setting power and the ability to regulate access of participants to a great degree. By setting the agenda the Commission may shape the states' own agenda and national positions. The states will take into account the EU-level activity and likely strategy when they make their own.

Turning to the *actor* roles of the Commission, there exists as discussed above formal autonomous powers to act in certain policy areas. In competition policy the Commission has the formal autonomy to act in a way that also has direct applicability and thus effect in and on member states. The DGIV does intervene very forcefully in cases of hindrance to competition. The ECJ often supports Commission moves against companies and member states.

Together these two institutions act autonomously: the Commission has formal autonomous acting powers in selected policy areas. It can use para. 90 of the Treaty of Rome to pass directives without Council approval; it can fine companies suspected of cartelisation or price fixing, and can intervene as an antitrust actor (Jacobs and Stewart-Clark, 1990; Louis, 1990).

Summing up, the Commission can *apply* policy *directly* in member states, and it can *issue binding directives* in some policy areas on its own exclusive authority. It thus has formal actor capacity, and several occasions for using its formal powers. These serve to enhance its role in informal ways. In the policy-making phase, the Commission can use its skills in *timing decision-making* and in presenting *better informed proposals* than member states. As any bureaucracy, it represents *profound knowledge* about the issue areas in question, although the importance of knowledge in policy-making is a contested one. Further, the Commission can utilise its skills as *broker between national styles* and interests to steer outcomes to its own preferences, yet the actual importance of this in terms of outcomes of policy is undetermined.

The role of the ECJ

In areas where the EU shares competence with the states or has exclusive competence, we expect the importance of EU actors to be a major one. Where the EU has exclusive competence, such as in the CCP and CAP, as well as in the prospective EMU, the formal role of the Commission is well established.

There is a growing literature which shows that the Commission and the ECJ both use formal and informal powers to make an impact and to enhance their institutional roles vis-à-vis the states. We will not discuss this literature here in any comprehensive way, but highlight the types of influence and the issue areas that are relevant to the human rights regime.

The history of the expansionism of the ECJ is well documented. Throughout the 1970s it has ruled to expand its role and implicitly that of the Commission by establishing legal supremacy over national legislation as well as the so-called direct effect of EU legislation (Burli and Mattli, 1993; Weiler, 1996). In famous cases like *Van Gend en Loos*[2] the court has stated that not only states, but also citizens are its subjects. It is more 'than an agreement which merely creates mutual obligations between the contracting states . . . the Community is a new legal order of international law for the benefit of which states have limited their sovereign rights'). Further, in the same case judgement the major principles of sovereignty are defined: citizens, and not only states are subjects of the EU treaties: the 'new legal order' has subjects 'which comprise not only Member States but also their nationals' (Weiler, 1996), while the

EU not only interprets the treaties as decided by member states, but also confers rights on citizens: 'Independently of the legislation of member states, Community law . . . not only imposes obligations on individuals but is also intended to confer upon them rights which become part of their legal heritage' (ibid.).

Thus, unattended by political public opinion, the major steps towards making a European constitutional order were taken by the court in its case law throughout the 1960s and 1970s. This legal development is well documented by a number of major legal studies but its political implications have not been discussed very much by political scientists. The EU is a halfway house between intergovernmental and a federal-type union, where the doctrine of legal supremacy over national law as well as its direct effect is well established, notwithstanding the ruling of the German constitutional court.

Weiler has also shown how the court has gradually embraced human rights and ruled on them in cases where, for example, the right to property is disputed (Weiler, 1999). It has been impossible to rule without interpreting and upholding human rights, even if the court has no human rights basis in the treaties. The ECJ has, however, acted as if it has a basis in a constitution, including a human rights basis. This practice over many years now helps to consolidate the importance of the EU Charter of Fundamental Rights, as will be discussed below.

Politically there is not a problem when one enounters inconsistency, such as on the one hand speaking of a European Union, but on the other upholding national foreign policies. In the EU, this 'logical' inconsistency means little and ensures support for an EU foreign policy that one can opt out of. But this kind of inconsistency is bound to be a problem for lawyers, because two contradictory principles cannot coexist in international law: an IO is either fundamentally intergovernmental, or fundamentally supranational. In the case of the EU, case law has laid down that the EU is indeed supranational because the ECJ acts as a supranational court, and the states, as the political actors, have largely accepted this. This political practice naturally entrenches this norm. In addition there is the fact that no state has yet seceded from the union – or exited from the organisation – even the terminology here makes for political choices; thus, it is also unclear whether a state can leave the EU. The treaty does not speak about this eventuality. This *inter alia* entails that national courts often ask for a preliminary judgement from the ECJ, which in turn means that the ECJ is the sole interpreter of who is 'der Herr der Vertrage'. Lower national courts may thus circumvent higher national courts, creating direct links with the ECJ.

The competence of the various EU institutions is not well established in the treaties, and the interpretation by the ECJ has not been contested until the *Bundesverfassungsgericht* contested the legality for Germany to accede to the TEU. However, in most instances the supremacy of the ECJ is not contested. The ECJ has often ruled in favour of the Commission's views in cases where the latter has been challenged. Burli and Mattli argue that the ECJ often employs a strategy which she calls a 'testing the waters' scheme which gradually widens the competence of ECJ rulings: first a general principle is established in one ruling, later it is applied specifically (1993: 67).

ECJ rulings have direct implications for member states, and the so-called 'constitutionalisation' of the treaties is the basis for *polity*-building in the sense that firms and individuals can appeal directly to the ECJ, bringing cases before it. This consolidates the direct relationship between the citizen and the EU and thus contributes to the institution-building of the latter. The 'mutual recognition' in the *Cassis de Dijon* case (1979) meant a tremendous increase in leverage to the Single Market project. *This evolution has enabled the Commission to act with the backing of the ECJ when there have been conflicts with member states over interpretations of competences.* The institutional setting of the Commission is therefore a favourable one, not only in terms of formal powers, but also in relation to the ECJ.

The ECJ itself has consolidated its power gradually, aided by landmark rulings like the one mentioned above. Against this history and actor pattern we can expect the human rights regime in the EU to be practised *as if* the charter were legally binding. As discussed in Chapter 6, this is indeed what we see in the first references being made to the charter itself where it is being cited as the major source on human rights, in a manner akin to a legally binding text.

The human rights regime: embeddedness and regime tools

The issue of human rights has come to the fore of EU policy in latter years, although the ECJ has ruled on human rights in cases which involve such rights. They have usually been economic cases, involving cases of property law or cases about employment rights. It is obvious that such cases often require principled judgements about what a specific human right means. As discussed, Weiler points out that the

ECJ has assumed a role of constitutional court over the years, introducing the doctrine of direct effect and legal supremacy (Weiler, 1996). This is a well-known fact of EU research, and Graver adds that the ECJ operates with what scholars term a *Wirtschaftsverfassung* – that it accords citizens of the EU with individual rights (Graver, 2000).

But also in the realm of foreign policy proper, the CFSP, the human rights regime, has been inserted with much force. In an assertive speech, EU commissioner Chris Patten, responsible for foreign affairs, stated that 'we have a legal framework for human rights in our external policy', and goes on to analyse the tools of human rights policy that the EU has at its disposal (Patten, 2000). They include the inclusion of human rights in the Maastricht Treaty in 1992 and their elaboration in the Amsterdam Treaty, which stipulates that 'the Union is founded on the principles of liberty, democracy, respect for human rights and fundamental freedoms, and the rule of law' (art. 6), while para. 2 asserts that 'The union shall respect fundamental rights, as guaranteed by the ECHR.'

In the Amsterdam Treaty there was also a sanction possibility inserted, in a new article 7, which states that the Council, meeting in the capacity of heads of state or government, and with the consent of the EP, 'may determine the existence of a serious or persistent breach of the principles mentioned above'. This article was further extended in the Nice Treaty of December 2000.[3] This tool, which may ultimately result in the revocation of the voting rights of a state, has to date not been used, but its existence means that the EU takes human rights so seriously that it has acquired policy tools in this area.

In the Amsterdam Treaty it is noteworthy that human rights, democracy and the rule of law figure prominently in its goals: 'The Union shall define and implement a common foreign and security policy covering all areas of foreign and security policy, the objectives of which shall be: ... to develop and consolidate democracy and the rule of law, and respect for human rights and fundamental freedoms' (art. 11, TEU).

Whereas the founding treaties of the EU made little reference to human rights, the treaty revisions starting with the Single Act, and also the TEU and the Amsterdam Treaty were all concerned with developing the EU's legal and political basis with regard to this area.

The EP has pushed for such a development for many years, being actively involved in human rights work in the form of both public and secret dipomacy. In 1984 it established a Human Rights Subcommittee, and this in turn drew up reports for plenary debate in the EP. With the advent of the Amsterdam Treaty there were also several areas that were lifted from national competence to Community level, especially in the field of justice and home affairs. Much of this is human rights work, and the EP thus found itself with influence in this area through the co-decision procedure.

The development of an explicit human rights basis marks, according to Patten, the 'transformation of the EU from economic entity into political body' (2000: 2).

The human rights charter

As discussed in Chapter 3, it was decided in 1999 to develop a charter for human rights in the EU. This charter was not incorporated into the treaty at the Nice summit, as proposed by a large group of states, because this was opposed by *inter alia* the UK and some of the Scandinavian states. Instead it was adopted as politically binding, which in itself is a major achievement for those who want to make the EU a fully fledged international actor.

The question of incorporation will again be discussed at the next IGC in 2004. As we know from similar EU processes, time and the slow work of the Commission and other EU actors often lead to an integrative outcome in a 'path-dependent' development (Pierson, 1996). At IGCs, one vote is enough to stop a proposal, but in the course of time such opposition is often diminished, and when EU practice, such as the legal practice of the ECJ, continues to take the charter into account, obeying it in actual policy-making and the rendering of judgements, one may see that the inclusion in the treaty eventually comes as a 'natural' consequence of political practice, as a codification of the latter. This has often been the case with controversial proposals in EU history, such as the small but gradual steps of codifying and extending EU foreign policy, as discussed above.

Legal codification in the future will in turn mean that both the COE and the EU will have legally binding and highly enforceable human rights legislation through their own courts, which both represent the most supranational of all international legislation in this area if one considers the direct effect and the right of petition.

The charter was thought necessary because the EU needed to show its citizens what their rights are (Introduction, draft charter) at 'the present stage of development' of the union (ibid., p. 2). In other words, the EU cannot be a real union without a constitution, as it were, and the charter sets out to provide such an element in a policy development which also includes most other policy themes of a nation-state.

The charter is, as discussed, part of the constitution-building of the EU, and acquires its importance in this perspective.

The charter is, however, not without controversy. The COE clearly fears that its role is being undermined by this new charter, especially if it becomes part of the treaty and thus legally binding. COE representatives stress that there is no need for the EU to possibly duplicate the ECHR.[4] COE secretary-general Schwimmer underlines the danger of duplication: 'Complementarity of human rights activities is best served by a strong human rights hard core, risks of dispersion and centrifugal forces should be countered by through creating a stronger centre' (Schwimmer, 2000). It is an open secret that the COE's *raison d'être* is uncertain if the EU develops a legally binding treaty that basically mimics the ECHR.

The charter, as laid out in Chapter 3, contains the same rights that we find in the ECHR and in the Social Charter, apart from some small adjustments and additions. The drafters were consciously following the ECHR, and chose to make shorter paragraphs with the essence of the latter. Quickly recapitulating Chapter 3, we recall that the EU charter starts with the dignity of the human person as the basis of human rights, then lays our equality before the law (art. 1), then the right to life and the moratorium on the death penalty (art. 2), the right to physical and mental integrity, including the prohibition of cloning (art. 3), the prohibition of torture (art. 4), of forced labour and slavery (art. 5), the right to liberty and security (art. 6), right to effective legal representation (art. 7), to a fair trial (art. 8), presumption of innocence and right to a defence (art. 9), no punishment without law (art. 10), and a right not to be punished twice for the same crime.

Thus, the rule of law is well defined here as it is in the ECHR and in the OSCE documents. These follow the other civil rights – freedom to marry and raise a family, freedom of religion and conscience, of expression and education. On democracy itself, it reads that 'all public authority stems from the people' in the preamble, while all citizens have the right to form political parties and to stand as candidates.

The social and economic rights include the customary rights to work, to a fair wage, to paid vacation, to form trade unions, to safe working conditions, and the right to maternity and parental leave. They also include the right to social security and assistance, environmental and consumer protection.

With the adoption at Nice of the charter as politically binding in the EU, we can at least conclude that this implies more coherence in EU policy in this field. It naturally remains to be seen how the EU will use its new charter. However, also in and of itself, as merely a political statement of values, the charter is important. It defines the standards and goals of the EU and candidate states, and it reinforces the common stance in both the COE, the OSCE and the EU with regard to these values. The human rights regime of Europe is complete with this charter – it sends a strong signal to all states within or aspiring to get within these organisations that they must comply with the elements of the regime.

The regime tools

The EU, however, has explicit policy tools with which to promote human rights and democracy. As stated, it can in extreme cases revoke voting rights for a state. However, most 'stick and carrot' tools are much more subtle and process-oriented, emphasising the 'carrot'.

First, the European Parliament (EP), like the COE's Parliamentary Assembly, has developed human rights tools of its own. It conducts *hearings* on controversial human rights situations, such as on for instance, East Timor and Algeria, and it was the first parliament to invite the Dalai Lama to an official meeting on Tibet. A hearing on Romania led to the suspension of negotiations for the renewal of the EC agreement with the latter, thus testifying to the importance of such public diplomacy.[5] The EP also conducts silent diplomacy, often aimed at the release of prisoners or looking at the cases of persecuted persons. As is customary in bilateral talks and visits, lists of prisoners are handed over, and this may often have more effect when brought to the attention of the press afterwards. Thus, this type of classical diplomacy is combined, when feasible, with public diplomacy where pressure is mobilised. The EP records that 'response from governments indicates that there is a very definite sensitivity to the EP's criticism' (ibid.: 6).

Stronger tools like sanctions are sometimes useful. Often the EP is the main cause of EU sanctions, which in recent years include *inter alia* Nigeria, Sudan, Togo, Burundi and the FRY. As a result of the treaty amendments from the SEA onwards, the EP can also reject agreements with third countries, which gives it considerable power.

The EP also monitors elections and supports various democratisation projects, like its 'sister' organisation, the COE's Parliamentary Assembly (PA).

The tools of the *Commission* and the *European Council* contain the suspension clause mentioned above, but this is a tool of last resort. Usually results will be achieved by positive measures. The EU as a whole has stipulated the conditions that must be met by new member states when they accede to the union. These so-called 'Copenhagen criteria' are very specific and straightforward, placing the emphasis on the duty of the applicant state to comply before being admitted. This is notably a different approach from that of the COE, which has practised 'therapeutic admission' throughout the 1990s.

The 'Copenhagen criteria' were adopted in 1993, and stipulate that candidate states must have stable institutions guaranteeing democracy, the rule of law, and human rights as well as respect for the protection of minorities; a functioning market economy together with the capacity to cope with the competitive pressures and market forces within the EU, the ability to adopt the EU's *acquis*, while the EU itself must be in a position to absorb new members while maintaining the momentum of integration (MacManus, 1998: 119).

These criteria not only place the burden of adaptation and democratisation on the new members themselves – they are not admitted before they are real democracies with market economies – but also gives a safeguard to the EU: it is not *obliged* to admit new members even if they are ready, unless the EU itself is ready in the sense of having accomplished the necessary reforms.

The 'mantra' of human rights, democracy, rule of law is, as we have seen, a major part of the admission criteria. This underlines the commitment of the EU to these values, also evident in the mission statement of the CFSP, of the treaty text itself as the basis of the EU, and in the admission criteria. It remains to be seen how this will be applied when the date of the first new entrant approaches, but at the outset it is clear that it will be much harder to enter the EU than the COE and the OSCE.

Human rights impact: the case of Austria

The relevance of human rights to the EU's new comprehensive policy was evidenced in the reaction against Austria's new centre-right government in 1999 and 2000. The alliance between the ÖVP (Austrian People's Party) and the FPÖ Party led by Jurg Haider led to sanctions from all the rest of the EU. The sanctions included a political boycott of Austria with regard to bilateral political contacts and visits as well as the non-promotion and non-support of Austrian candidates to international posts. As there was no breach of human rights in evidence – just the unacceptable xenophobic rhetoric and racist populism of Haider – there was no basis for a common EU action. In fact, the sanctions were legally speaking 14 *bilateral* moves which had basis in EU treaties or the *acquis*.

The background to the sanctions was dubious, as it appeared that only two or three of the EU leaders had staged it – Germany, Portugal, which held the presidency, and France. Belgium was, however, the harshest critic of Austria, along with France. Suspicion was raised about the real reasons for the boycott – was it the left, dominant in the EU, punishing the right? Whatever the real cause, the sanctions were followed by the most other Western states, including the USA, Canada and Norway. In Norway's case, it was a 'reflex' to follow the EU's foreign policy moves.

The actions against Austria were justified on grounds that if the EU places major stress on human rights in the admission of new members, then it must certainly have its own house in order. The Haider stances were seen as being on a collision course with respect for human dignity and equal treatment of all, regardless of race and nationality. Undoubtedly this was a correct analysis of the ideological statements made by the party leader, and the FPÖ's government role continued to embarrass Europe. Belgium and France even boycotted Austria in international fora such as the OSCE and within the EU ministerial meetings, making it hard for 'business-as-usual' to be conducted.[6]

The stigmatisation of Austria as such was monumental. There were boycotts by artists and tourists, and planned conferences were cancelled. The cost in money must have been formidable, while the cost in terms of Austria's reputation as a modern democracy is staggering. The boycott has in that respect been a 'success'. It has made a benchmark for the lower limit of what is acceptable for a European state and may thus act as a preventive measure. Populism, racism and shadows of Nazism in combination will not be acceptable, even if the people vote for it. Clearly the lack of Austrian self-criticism about its role in the Second World War is the central factor here. Had there been a similar process to that in Germany, the Austrians would probably not have given support to Haider. Statements by Haider about Nazism in Austrian politics would be impossible to make in other states. But the Austrians seemed surprised that there were reactions.

However, the boycott was sloppy from a diplomatic point of view because there was no 'exit strategy' and no goal for the action taken. Was the goal to topple the Austrian government? Or to change Haider's party programme? Was the 'progress' to be measured by actual politics? The Austrian government signed a government declaration that contained everything anyone could desire in terms of human rights, and did nothing that could be interpreted as contrary to those goals. Nonetheless there was much discussion about whether to lift the sanctions. The EU, although acting bilaterally, had to act unanimously. The Christian-Democratic and Conservative parties (European Peoples Party) in the EP called for a lifting, and the European Council in Feira in Portugal in June 2000 was marked by the conflict over what to do. Opinion moved towards finding some solution, while Austria threatened to boycott, for its part, all decision-making in the EU and to hold a referendum on whether Austria should remain in the EU, worded differently, but clearly aimed at the providing legitimacy for eventual secession.

Finally it was decided to send a 'wise men's group' of three independent experts to Austria to make an assessment. The result was that there had been no breach of human rights in Austria, and the sanctions were lifted.

The Austrian case is interesting and important in several respects. First, it signals that human rights concerns are of overriding importance to European and international politics. No state can afford to sow doubts about its 'political soundness' in this regard. International public opinion will easily be mobilised on issues of racism and discrimination. International norms in this area have a *real effect* in domestic politics, as in this case: here other states intervened in Austrian politics against a democratically elected government, thus disregarding *two key norms: non-intervention and democratic legitimacy*. These states, each acting on its own, although in concert, said that the politics of the FPÖ are unacceptable because they go against human dignity, even if democratically willed and taking place inside a Western democracy.

Here one has *crossed a threshold of intervention* in a Western democracy – not a 'rogue' state in the Third World; and one has placed *human rights norms above the norms of both non-intervention and democracy*. Values matter, and the international human rights regime matters. As mentioned, the cost to Austria of this boycott has been enormous in more than one respect. Even if the real cause of the intervention were a left-wing action to punish the far right, the *effect* of the shaming was real enough and showed beyond doubt the power of human rights in public diplomacy.

Enlargement: the impact of the Commission

The work on enlargement has become embedded in the human rights regime in a major, new way. Democracy itself – to establish it and promote it – is perhaps the major reason for enlargement. As Schimmelfennig has shown in his analysis of the political statements on enlargement, the EU member states all agreed on the need to extend the values of democracy, rule of law and human rights to the newly independent states of Europe (Schimmelfennig, 1999).

There were no economic reasons why enlargement had to happen, apart from the long-term prospects for trade. Although the geopolitical security interest certainly was present, in integrating Central and Eastern European states into Western political organisations for good, the issue of enlargement was debated in terms of the very *raison d'être* and values of the EU. Thus, one could make the argument that these values explain why enlargement was agreed to, despite traditional national interests to the contrary. Schimmelfennig shows how the agenda-setting was done by the Commission and key member states in an act of public diplomacy which left the recalcitrant states unable to stop the process. This is in fact an excellent case which illustrates the impact of the human rights regime: no one could oppose the discourse based on values with narrow, national interests. It was simply so inappropriate that no state would risk the shaming involved. One could prolong the process of enlargement and procrastinate over it, but it could not be halted. This agenda-setting took place in the public sphere, where the terms of discourse are the values of the EU, not the national interests of the member states. Schimmelfennig traces the agenda-setting on enlargement, mostly carried out by Germany and the Commission, showing how it became impossible to change this agenda once set.

But also in terms of *impact* on the part of the EU on the candidate states we see a major impact by this regime. Here the regime has become embedded in the specific pre-accession strategy for each candidate, in terms of goals to be achieved and ways to achieve them. The PHARE programme, the EU's general aid tool for Central Europe, was in 1997 changed into a specific democracy programme, thus acting in addition to the conditionality based on market economic criteria alone. About 30 per cent of PHARE money is to be spent on 'institution-building' in terms of democracy and rule of law, an amount per year of about 500 million euros. Institution-building means 'designing management systems and training and equipping a wide range of civil servants, public officials, professionals and relevant private sector actors: from judges and financial controllers to environmental inspectors and statisticians'.[7]

Examples of PHARE projects include strengthening the functioning and independence of the judiciary in the Czech republic, twinned by the Netherlands as the principal country; modernisation and development of anti-fraud measures in the taxation system in Hungary, twinned with Austria; reform of the court system in Latvia, twinned with Germany, and police training in the Slovak republic, twinned with the UK.[8] Thus, the democracy and rule-of-law measures vary between applicant states, and are tailor-made to the needs of each one. The twinning mechanism means that officials from EU states will reside and work in the applicant state for at least 12 months, inside its public adminsitration, so that transfer of competence and best practices will be optimal.

It is too early yet to assess the impact of these ongoing projects, but it is notable that *the funding provided for this work far exceeds the money made available by the other two IOs in this study*. Thus, the EU human rights regime both has regime-specific tools in the form of funds, and an institutional embeddedness in the pre-accession strategies of the EU which ensure specific surveillance and expert assistance through the twinning mechanism. Further, it is very hard to escape this impact as long as it is presented as a *de facto* conditionality for membership.

Grabbe's detailed work on conditionality in accession notes that there was a first period of conditionality between 1989 and 1993 which applied conditionality to third countries' aid and trade programmes in general (Grabbe, 1999). In this period the EU inserted a suspension clause based on failures to develop democracy, rule of law and human rights into the Europe Agreements (EAs) to further enable it to put pressure on applicant states. At this time – 1992 – the EAs were still the major tool for enlargement. The criteria for entering into an EA included human rights, rule of law and 'free and fair elections', in addition to market economic criteria. Thus, the human rights regime was fully embedded in the most important EU tools for shaping other states. As Grabbe notes, accession to the East is the most 'unequal' bargaining situation in EU history: the entire *acquis* must be adopted by the new states, without the customary derogations, and the conditions on both politics and market preparedness – the so-called Copenhagen criteria – must be fully met *prior* to accession.

The Essen European Council in 1994 launched the more intensified accession work, called pre-accession strategies. These included the EAs, PHARE and also the Single Market White Paper, which, as Grabbe remarks, represents a curious step: this White Paper, not part of the treaties, assumes the role of binding obligation on the candidate states, thus contributing to building an extended formal role for the EU (Grabbe, 1999: 14).

The contents of each applicant state's pre-accession strategy is comprehensive: specific political demands on democracy and rule of law, specific demands on the institutions of the market economy, and detailed provisions on what is needed in fields like transportation and the environment, agriculture and industry; for this two funding programmes have been erected in addition to PHARE: ISPA for the former fields, with an annual budget of 1040 million euros, and ESMOD for the latter fields, with an annual budget of 520 million euros.

It is evident at the outset that the human rights regime in the EU is embedded in a way that defines conditionality in both political and economic fields very clearly, with both regime tools in terms of money and expertise to accomplish the goals, but also with strict surveillance and deadlines. The EU enables the states to catch up, but makes strong demands on them in the process.

What evidence is there that the values of the human rights regime mean much, compared to the market criteria of the EU? There are as yet far too few cases to really answer this question, but indications of the independent importance of political conditionality are provided by the clear use of the latter in the enlargement assessment.

The EU has used political conditionality to criticise Slovakia in particular. There were several critical démarches about the Meciar government in 1994 and 1995, and the process towards accession for Slovakia was delayed until a new, democratic government came into power. Also Turkey, classified as a 'candidate country' so that pressures may be applied more effectively, is being severely criticised on political and human rights grounds, and Turkey has responded with a pre-accession programme that goes further in terms of 'talking the talk' of human rights than any former response to human rights criticism.[9] In the Commission's regular report on progress for Turkey in 1998, there was harsh language on 'persistent human rights violations and major anomalies in the treatment of minorities. The lack of civilian control of the army is a concern.'[10] With this point of departure, the Commission goes on to examine, in detail, political and economic progress that has been made since this time. These reports, one for each country, is both a platform for 'shaming' as well as conditionality for admission to the club. Thus, 'shaming' appears as part of conditionality in this case. The Commission's evaluation of each candidate state is the most detailed and comprehensive 'grade book' that exists among the IOs under study here.

Regime-specific tools: a summary

The EU commands a number of policy tools for dealing with human rights, more than the COE, and with more power than the OSCE.

Persuasion/learning tools

Here the EU conducts a lot of activity, especially in applicant states. As stated, experts are seconded from the Commission in the various ministries in these states, teaching how to adjust legislation and institutions to EU standards and rules. The impact of this is direct and unquestioned: it is a matter of necessity for an applicant state to adjust to this.

Furthermore, the EU has seconded experts in other states as well, such as the Balkans. Here both technical and in-kind help may be given. For instance, the WEU and the EU conduct police training in Albania.

For general democratisation there are funds and programmes, but the amounts are not very big: *the European Initiative for Democracy and the Protection of Human Rights,* a special fund, amounted to approximately 100 million ECU in 1999, which will decrease slightly for the period ahead. This is only a small part of the external development budget, yet is a relatively new part of the budget.

The EU also has election observers in many states, and training programmes of various sorts.

Monitoring tools

Unlike the COE and the OSCE, the EU does not have its own offices and missions apart from the normal diplomatic ones. But there are exceptions, such as the ECMM, the European Commission's Monitoring Mission, which plays a very important and well-appreciated role in the Balkans. Known by their white uniforms, these unarmed observers collect detailed data on local conditions all over the Balkans. This information is not 'processed' into streamlined reports, but is on the contrary distributed to member states as is. For experts on Balkan affairs, these raw data are invaluable. The observers are respected by the local population for their impartiality, and they know the local area they patrol better than any other expatriate. Thus, at an early time they can spot developments that may later erupt into violence.

Legal tools

The EU is a community based on law. As discussed, the use of the ECJ to judge on human rights cases is well established as political practice.

Weiler, perhaps the foremost scholar of the EU's legal status, has pointed to the 'creeping consitutionalism' that created legal supremacy for the EU in the form of direct effect (Weiler, 1996). This means that the ECJ has interpreted its mandate to be supranational in making its judgements apply directly to all states and citizens of the union.

In short, the EU is unlike other IOs in its being a hybrid between intergovernmentalism and a federal union. The court has been the major actor in the process of making the EU's treaties into a constitution.

On this view, it is essential for the human rights regime and its impact that the human rights charter becomes part of the treaty. Only thus will the court have it within its mandate, and become a truly constitutional court for Europe.

But the the impact of legal tools is not only through case judgements. EU law, and the entire *acquis*, is the basis for accession to the organisation. It is required of new member states that they streamline and adjust their own legislation to that of the EU. Here we have a direct impact of the EU's legal tools.

Conditionality in aid programmes and trade agreements

The EU's development policy has as its aim that 'Community policy in this area shall contribute to the general objective of developing and consolidating democracy and the rule of law, and to that of respecting human rights and fundamental freedoms' (TEU, art. 130u). Thus, there is a conditionality clause in all aid, save that of emergency aid.

This kind of conditionality is a typical trend of both the UN and other Western states in the present period. But this was not always so. Smith notes that EU aid was supposed to be apolitical, despite EP pressures to the contrary: 'Using trade agreements or development aid to punish human rights abuses was not acceptable' (Smith, 2000: 2). There was until the 1990s a clear reluctance to use coercive policy instruments, and to mix politics and trade. The EP continued to advocate a different view all this time, but only gained a hearing in the Commission in the late 1980s. The EP's powers were then increased by the new assent procedure under the EA which allowed the EP to refuse assent to third country agreement. In 1987 and 1988 the EP used this new power to refuse ratification of financial protocols with Israel and Turkey on human rights grounds, demonstrating that the little power the EP possessed, it would use actively.

But the main impetus for the conditionality in third country agreements came with the demise of the Iron Curtain and the need for democratisation in the eastern part of Europe. In 1991 the European Council decided that the promotion of human rights and democracy are aims of the EU, and this is also to be achieved through political conditionality in third country economic and cooperation agreements. The TEU from 1992 reflected this change. While politics and economics had been quite distinctly separated until this time in EU history, they were now reinforcing each other and economic weight and pressures were used to promote the human rights regime.

Suspension of membership and partnerships

The new member states must fulfil a so-called 'human rights clause', adopted at the Copenhagen European Council in 1993. The positive conditionality from 1992 was supplemented here by negative conditionality, viz. the rights of suspension if parties did not meet obligations.

Since 1995 more than 20 agreements containing human rights clauses have been signed, including the revised Lomé convention. To date no suspensions have been made, and there is a 'clear preference for . . . a positive approach' (Smith, 2000: s. 8). The desire is for constructive engagement and to keep cooperation going as long as possible, and the Council will increase aid to reward good behaviour. However, in grave cases the EU has suspended cooperation and aid (Smith, 2000).

Shaming in public diplomacy

The EU has one voice at UN, in the UN Human Rights Commission as well as in the UN's Third Committee which deals with human rights. Apart from the USA, the EU is the most important actor on the world scene. Its stance on human rights resolutions is of key importance.

Also, the various démarches and public statements made by the EU matter a great deal to international public opinion. It is customary that non-EU states like Norway, as well as the candidate states, align themselves with the EU – this makes for more impact.

The EU has also developed its own human rights norms, such as the Code of Conduct on Arms Exports, 1988, which gives rules for arms brokers that are to be followed by EU member states.

Hard power tools

Sanctions

The EU has also used hard power, such as sanctions. Like the USA, it is big enough to have a real impact with this tool. It undertook, *inter alia,* sanctions against South Africa in 1985 and 1986; an arms embargo and economic and diplomatic sanctions against China in 1989; diplomatic – but not economic – sanctions against Nigeria in 1993 after the cancellation of presidential elections and also in 1995 after the execution of the author Ken Saro-Wiwa. In this case development cooperation was also suspended. In 1996 the EU adopted stronger sanctions against Myanmar because of human rights violations, and the oil sanctions against Serbia were only lifted after the regime change in 2000.

Military power

As of 2001, the EU 'commands' a force of up to 63 000 personnel for crisis management operations. This is at least a potential hard power resource, although there are no instances of this force being used as yet, and the relationship to NATO is still undecided. But this tool supplements other EU tools and makes for a comprehensive foreign policy.

Conclusion: the impact of the EU human rights regime

The EU developed political conditionality in the 1990s, first in relation to third countries in general, later in a variety of increasingly more specific instruments for accession. The legal tools for political conditionality have gradually been inserted into the treaties, from the TEU's art. F which stipulates the goals of human rights and democracy, to later insertions of suspension clauses for breaches of the former; from the inclusion of human rights and democracy as conditions for closing third country agreements, to the tailor-made conditionality of the pre-accession strategy, suited to each applicant state.

The record on the EU praxis of conditionality is, however, mixed. There is a lack of consistency, as Smith (1999) notes, in the frequent use of 'shaming' and aid suspension vis-à-vis remote and insignificant African and Asian states with known human rights and democracy problems, compared to the lack of political will to address the human rights problems of major trade partners such as China. This kind of problem is, however, not unique to the EU, but is typical of almost all Western states. Research on aid conditionality in the period up to 1995 shows no significant application of such in either the major European states or the EU (Zanger, 2000).

The EU-managed, but bilateral, political boycott of Austria showed a new political will to grapple with xenophobia in its own ranks, although the action was poorly handled and undertaken without any exit strategy. Nonetheless it showed sensitivity to human rights issues and the conviction that there are higher, universal norms of human dignity than either sovereignty or democratic procedures for elections; in and of itself a very significant development.

The *conditionality of accession* is, however, the most important so far. From the stipulation of the Copenhagen criteria of political and economic conditionality in 1993, the Commission has assumed a key role in defining each applicant state's status in meeting these criteria, in defining how to meet them and also in funding much of the work in meeting them.

The *avis* on each state was published in 1997, defining Slovakia as too undemocratic to be ready for accession negotiation, but included again later when a new government was in place; while Turkey received continuous critical evaluations on account of the treatment of the Kurds and the role of the military in government.

After the *avis* in 1997, the conditionality became stricter, being embedded in each state's association agreement. The PHARE set-up was designed by twinning and contained benchmarks for success, but also short time spans and no leeway for compromises. The APs are not negotiated between equals, but rather the Commission plays the pivotal role, both as standard-setter and as judge of whether the benchmarks have been met. Although the member states in the European Council make the formal decisions on the status on membership negotiations and ultimately the decision on new members, it is the Commission which sets the AP agenda in detail, makes evaluations and deals with the applicants. The power of the Commission – a non-state actor – is therefore almost unparalleled. Its role in the human rights regime is far more than an arena function – it is in fact the principal actor.

The scant research that exists on the relationship between the Commission and the applicant states (principally Henderson, 1999; Grabbe, 1999; Seidelmeier, 2000) shows that the applicants all favour membership as their primary political goal, and that they are in need of funds and help for change. Their 'newness' as democracies and market economies naturally leave them weak as negotiation partners, and the EU is deemed to have become the key motor of impact from abroad on these states from about 1997–98: 'The AP represent a large policy-making agenda that pushes some fundamental reforms rather quickly. For most of the applicants, it means that the EU is taking over as the key external driver of reform' (Grabbe, 1999: 19). Grabbe also makes the point that these states have to adopt the entire *acquis* as well as the Single Market White Paper, in and of itself not legally binding. This is also one of the reasons why it is the states and not the Commission which make formal decisions on the process, because the Commission actually administers conditions for which there is not always a strict legal competence in the EU.

The impact of the PHARE programme through twinning has been considerable, through learning and through decentralised implementation (Rupp, 1999). Rupp finds that the impact of PHARE has been much larger than that of 'political dialogue', which mainly refers to foreign policy. Here the applicant states simply align themselves with the EU actions and statements. But in the PHARE framework there occurs extensive training of civil servants and institutional learning. This is supported by my own interviews in the Polish MFA, where the concrete projects in management and rule of law are highlighted as the most important drivers of change.[11] Hungarian civil servants agree with this conclusion.[12]

The EU's human rights regime has impacts in several ways: in the direct impact of conditionality, as discussed above, but also in the impact towards other IOs, towards the member states and towards the general profile of the EU as a foreign policy actor.

Finally, the EU human rights regime has an important function as the very cornerstone of the CFSP. It defines the goal of a fully fledged EU foreign policy, worthy of a political union, not only a common market. Now the EU has the same lofty foreign policy goals as any nation-state, and it has gradually established many foreign policy tools for itself. The coupling of political conditionality and aid will render the human rights regime increasingly important, as will public diplomacy, often couched in human rights terms, where the EU plays a considerable role in the world. The two main Western actors on the global scene are the USA and the EU. What the EU says about human rights, will resound. This means that shaming and shunning will receive maximum effect.

8
Human Rights and Hard Power: a New Norm for Intervention?

Throughout this book we have analysed the use of soft power tools for the promotion of human rights, democracy and rule of law. The argument has been that these values increasingly matter in foreign policy, not only as justifications, but also as real moving forces of policy. We have seen how the OSCE's tools are based on soft power, and how this organisation works in a very practical way to promote democracy in states with weak political traditions in this respect, and in states that are ridden by violent conflict and great tensions. Further, we have seen how the COE has an impact through its admission procedure and monitoring mechanisms, as well as through its court rulings that have a direct effect in the member states. Also, the fear of being 'shamed' is a very real one.

Finally, we have outlined the human rights charter of the EU, adopted as politically binding at Nice in December 2000, and the admission criteria, the so-called Copenhagen criteria, which make it imperative for new members to be democratic states. No new EU member is admitted that does not abide by the rule of law and multiparty democracy, although it naturally takes time before practice corresponds to the letter of the law.

It seems clear that the values we have analysed in this book form the basis for acceptance of states into the 'good company' of IOs. It has become extremely important for any state to have a good record in this regard. Turkey's problem regarding EU membership concerns the degree of democracy and its institutions – the unacceptable power of the military in political life, the denial of minority rights to the Kurds – and these are the issues that hinder membership.

Thus, we have made the case that the values of human rights, democracy and rule of law are more than just window dressing and are indeed of critical importance in the foreign policy of Western states. We have also argued that these states and their organisations primarily employ soft power in order to achieve these goals. However, at the outset of this book we ventured to say that the military intervention in Kosovo and Serbia in 1999 was at least partially based on the same values, in fact, on their transgression and violation. This claim is the second argument of this book: that hard power intervention is also increasingly value-based.

As discussed in Chapter 4, the main motivation for value-based intervention is probably an *instrumental* one: states that want membership in the COE or the EU adapt to the political conditionality of the latter, while politicians who want to be re-elected have to respond to popular and press calls to 'do something' when they see massacres unfolding on the TV screen. Without the effect of the media and transparency of modern communications, it is not very probable that intervention of the Kosovo or Bosnia type would have happened.

The hypothesis of the importance of instrumentality does, however, *not* rule out the possibility that politicians are really motivated by the values of human rights, democracy and rule of law – to such an extent that they even run the risks of hard power intervention in order to assist a population or ethnic group – but simply says that *instrumentality as an assumption is sufficient to explain why even hard power value-based intervention takes place.*

This is important for two reasons: first, most theories of international relations – neo-realism as well as neo-liberalism – assume such instrumental behaviour where self-interest or narrow national interest is most important. Showing that the values of the human rights regime have an independent impact under these assumptions is therefore of key importance, because it shows that *there is a new logic of public diplomacy at work even in the* Realpolitik *of international affairs.*

Second, it is almost impossible to detect the real motivation behind political behaviour: politicians will often claim values, but act on interests. Claiming values as the motivation for political action is necessary as part of the justificatory rhetoric of public diplomacy. But we may also see it from the inverse angle: when really motivated by values, politicians must often justify by recourse to national interests, when this is appropriate, as is often the case in security policy. The logic of public diplomacy differs from one policy area to another: in the Norwegian EU debate, it has never been appropriate to talk about Norway's contribution to the values of Europe. The discourse has always been in terms of strict interests, whereas the Norwegian foreign policy discourse on the

UN and the OSCE has been cast in terms of values. The point is that in both kinds of cases – when the appropriate terms of discourse are values and when they are interests – none of the public diplomacy utterances by politicians can be taken at face value. They therefore do not say anything about the real motivations of actors.

In this chapter we investigate the thesis that hard power intervention for human rights really takes place. The record of the UNSC in the 1990s is analysed, and it shows that the official mandate for both sanctions and interventions increasingly takes these values as their justification. In two cases – FRY and Rwanda – the council has erected supranational courts to judge war criminals. In almost all cases the council has relied on humanitarian reasons for intervention. The evidence from the practice of the UNSC is that value-based intervention is a reality in international politics today. We also discuss in detail the importance of the human rights regime in two interventions, Bosnia and Kosovo, in order to assess the causal factors that led to intervention. Here we contrast a narrow national interest in power enhancement and geopolitical improvement in power status – a neo-realist approach – with an explanation based on the new logic of values in public diplomacy.

First we shall look at the historical practice in this field, and ask whether there is really anything new.

Value-based intervention historically

The term used to denote military interventions is usually 'humanitarian intervention'. This is an imprecise term, legally as well as politically. In international law there is a body of law called 'humanitarian law', which refers to the rights of civilians and the duties of military commanders in times of war, the Geneva Conventions of 1949[1] and their ensuing protocols. These norms of warfare and the treatment of civilians are variously respected in practice, but are well known and disseminated. They have nothing to do with the reasons for intervention, however.

'Humanitarian' here is used in its precise meaning, referring to humanitarian minimum standards and to conduct of actors that aid or may hinder aid to civilians. However, it is misleading to use the word 'humanitarian' to refer to ordinary military interventions that are justified by massive human rights violations, as this can easily be confused with the subject matter of the Geneva Conventions. We therefore refer to 'value-based' interventions instead of 'humanitarian' intervention to denote military actions that are based on the claim that they are to stop massacres and massive human rights violations. This naturally in no way means that the justification given for the intervention – the values of human rights – is the real reason for it. In each case this is an empirical question to be determined by analysis. This is also consistent with our usage of the three types of political interests discussed in Chapter 4: security, economic and value-based interests. A 'value-based' intervention is one that is caused by massive human rights violations and abuse.

There is much talk about 'value-based' intervention today, as if this were a new phenomenom. But this concept had been used and discussed much earlier (Caplan, 2000). The discussion about the 'just war', referring to the criteria for intervention and warfare, is as old as political philosophy and international law itself. The 'just war' tradition was based on natural law argumentation as it was developed in the Middle Ages and before that. St Thomas Aquinas is known for his principles of a 'just war', and the 'father' of international law (*Volkerrecht*), Hugo Grotius (1583–1645), argued that in extreme cases, the subjects of a ruler were entitled to revolt against him if he were a tyrant.

The ancient tradition of a 'just war' can fruitfully be seen as a precursor of what was later defined as the human right to security of person, or 'human security'. The core criterion was that of justice: an aggressor can and should be unarmed; but the use of force should be proportionate to the goal to be achieved. In such cases it was legitimate to be aided by another state, thus making for a 'value-based' type of intervention. Grotius' thesis about the right to a strongly conditioned intervention was built on by international jurists well into the nineteenth century, and at this time there were several interventions based on values such as the violations of the individual right to religious freedom of Christians in Muslim countries.

The following interventions, which were all collective, were justified by human rights violations:

- The UK, France and Russia intervened in Greece in 1827 in order to stop the massacres of Greek Christians
- The French intervention, monitored by the five European great powers, in Lebanon in 1860, in order to stop the massacres of the Christian Maronites carried out under Turkish leadership

- The European great powers intervened in Turkey's adminstration of Crete in 1866 in order to protect the suppressed Christians
- Again, the great powers of Europe intervened in the Balkans in 1873 to protect the Christians in Bulgaria and Bosnia-Hercegovina who were being massacred by the Turks
- The European powers intervened in Turkey in 1903–8 in order to help the suppressed Macedonian Christians

Krasner has analysed these interventions in his book *Sovereignty: Organized Hypocrisy* (1999), and makes the point that intervention was relatively frequent and mostly based on arguments about the need to protect Christians, i.e. on minority rights. They were 'value-based' in terms of justification.

He also notes that sovereignty has never been an absolute norm, and that it has not only been practised variously and inconsistently, but has also been circumscribed in international law as early as in the Treaties of Westphalia – the very bases of territorial, state-based sovereignty – which allowed for religious minority rights. A conclusion is thus that value-based intervention has been a persistent and important theme both in Western political thought as well as in political practice. There is nothing new in the discussions today about the reasons for legitimate intervention. However, atrocities today are broadcast globally, and foreign policy is democratised. These trends discussed in Chapter 3 make for an acute interest in the reasons for warfare, and the new norms that circumscribe the use of war as a political tool in the twentieth century make for a decision-making context markedly different from earlier ages.

However, in the twentieth century there was a major change in the political and legal norms regarding war as a political instrument. Whereas the doctrine on *value-based intervention was accepted by perhaps the majority of international jurists in the first half of the twentieth century*, there came at this time major advances in prohibiting war as a political tool, such as the Kellogg–Briand Pact of 1928. The degree to which value-based intervention was really accepted among legal scholars of international law is contested (DUPI, 1999), but it is a fact that the number of interventions with this justification fell during the first part of the twentieth century. States also vary in their view of this: the major powers, such as the USA, maintain this right, as do France and the UK, whereas smaller states want to deny that such interventions are valid tools of international politics. Not surprisingly, the smaller states are those that could be the objects of intervention but which could never launch an intervention themselves.

The post-war period

In the post-war period the UNSC was largely unable to function as intended, although it holds the global mandate for maintaining international peace and security. The Cold War de facto defined security policy, also beyond the two superpowers. Ethnic conflicts did not break out because they were quelled before this stage, being contained by communism in Eastern and Central Europe, within the Soviet Union and in the Balkans. When wars erupted in the Third World, they were 'managed' by the superpowers, and the same two actors maintained their proper 'sphere of influence' where the other did not intervene. The Russian and American veto in the UNSC would have stopped any real 'interference' by the council in this security structure.

However, there were a few interventions by the council in this period that signalled an emphasis on human rights and humanitarian concerns. Chapters VI and VII of the UN Charter[2] form the basis for council's actions. In Chapter VII, art. 39 and 42, we find the paragraphs that endorse the use of hard power in cases where there exists a threat to 'international peace and security'. One first employs other types of hard power, such as sanctions or embargoes, and only if they are insufficient, is the council able to resort to the use of military power. The charter further establishes a military committee and calls on states to supply permanent military resources to the UN. This has, as we know, never happened, and seems most unlikely to become reality.

The UNSC has to rely on the member states to provide military resources on a case-by-case basis. This means that the council provides the mandate, but not the actual force. This also means that some interventions take place, others do not, or only much later than the time of mandate and the diagnosed need for intervention. For instance, there was little or no willingness to intervene in Rwanda despite the council's resolution that mandated such an invasion: the secretary-general asked 21 states for contributions and got none. In Bosnia there was a mandate to intervene two years before the actual NATO air campaign.

The council mandates a group of states or a regional organisation to undertake the military intervention in cases which are not a question of self-defence. The intervention must follow international humanitarian law, as laid down in the Geneva Conventions, and must follow the mandate of the UNSC.

The Cold War period was, as mentioned, one of low-level activity by the council. However, there were at least two cases where human rights violations were the main cause of council action: in 1966 in Southern Rhodesia (Zimbabwe) the council for the first time regarded breaches of human rights as a threat to international peace. In 1965 the white minority had declared the territory to be independent against the majority of blacks. In res. 217 (1965) the council declared this situation to be a threat to international peace and security and encouraged economic sanctions against the regime. When this had no effect, another resolution, 221 (1966), asked the UK to lead the blockade of ships carrying oil to the regime, and in doing this, use military force if necessary.

The second time the council invoked human rights in the Cold War period was in 1977, against the apartheid regime in South Africa. In res. 418 (1977) the council, after repeated condemnations of this policy, mandated a weapons embargo against the country.

There were thus some precursors for the UNSC practice in the 1990s in terms of reasoning about humanitarian factors, but there were few cases. With the changed security picture after 1990, this changed as well: now ethnic conflicts in Europe and in the newly independent states had no 'lid' on them, and the wars in Africa continued to flourish. The superpowers no longer 'divided' these conflicts between them, and in the absence of any hegemonic actors to deal with such conflicts, the UNSC found itself in the role it had been intended for.

The 1990s and beyond

The type of war we see today is mostly in the form of armed conflict inside a country, brought about by conflict entrepreneurs and warlords, and involving civilians as the main protagonists and victims. The military component is often paramilitary or guerrilla forces, or even mercenary soldiers (Wallensteen and Sollenberg, 1998; Smith, 2000).

It is clear that both the Geneva Conventions and human rights norms are very easily violated in this type of war. It is hard to see how they can avoid being violated when the civilian population in practice has no protection. The UNSC was, however, never intended to deal with this type of conflict, as the wording in Chapter VII refers to *international* peace and security. There was not the anticipation of modern internal wars, nor of the fact that civilians would make up about 90 per cent of casualties in the latter.

The first major intervention mandated by the council in this period was in Iraq. In res. 688 (1991) the council decided that the Iraqi suppression of the Kurds in the north, where Saddam Hussein even used chemical weapons on whole villages, represented a threat to international peace and security in the region. The council demanded that humanitarian organisations be given free access to Iraq at once, and based on this resolution and the previous 678 (1990), which had mandated the first value-based intervention ever, giving a green light for an intervention to force Iraq out of Kuwait – many such organisations went to Iraq with military protection.[3]

Resolution 678 concerned Kuwait, and assistance to remove the aggressor who had invaded the country, and did not as such mandate an intervention into Iraq to protect and assist the civilian population. Legal views on whether the UNSC mandated the intervention into Iraq are divided, and some maintain that this case is similar to that of Kosovo, discussed below. In this case there was a heavy argument for intervention, although no one resolution explicitly mandated a military intervention, only the use of hard power to safeguard humanitarian supplies. The invasion of Kuwait by Iraq prompted Kuwaiti demands for assistance in its self-defence. Such assistance need not have a council mandate.[4]

The next 'hot spot' for the council was the FRY. Here the civil war was at its height from 1991 onwards, with the siege of Sarajevo and the massacres of civilians in so-called 'safe enclaves' of the UN from 1994. The worst examples of massive human rights violations imaginable were seen in Europe itself when more than 7000 boys and men were executed in the UN 'safe area' of Srebrenica.

The international community was, however, slow and unwilling to intervene. Driven by events and the media, there was a clear pressure that 'something must be done'. The first step was economic sanctions against Serbia and Montenegro, mandated by res. 757 (1992) and based on an assessment that the situation represented a threat to 'international peace and security'. A later resolution (770/92) the same year mandated a military intervention to protect convoys with humanitarian aid, while the UN called on NATO to protect its so-called 'safe areas' in 1994. Finally, the council set up the war crimes tribunal, ICTY,[5] in res. 827/93, to judge war criminals from the FRY. The mandates for hard power intervention in the FRY followed the pattern of embargoes first, and then assistance to protect the UN peacekeeping force UNPROFOR and the civilian population in UN 'safe areas'. The actual hard power intervention amounted to air power, and is discussed in detail below.

Another difficult case in the same year was Somalia. Here the council again mandated, first, a weapons embargo (res. 733/92), and later, a military intervention (794/92) because the humanitarian tragedy caused by civil war represented a threat to international peace and security. In this resolution, which is a key one showing that the human rights values were gaining in importance, the council did not speak about any border spillover of the security threat. It was simply caused by and confined to the situation inside Somalia alone. As the council's mandate is that of 'a threat to *international* peace and security',[6] we see here that the intervention in this case was mandated without any reference to this international context. This is a significant departure from the main basis for intervention on the part of the UNSC. It was also in the Somalian intervention that the USA suffered heavy and outrageous losses of their military personnel; the direct cause of the political restriction on land force intervention in US security policy.[7] In the Somalian case the intervention was, however, also a reluctant one, spurred on in the end by the massive humanitarian tragedy caused by the civil war.

The next resolution of importance to our argument is on Haiti. Here the USA in particular sought a mandate for the reinstallation of president Aristide, democratically elected under UN supervision in 1990. However, a military coup in 1991 exiled him, and toppled his government. Again the council adopted economic sanctions at first, but when they had no effect, mandated a military intervention because the coup and the humanitarian situation represented a 'threat to international peace and security' (res. 940/94). In this case the threat of intervention worked: the regime reinstalled Aristide.

What is remarkable is that this intervention was mandated with a reference to international threats to peace and security, while the fact remains that this threat was made up of the form of government: it was not democratic, but a military dictatorship. But the principle this would create, would mean that hard power intervention is allowed in all cases where the form of government is not a democracy. The resolution explicitly states that this is a unique case, but it is nonetheless a case which may create precedent. Almost all the cases of the UNSC in the 1990s are presented as unique cases with unique mandates, but this raises the issue of when a row of 'exceptions' make for a new practice and a new canon of interpretation.

The next case was Rwanda, where the civil war reached huge proportions in 1994. Again the council mandated a weapons embargo, based on a humanitarian situation which was diagnosed as a threat to international peace and security (res. 918/94). When the situation deteriorated, the council mandated a military intervention to alleviate the humanitarian situation (res. 929/94), and finally a tribunal for war crimes, crimes against humanity and serious breaches of international humanitarian law was established later in the same year (res. 955/94). This was a further recognition of the human rights basis of security policy, despite the fact that none of the 21 states that were requested to send military personnel to intervene, came forward with troops.

From 1998 onwards, the UNSC became involved in Kosovo. Here it became clear that China and Russia would use their veto, and it would therefore be impossible to achieve a mandate for an intervention. The council came as close to this as possible, however. First, it passed a resolution, 1160/98, which condemned the use of force against civilians by both the Serbs and the Kosovars. Then the council adopted a weapons embargo against the FRY, and also advised that the situation represented a threat against peace and security in the region (res. 1199/98). Finally the council warned that further measures would be taken unless the demands set out in res. 1160 were implemented.

The next resolution on Kosovo was, however, not a mandate for intervention, but the settlement with the regime in Belgrade about peace implementation and the establishment of UNMIK in Kosovo (1244/99). There had been no explicit mandate for intervention, but NATO member states, including Norway, interpreted the situation such that there was sufficient reason to intervene: the two resolutions that had diagnosed a threat to international peace and security, the exodus from Kosovo of 850 000 Kosovars, the evidence of massacres on civilians, etc. Thus, NATO attacked in an air campaign that lasted from 26 March to 10 June 1999, the first such NATO operation in its history. The official reason given was that of 'halting a humanitarian catastrophe and restoring stability in a strategic region', thus wedding human rights and security policy.[8]

Political vs. legal issues

What can we conclude from this survey of UNSC action in the 1990s? First, it is clear that the action itself is dependent on political will, not legal arguments: the council is a political body which does not act without member state will. Thus, some internal armed conflicts have received scant attention, while others have been 'adorned' with military forces and peacekeeping operations. As Oudraat points out, the UNSC is a political body, not a legal court (Oudraat, 1996: 514).

Second, there is no consistency in the council's attention to conflicts: those in Europe – Bosnia and Kosovo – have received much more attention and action than the many wars still ongoing in Africa. Also this underlines the essentially *political* character of the council. Were it governed by law, one would expect a certain consistency of behaviour.

However, it is clear that despite this uneven practice, all the major conflicts dealt with in the 1990s have had major humanitarian consequences. The humanitarian situation has remained a constant cause for diagnosing a situation as being in accordance with Chapter VII's criteria as a threat to international peace and security. Every modern armed conflict does involve such threats, and it is therefore not surprising that *human security* is at the core of the council's actual mandates for intervention. But the intention of the charter was not that of intervention in sovereign states. The traditional norm of state sovereignty and non-intervention was preserved in art. 2 (7) of the charter, and defined when force was allowed between states as the exceptions: only in the case of being attacked, in self-defence, and in the case of being asked to assist a state in such a situation.

Further, the practice of intervention *in another state* is not anticipated in the UN Charter. The same applies to the concept of security: the 'threat to international peace and security' is written with *state security* as the model.

The dilemma is the following: the UN Charter was written at a time when human security as a concept was an unknown, and when wars were mostly inter-state. The mandate for intervention was furthermore not the province of a court, with legal experts deciding, but that of a highly political body where five states even have a veto. This in itself ensures that the spirit and letter of the law are not given the key role they would have in a legal body, but that national interests are the main variables along with the rules for interpreting the charter. Thus, both the charter and the body that uses it, are highly 'imperfect'. However, this is the most 'legal' and impartial basis we have for the use of force. The alternative, viz. the use of force as a tool of bilateral foreign policy, is much worse.

However, as the critics of 'sola concilium' would be quick to point out, even international law is dynamic, and there are later developments than the UN Charter: the 1948 Genocide Convention – never having been implemented, but giving a basis for crimes against humanity – and the 1949 Geneva Conventions, which define humanitarian law. These conventions do not provide mandates for military intervention, but they define 'human security' as it is also laid down as the right to 'security of person' in the general human rights instruments.[9] This definition of security, based on the individual, is thus much closer to the modern type of armed conflict than the situations envisaged in the UN Charter, largely inter-state wars. One may say that the human rights definition of security rights is well established and consistent, but it has not until now been utilised in security policy. There is no *formal* link between human rights and the UNSC's basis for the granting of mandates, however. The *practice*, even so, is one of increasingly using human rights violations as the basis for hard power intervention.

This is a development with revolutionary consequences in terms of the norm of state sovereignty. The superiority of this norm to that of the human rights logic has been well guarded, and still is. The majority of UN member states are highly sceptical of any kind of intervention, especially hard power intervention. This is quickly seen as a new kind of Western imperialism. This aspect of the human security agenda makes it hard to advance politically, especially in the UN system.

But there is also the question of Kofi Annan: what happens when the UNSC does not act and there unfolds a major human rights tragedy?[10] The Korean 'Uniting for Peace' resolution adopted by the UN General Assembly (UNGA) was the example that showed that the UN had to act when the council could not: during the Korean War, the UNSC could not reach a resolution on action, and the USA brought the issue to the UNGA which provided the mandate for intervention by majority voting. This resolution sets a precedent for similar actions by the UNGA.[11]

But even beyond this, there are arguments that international law provides a basis for military intervention. The UK issued a memo to all NATO allies where it argued that 'Security Council authorisation to use force for humanitarian purposes is now widely accepted . . . but force can also be justified on the grounds of overwhelming humanitarian necessity without a UNSC resolution.'[12] The following criteria would need to be applied: there must be evidence of 'overwhelming humanitarian necessity', of 'extreme humanitarian distress in a large scale', and the force used must be 'proportionate' and 'limited in time and scale'.

These UK proposals, although well intended, run the risk of divesting the use of force from an international and collective context, placing it again, as before in history, in the hands of the individual state.

The debate on the whether international law allows for intervention without a UNSC mandate remains undetermined (Caplan, 2000). There is the open question of whether the 1955 'Uniting for Peace' resolution of the UNGA can be used again (Roberts, 1995), but there is also the recognition that state interests lie at the heart of any decision by both this body and the UNSC. The legal issue is important because it confers legitimacy on an intervention, and the UNSC remains the only body to confer such legitimacy. This is one of the reasons for seeking a mandate for intervention from this body, and it is likely that the USA reasoned in this manner when seeking mandates for both Haiti and Iraq (Cortrell and Davis, 1996).

However this issue develops in the future, a major and important conclusion is that the *definition of security policy and intervention in the 1990s has been extended to internal conflicts where major humanitarian issues are dominant as reasons for security threats*. The original intention of the UN was to be a collective security organisation with its own intervention force: a military committee and a multilateral army was to be set up (Roberts, 1995). For various reasons this never came to be, and the intervention capacity has remained that of the willing and able member states. Gradually the UN practice has evolved into two modes of peacemaking: the peacekeeping operation, impartial, using force only in self-defence; and the military interventions aimed at assisting peacekeeping operations and humanitarian aid efforts. There has never been any sharp line between pure peacekeeping and peace enforcement, as the term has been coined, and it has been impossible in many cases to uphold such intended distinctions (Minear, 1994).

In sum, the mandate for using force was originally clearly aimed at traditional inter-state conflicts where one aggressor could be clearly defined, and when the latter would attack another state. The rules of engagement in the Charter's Chapter VII are written with this situation in mind, and not with armed internal conflicts where massive attacks on civilians are the key problem.

This explains why the UNSC has had to link traditional security policy with the current humanitarian issues as the *formal* basis for intervention in their resolutions in the 1990s. There is simply no other basis to use than the one that stipulates a threat to 'international peace and security'. In most of the resolutions cited above, there has been this explicit link whereby it has been said that the humanitarian situation represents such a threat. This can be substantiated by citing spillover danger, large exodus of refugees, instability in the region of the conflict, etc., but the only truly security-policy implication among these is the spillover thesis. Thus, *the UNSC had in fact widened the definition of security policy by including human security concerns as reasons for intervention.* Caplan goes as far as concluding that 'we are witnessing the emergence of a customary law of humanitarian intervention' (Caplan, 2000: 36). This seems an overstated view, because the requirements for calling something customary law include the belief in the legal validity of a political rule or norm (Buergenthal, 1990), but Caplan is right in pointing out that the norm for intervention is changing in this direction.

This in itself is significant, because the UNSC is the sole organisation with a mandate for hard power intervention. This practice, however, tells us nothing about the real reasons for interventions: were they driven by traditional, narrow national interests, or were they increasingly driven by human rights and humanitarian concerns? Were they value-based or not?

This is the central issue of this study, and we have seen that soft power interventions have had the core values of the human rights regime as important drivers: the COE, the OSCE and the EU have all recognised the importance of a functioning democracy and respect for human rights as the very basis for both investments and stability, thus making the traditional distinction between values and interests a more spurious one. The importance of public diplomacy means that legitimacy increases in importance, and also for this reason the human rights regime has gained in impact and importance. Both Western states and Western IOs impose the values of the regime on new members and candidates for membership, as a sine qua non.

Value-based intervention? The cases of Bosnia and Kosovo

If we are looking for clear and indisputable evidence of value-based intervention, we will not find it. But when analysing the cases of UNSC intervention in the 1990s, in most cases there is no trace of traditional narrow national interests. We are interested in determining *how much* the values of human rights and democracy 'weigh' in decisions about intervention, and if found to be significant, to explain *why*. We have argued that states pursue both security-based, economic and value-based interests. In order to answer our question, we have to contrast the 'value' explanation with other explanations.

The 'null hypotheses' of this study are neo-realism and neo-liberalism as explanations for both soft and hard power intervention. The neo-realist security interest is by definition 'narrow' in the sense that there must be a threat to *national* or *regional* security if we care enough to act on it, while the neo-liberal economic interest says that only in cases where there is an economic advantage to intervention, will it happen. In Chapter 4 we argued that we could explain intervention with these models only if we define the national interest much more widely: such as instability in the Balkans or the Middle East as a threat to national security; or the advantage of democratisation in Eastern Europe as the advantage to national economic interests. In thus widening the national interest we could argue for both hypotheses, but then we would have to add 'in the long run'. In the long run it is true that both democracy and human rights benefit the market economy regionally and internationally, and it is equally true that stability on the edges of Europe will benefit national security in core Europe.

But it makes little sense to operate with such broad definitions of 'national interest' that everything can be explained by them. After all, it is not obvious that such a broad definition will lead to a national commitment to problem-solving and funding for projects. For example, even though Norway recognises that human rights and democracy lead to both stability and a functioning market economy, it does not follow from this that the country will feel obliged to work to bring this about, especially if it commits money and resources, and perhaps demands hard power intervention. *The national interest, defined this broadly, is too vague here to act as a trigger of commitment.* Only the narrowly defined national interest in both these models will do as an analytical model suitable for empirical testing.

On such narrow definitions, it becomes possible to contrast a national security interest, a national economic interest and a value-based interest. Which one of these explains hard power intervention in Bosnia and Kosovo? Which interests explained hard power intervention in Somalia, Haiti, Rwanda and Iraq?

The latter four cases, discussed briefly above, yield some interesting indications: in Iraq, we find an economic national interest on the part of the USA, viz. the continued secure oil supply from the Middle East. This interest probably explains why the USA elected to intervene. There is in addition the security interest in the fact that Saddam Hussein commands and uses both biological and chemical weapons, in addition to probably producing nuclear weapons.

Thus, both security and economic interests on the part of Western states are abundantly evident in the Iraq case. It is quite inconceivable that the intervention would have been undertaken for humanitarian reasons. However, the USA still opted for a UNSC mandate in a case where the Kuwaiti government asked for help and such a mandate was not strictly necessary (Cortrell and Davis, 1996).

But in the other cases of hard power intervention in the 1990s there was often not such an economic or security interest. Haiti is one example where the concern to the USA was one of restoring democracy, while Somalia is another case of intervention faraway from home in a conflict where one would be hard pressed to find any narrow national interest. In Rwanda there was a lack of political will to commit resources to an intervention for exactly this reason, although the French intervened briefly, mainly because of old colonial ties and interests, but all in all this intervention never got going because UN member states did not want to participate in it. Thus, some of the hard power interventions were undertaken for traditional national interests, some were not undertaken at all despite the mandate given, and some were undertaken without any such national interests present, but with a major humanitarian disaster at hand.

In order to analyse the drivers for intervention, we will look in more detail at the Bosnian and Kosovo cases.

Bosnia: Reluctant intervention for humanitarian reasons

The Bosnian case is one where the 'moral' argument became increasingly prominent in Western Europe and the USA, but where these states were bewildered as to what to do because there were no clear national interests of a traditional kind at stake. Burg and Shoup (1999) recount how US policy-makers decided that the USA should not get involved because national security interests were not at stake, but these were policy-makers and advisers used to the closed circle of diplomatic deliberations. To them, the case was an easy one: no direct national interest at stake, so no involvement beyond peacekeeping.

In Bosnia, events on the ground gradually led to Western hard power involvement, but only very reluctantly. There was clearly no intention of hard power intervention in the first place, neither by the Europeans nor the Americans. The UN authorised several mandates to use force in order to escort humanitarian convoys, protect civilians and enforce embargoes, and established a large peacekeeping mission. All this was done with impartiality as the guiding principle: the UN forces were not going to take sides in this conflict, but remain neutral. The 'moralists' in Western public opinion called for intervention against the Serbs, while UN neutrality led to disaster for the Bosnian population whom it was intended to assist. The impossibility of being neutral while being engaged appeared increasingly obvious to the Western public, which demanded intervention to prevent further massacres. Yet the Western political elites decided against this. Hard power intervention from the West, led by the USA, only came after the massacres of 7000 civilian men in Srebrenica and the Serb attack on the Sarajevo food market which killed 64 people. Public outrage and pressure for action at this point were decisive (Burg and Shoup, 1999).

The story of Bosnia shows how difficult it is to get hard power intervention accepted when the risk is high and there are *no clear national interests* at stake. The lesson from Somalia had been very effective in the USA: the so-called 'body-bag' syndrome was a reality. No political leader could risk TV coverage of US soldiers' bodies being pulled through the streets of a foreign capital and survive this politically. This had created a barrier against hard power intervention abroad. If it were to happen, it had to be risk-free. That meant air power and no land forces.

As the Balkans and especially the Serbs were notorious for guerrilla warfare techniques, any intervention into a war here would certainly mean great losses. The UN has been harshly criticised for its inaction in Bosnia, and also by its own assessments, but it is a fact that none of the major Western powers wanted to intervene and thus left the issue to UN peacekeeping. Never was it more evident that the UN commands no resources beyond those of its member states.

Intervention was not wanted, but intervention gradually happened because of human rights and humanitarian reasons. But this intervention was designed to be as risk-free as possible, and came very late in terms of preventing human suffering. As we shall see, the trauma of Bosnia left a major legacy for later action. Kosovo did not linger on like Bosnia because one had learnt from experience.

In the Bosnian case, the point of departure for the Western states was *non-intervention*. They agreed to establish a peacekeeping mission, UNPROFOR (United Nations' Protection Force), which was wrongly labelled as a 'protection force'. It was not equipped to protect anyone against military attack, and was later to be exposed as impotent in the face of Serb attacks on the very civilians the UN had set out to protect.

As mentioned above, there were several UNSC resolutions related to Bosnia. Once UNPROFOR was in place, the council adopted sanctions against the FRY – or what remained of it, viz. Serbia and Montenegro. These were both oil and weapons embargoes, and the council mandated the use of force to monitor the Adriatic in these two areas. Operation Sharp Guard started in July 1992, and was successful in the area of oil shipments, but not regarding arms. Clearly there were other ways of transporting arms than the sea route. However this may be, this was hard power use which was easy to handle.

Already at this time it was clear that UNPROFOR could not retain neutrality and carry out its mission. The Serbs did not respect humanitarian law, and shelled food supplies to Sarajevo as well as its inhabitants. The UNSC therefore tried to assist UNPROFOR by mandating a 'no-fly zone' later in 1992, Operation Sky Monitor. But this no-fly zone was violated, and led to further flight monitoring. The UNSC mandated the use of force to ensure compliance with the ban on flights, and Operation Deny Flight was launched in 1993. This was an operation which was difficult to carry through, but for the first time in its history NATO used force and shot down four Serb planes. This was no longer a neutral operation, yet the UN continued to oppose any taking of sides. The Serbs retaliated by taking UN hostages.

After this the UN declared its so-called 'safe areas' of six towns in Bosnia. UNPROFOR was to protect these areas, but only use force in self-defence. Yet the civilians here were supposed to be safe. This was a major mistake on the part of the UN, and one that showed that it was impossible to retain a neutral peacekeeping operation. Again there was the provision of a UN mandate to use force to protect UNPROFOR, but it was quite unclear whether any state would send forces for this purpose. The West did not want to intervene with ground forces, and seemed prepared to let the warring factions continue on their own. Sarajevo had been under siege for almost two years, and nothing was done by the West apart from sanctions and humanitarian aid. The actual hard power use was not easy to embark upon: any land force would involve large losses. Which democracy would sustain that?

The moral debate about the injustice done to the Bosniacs and also the Croats continued in the Western press, with calls for hard power intervention to assist them. US politicians led by Bob Dole wanted to arm these two groups and to lift the embargo, an initiative called 'lift and strike'. This eventually became the US position, but was resisted by the Europeans, who manned UNPROFOR. They naturally feared retaliation against the peacekeepers, who had been taken as hostages by the Serbs on several occasions.

The decisive turn came with human rights atrocities shown on the world's media. The Bosnian war was uniquely covered by the media, especially the siege of Sarajevo.[13] The fresh food market in Sarajevo was shelled on 4 February 1994, killing 64 people, and this provoked a response from the UN for a NATO attack on the Serbs on Mount

Igman. NATO acted with immediate pressure on the Serbs, which led to a ceasefire. But the Serbs continued with attacks on the so-called safe areas: Gorazde, Bihac, and later, in 1995, Zepa and Srebrenica.

When the pictures of long rows of men taken away to be massacred after the fall of Srebrenica reached the Western media, there was no longer any choice: hard power intervention had to be undertaken. Operation Deliberate Force came in 1995. But by this time the massacres of Srebrenica were complete. The air power intervention came too late, and was too limited. There was never any contemplation of the use of ground forces, despite the rapid reaction force deployed by the UK and France to serve around Sarajevo.

The USA secretly helped the Croats win back lost areas in Krajina and Knin as well as East Slavonia in 1995, marking a turn in the war. This induced a Serb willingness to negotiate for a settlement, which became the Dayton agreement.

The hard power intervention in Bosnia was both limited, late and reluctantly carried through. *However, the Bosnia experience changed the view of intervention in Western states.* They had not intervened because there were no real threats to national interests and no one wanted to get involved in the risky warfare in the Balkans. Yet public opinion had become involved like nowhere else in the plight of the civilians, first as victims in Sarajevo, then as objects of brutal massacres that had only been seen during the Holocaust in the Second World War. This modern and atrocious massacre, coupled with modern media coverage, showed the new dynamic of value-based *Realpolitik*: something had to be done.

The UN was shown up in a more and more impotent and shameful light with its insistence that it was impartial as a peacekeeper when there was no peace to keep, and the Serbs manipulated the UN personnel. The nightmare of Srebrenica was that the TV cameras recorded the drama of General Mladic's playing cat and mouse with the Dutch commander Kerremans, toasting him on the infamous picture that has plagued the Dutch national consciousness ever since, while mocking the UN and moving into the 'safe haven' to separate the boys and men from the population. They were escorted to their death outside the town. All this happened while the UN still tried to stop the use of force to prevent the massacre: the UN special representative Akashi did his best to retain the 'impartiality' of the UN to the very end. When the NATO attack came, the worst massacre since the Second World War had already been carried out.

The Bosnia intervention was a non-intervention for four years while the war was going on, only to become a reluctant and belated hard power intervention when human rights abuses became as bad as they could possibly become. Even then the intervention was reluctant, and half-hearted. But *what finally triggered it to happen, was not strategic or economic interest – it was concern for the humanitarian situation and for massive human rights breaches*. Political elites did not elect to intervene; but media coverage and public outrage forced them to act.

Kosovo: hard power intervention for human rights

The Kosovo intervention from March to June 1999 happened at a swifter pace. Roberts, an expert in Western interventions and the UN, states that Operation Allied Force (the Kosovo intervention) marked a high point in the increasing emphasis on human rights and humanitarian issues which has been a striking feature of international relations in the post-1945 era. For theoreticians of international relations it represented a 'further remarkable twist in the strange and long-running association between the supposedly hard-nosed and "realist" factor of force and the supposedly soft and "idealist" factor of international humanitarian and human rights' (Roberts, 1999: 102). He further remarks that the launching of this operation took place on the same day as General Pinochet was found to be able to be extradited to Spain by a UK court, another sign of the salience of international human rights norms over traditional state sovereignty.

Why did NATO act, even without an explicit mandate from the UNSC? Roberts, usually a 'hard-nosed' realist himself, is in no doubt: 'the NATO states were united by a sense of shame that, in the first four years of atrocious wars in former Yugoslavia, they had failed . . . to devise coherent policies and to engage in decisive actions' (1999: 104). Further, 'the available evidence suggests that the critical considerations impelling NATO to take action were those of humanity and credibility' (p. 109). Robin Cook, as one of many NATO foreign ministers, spoke like this: 'The first reason why we took action was that we were aware of the atrocities that had been carried out . . . not to have acted, when we knew the atrocities that were being committed, would have made us complicit in their repression.'[14]

Similar justifications for the intervention were presented by all the NATO leaders. It was primarily a moral argument, based on the duty to help the people escape massive human rights violations. Additional arguments were the credibility of NATO and the danger of instability in the region. The argument about NATO was clearly a valid one, once it has been threatened to use force, but the interesting issue is that the ACTORD – the official procedure towards mounting an intervention –

was released as such. In Bosnia the USA had threatened the use of force without following suit, but in the Kosovo case it seemed that political elites were willing to use this threat much earlier. The other argument, about regional instability, did not carry much weight, as this was a case of intra-state conflict where the only spillover was from refugees.

It is clear that the humanitarian factor was the key one in explaining intervention. Perhaps it was assumed that Milosevic would bow to pressure, but threatening intervention was no less a risky strategy. It also carried with it the disadvantage of alienating Russia at a time when a fairly good relationship had been built up between Russia and NATO. The Partnership for Peace (PfP) programme, the cooperative body between Russia and NATO, suffered as NATO never used it to consult the Russians on Kosovo, as they were obliged to do according to PfP rules. This angered the Russians greatly: they withdrew their NATO ambassador when the bombing started and cut all cooperation with the organisation. This was all very disadvantageous to NATO's plans for integrating Russia as much as possible save for accession.

There were thus no security or economic interests that would explain this intervention. The fact that 19 NATO countries agreed also testifies to this: they could not possibly have identical national interests in the Balkans that they sought to pursue.

The political logic of the preparations for intervention naturally also played a role. Once the threat of hard power had been launched, NATO credibility was at stake. But the willingness to threaten to use force is remarkable, also given the lack of a UNSC mandate. Why did 19 Western states risk this?

The lesson learned from Bosnia was that Milosevic like other Balkan leaders only understood this tough kind of politics. Without hard power as a credible part of the political tools, no results would be achieved. In Bosnia negotiations had been tried with a feeble or non-existent hard power threat, with fiasco as the outcome.

Given this, the question then becomes not that of hard vs. soft power, but of *involvement vs. non-involvement*. The alternative to involvement was simply to let the Serbs settle things within their own borders: Kosovo was, and is, a part of the FRY. But this option was no longer a viable one when reports of massive internal displacements of Kosovars came in the summer of 1999. More than 300 000 people fled their homes for the mountains when Serb paramilitaries started to harass the population. While the negotiations with Milosevic continued, Western states, through the KVM, recorded troop movements into Kosovo in violation of the

Holbrooke–Milosevic agreement. When several episodes of violent clashes and killings occurred, it was clear that an armed conflict was starting. The Kosovo Liberation Army (KLA) was by this time well armed and mobilised.

This was a classic civil war situation. The West could have pulled out at this stage, seeing the obvious danger of a land-based war. But it was elected not to. The willingness to continue into a scenario that more and more implied the use of force is remarkable, given the lack of security and economic interests in the area. In addition, this was not an international conflict with border spillover; it was an internal conflict inside a sovereign entity. Throughout 1999 it was, however, clear that Kosovo remained at the top of the Western political agenda, and that no Western leader would back down from the issue. This is a significant indication of the importance of human rights on this agenda. When the Rajak massacre happened in January of that year, it was absolutely clear that non-involvement was not an option. This is not to attribute moral motives to Western policy-makers – which probably did exist but which are not relevant to the argument – but simply to note that the public diplomacy logic worked. For a Western leader to avoid the question: 'What are you going to do about this?' with the answer: 'This is inside another state's borders and therefore none of our business', would have been political suicide. Whether Rajak was a Serb massacre or not, it acted as a trigger for full Western involvement.[15]

The Kosovo intervention happened despite the lack of an explicit UNSC mandate, and was a planned intervention in the sense that NATO used the threat of hard power early in the diplomatic confrontation with Milosevic. In September 1999 NATO's defence ministers decided to 'study military options' in response to the violation of the Holbrooke–Milosevic agreement, where there were large internal population displacements due to Serb aggression. In late October 1999, when the humanitarian situation worsened, and also because winter was approaching, NATO set in motion the ACTORD, which meant full and formal preparation for military action. Once launched, the threat to use hard power was in a sense 'binding', contingent on specific ultimata. These were not met in the Rambouillet negotiations between the two sides in Kosovo, ending with Serb refusal to agree in late February 2000. The troop movement into Kosovo continued; the KLA continued its military build-up, and the KVM had to be withdrawn when violence escalated in March. The Western fear of massive ethnic cleansing was a constant theme of the media and of political elites. The Rajak massacre was a trigger for action, but it was only one such trigger.

Alternative explanations for this intervention make little sense. Of economic arguments there were none; of narrow security arguments there was little beyond the danger of a massive exodus of refugees into neighbouring states, but this did not constitute a credible security threat to NATO states as such. The most likely explanation for the decision to threaten the use of force – the launching of ACTORD – was the escalation of internal displacement, harassment and violence in Kosovo. However, without the recent experience of inaction in the similar situation in Bosnia it is unlikely that the Kosovo intervention would have happened.

There is another case with constellations similar to those of Kosovo: the Chechen case. In two wars, 1994-97 and from 1999 to the time of writing, Chechnya has been the theatre of major warfare involving huge casualties and suffering on the part of civilians; massive deportations and flight from the areas of fighting, and terrible destruction of cities. There are no reports of ethnic cleansing in Chechnya, rather of disproportionate use of force against civilians by the Russians, and likewise of largely insufficient efforts to provide humanitarian aid.

The situation is also similar in the sense that both Kosovo and Chechnya are, legally speaking, 'internal affairs' – Chechnya is part of the CIS, and the Russians have a right to restore and keep order there, while Kosovo is part of the FRY, and the Serbs have the same legal right. It follows that intervention by a third party, especially hard power intervention, is matter for the UNSC as a general rule, and that such intervention should follow the criteria discussed above.

However, intervention in the Chechen case has been almost non-existent. There has never been any discussion of hard power intervention; here Kosovo stands out as a case where such intervention took place even in the absence of an explicit UNSC mandate. But the remarkable feature of the Chechen case is the weak international response and criticism: soft power intervention is also conspicuous by its absence. Apart from a few efforts on the part of the OSCE and the COE, almost no Western country or IO has been concerned with the humanitarian plight of the Chechens.

Lapidus, who has investigated this case in great detail, chronicles the Western response. It was in conformity with norms of 'old sovereignty', she concludes: the USA in particular accepted Russian descriptions of the 'bandits' and the need to impose law and order, and the 'response in European capitals was similarly restrained', she records (Lapidus, 1998: 144). This was despite the violation on the part of the Russians of many international commitments, such as for example the

OSCE norms and the Geneva Conventions. The US response was in fact an endorsement of the Russian military action when it started in 1994, and then Secretary of State Warren Christopher even defined it as an entirely internal affair where 'It's best to leave it to the judgement of president Yeltsin; . . . I'm sure he thought through what he was doing before he did it, and it's best we let him run such things . . . we would not like to see the disintegration of Russia'.[16] In the Western response, there was no mention of international humanitarian norms and human rights.

This cautious attitude has continued throughout the second Chechen war from 1999. There are two explanations for this: one based on neo-realism, the other premised on our argument about the importance of public diplomacy. The neo-realist explanation stresses the need to keep a good relationship with Russia because it is a major power, and also the common interest in avoiding new state formations and unrest in the Caucasus, where there are major oil and gas reserves. Also, this area is too far from Western Europe to be a traditional security risk, and any action taken against Russian interests here might lead to responses in other areas, such as in the High North. There are plenty of neo-realist reasons why the Chechen case has been ignored by the West.

However, it is precisely in this light that the importance of public diplomacy and the media become a key: there was no major media coverage of the Chechen war. The few journalists in the region had to leave for security reasons, including also the only international presence, the OSCE Assistance Group, which was until its departure in 1999 the only international actor in the region. During both Chechen wars – in which civilians have been killed in large numbers, deported and have had to flee, in which the city of Grozny has practically been razed to the ground – during this war there has been very little or no 'footage' and international reporting. Likewise, no NGOs have been allowed into the area, and all international humanitarian organisations, such as the UNHCR and the ICRC, have had to leave their supplies in Moscow or operate under stringent criteria laid down by Russian forces in Chechnya's neighbouring republic Ingushetia.

There can naturally be no conclusive evidence that the lack of public diplomacy is the 'cause' for this lack of Western soft power intervention, but it is probably a major reason why the neo-realist factors mentioned above have been allowed to work freely. As we have argued here, the human rights regime only has an impact when there is considerable public diplomacy at work, where 'shaming', democratic accountability and the logic of public discourse become central to political accountability, and where the agenda is set in these terms. Otherwise, we have argued, there will be no power behind the human rights regime.

This case illustrates this argument to the full: in the Kosovo case, the logic of public diplomacy was at work, setting an agenda based on human suffering and violations of human rights. The media were present, reporting at centre stage both in Bosnia and in Kosovo. Kosovo was widely seen as the 'replay' of Bosnia, and politicians in Western Europe had to address this agenda. They learnt from the Bosnia experience that they were left with the moral responsibility for the failure of inaction. The pressure was on from the very beginning in the Kosovo case that such a 'Bosnian' outcome would not be a viable one.

In the Chechen case there was no media coverage and no NGO mobilisation. Consequently international public opinion was not aroused, and Western politicians were allowed to resort to the 'old' sovereignty.

The present period: the politics of human security

The present period lacks good paradigms for the security policy that is actually carried out. On the one hand the UNSC looks for state security reasons for its value-based interventions; on the other the media and public opinion increasingly call for human rights to be considered legitimate reasons for both soft and hard power intervention.

One possible paradigm for security policy is that of human security, introduced in Chapter 1. State security has always been the cornerstone of the international system and of 'high politics' as such. It has been, as Lodgaard remarks, the hallmark of the state system (Lodgaard, 2000). However, in recent years there has been a development of a complementary type of security policy where the individual and the rights of peoples are the units. The security of persons and their right to security from their government is the key to this new concept. As was underlined in Chapter 2, the relevant international human rights instruments all contain a reference to the individual right to security. Today there are many states that do not provide such security, however, either because they are oppressive or because they are weak.

The concept of human security was first coined by the report *Our Global Neighbourhood* by the Commission on Global Governance in 1995. In the post-Cold War period there was much discussion about comprehensive security issues, but it seems that the concept of human security is gaining ground more permanently. The UN's political practice in the 1990s, as we discussed above, has centred much on internal conflicts in this period. These actions of collective security have been undertaken to enhance the security of peoples, not of states. All conflicts that have led to embargoes and/or interventions have involved massive humanitarian problems. Thus, the idea that security policy refers to individuals and not only to states is very relevant to the political issues that confront modern security policy.

Human security refers to the personal security each inhabitant has, and naturally confronts issues such as mines, small arms, child soldiers, how to create democracy and rule of law, and how to manage and settle violent conflicts. One could, as a shorthand, say that human security refers to every issue that pertains to the physical security of the individual.

But state security is linked to human security:

> State security is a means of providing human security . . . but outwardly aggressive or inwardly repressive regimes may be major sources of insecurity. This is also the likely effect of failed states . . . a high degree of human security may shed legitimacy on goverments, regimes, and states, whereas grave violations of human security may trigger international actions against them (Lodgaard, 2000: 5).

The Canadians have developed the concept in a publication from the Ministry of Foreign Affairs, *Human Security: Safety for People in a Changing World* (1999), where it is argued that the proliferation of internal, armed conflicts demands that security policy takes its point of departure in the individual, while being complemented by state security, which should also serve the individual. This trend, it is noted, is part of 'people-centred' foreign policy. Thus, we see a shift from the state focus to the individual focus, and also a 'domestication' of foreign policy: security policy now takes place within states.

Human security is premised on the right of the individual to personal security, and thus reintroduces the issue of what constitutes a legitimate state that we discussed in Chapter 1. The general argument is that only states that provide their people with security in terms of peace and general human rights, are legitimate ones. This notion invalidates traditional state sovereignty, but is an emerging norm in the practice of international politics today. The normative basis for 'intervention for human rights and democracy' we find in the OSCE norms, but also in UNSC practice in the 1990s. The ultimate basis for this norm is, however, to be found in the logic of human rights itself, as expressed in the traditional formulation of the right to security of person. A security policy based on 'human security' links human rights and soft power, but also hard power, the tool of traditional security policy. This is a development we can see happening today, although many states are opposed to this.

The human security network: international agenda-setting for a new norm

The human security agenda was launched by a group of like-minded states under the informal leadership of Norway and Canada. In 1998 the Canadian and Norwegian foreign ministers met at Lysøen island near Bergen where they signed a declaration which established a like-minded group and a partnership in the areas of human security (Lysøen Declaration, 1998). They agreed to hold a yearly ministerial meeting where NGOs would also participate. The following year ten states – Austria, Canada, Chile, Ireland, Jordan, the Netherlands, Slovenia. Switzerland, Thailand and Norway – met at foreign minister level in the same place, adopting plans for action in many of the human security policy areas. These included specific actions to be coordinated between these states in the areas of landmines, small arms, child soldiers, international humanitarian and human rights law, promotion of the ICC, work for conflict prevention and for the safety of humanitarian workers (Chairman's Summary, 1999). The following year the same states met in Lucerne, adding Mali and Greece to the group. This time they named the cooperation 'The Human Security Network' . The key speaker, Francis Deng, the UN's special representative for internally displaced persons, gave the keynote address where he defined human security as the 'normative meaning of sovereignty as responsibility and the basis for holding governments accountable' (Chairman's Summary, 2000: 1). Here sovereignty is no longer the supreme norm of international politics but rather a norm relative to that of human rights: only governments that honour human rights, here the right to security of person, are legitimate. Human rights are superior to sovereignty.

The ministers were joined by international NGOs such as the Red Cross, and dealt specifically with the trade in small arms and light weapons as well as non-state actors in war, such as guerrilla movements. They also devoted considerable time to strategic thinking about how to put human security on the international agenda, and agreed that the like-minded governments and the NGOs would seek to 'deepen their informal contacts with interested states and NGOs, promote further and sustained consideration of human security issues in international and regional fora, in particular the UN as well as within the framework of international financial institutions' (ibid.: 2). They also arrived at a common position and strategy for the UN World Conference on Small Arms and Light Weapons in 2001 (ibid.: annexe 1).

This group of like-minded states and NGOs, which is now officially called a 'network', is aimed at setting the international agenda in security policy. It works though informal contacts, conferences, meetings and public diplomacy to achieve this goal. For instance, the two leading states, Norway and Canada, have had their foreign ministers write articles in the international press on the topic.

The networking activity and the public diplomacy for human security fit in well with what Keck and Sikkink (1998) call 'advocacy networks in international politics'. Noting that these networks are

> motivated by values rather than material concerns . . . advocacy networks often reach beyond policy change to advocate and instigate changes in the institutional and principled bases of international politics. . . . What is novel in these networks is the ability to mobilize information strategically and to create new issues and categories and to persuade. . . . Activists in networks try not only to influence policy outcomes, but to transform the terms and the nature of the debate (ibid.: 2).

These networks are particularly successful in policy areas such as human rights where values play a key role. Examples of successful networks, involving both NGOs and states, are the landmine convention campaign (Price, 1998), how gender was put on the international agenda, and also how the environment was launched as an international issue. Currently human security is a candidate for such agenda-setting. The Human Security Network plays the pivotal role in this process, working transnationally with both states and NGOs, seeking to launch the concept in public debate as well in IOs. It appeals to the human right of security of person, and defines the concept as one that includes every issue related to the physical security of people, such as small arms and landmines.

It remains to be seen how human security will develop as a key security concept, but it is already clear that it is being increasingly used. For instance, the Canadian foreign minister launched it during Canada's chairmanship of the Security Council, requesting the secretary-general to write a report on civilians in armed conflict for the council to discuss and to take action on. The report[17] essentially recommended that the Security Council get involved in the whole range of human security activities. In the ensuing debate, most states welcomed the suggested points of action, and thereby agreed that security policy – the competence of the council – also includes the protection of civilians in armed conflict. Some states, like Egypt, criticised the report for putting human rights above national sovereignty, while India went further and warned the council not to transgress its mandate (national interventions, Security Council, 16-17.9). Thus, the human security concept is easily seen as a challenge to national sovereignty.

In the general debate at the UN's general assembly, Canadian Foreign Minister Axworthy called for the establishment of criteria for humanitarian intervention, which would be based on 'fundamental breaches of international humanitarian and human rights law' (Canada's intervention, 23 September 1999, p. 2), thus changing the basis for Security Council intervention from 'a threat to international peace and security' to a human rights basis. The same direct link between human rights and intervention was made by him in an address at Princeton University where the Kosovo intervention was justified on human security grounds: 'a new reality is emerging. The well-being of individuals – human security – is increasingly front and centre in how we define peace and security – the crisis in Kosovo is a concrete expression of this human security dynamic at work' (statement, 7 April 1999).

This radical statement was met by much opposition by developing states, jealously guarding their sovereignty, but also of course by states like China and Russia. However, the secretary-general himself had launched this debate as the key issue for the UN in the time ahead.

In his own address he had said: 'State sovereignty is being redefined by the forces of globalisation and international cooperation. The state is now widely understood to be the servant of its people, not *vice versa*. The inability of the international community in the case of Kosovo to reconcile these two equally compelling interests – universal legitimacy and effectiveness in defence of human rights – can only be viewed as a tragedy. It has revealed the core challenge to the Security Council and the UN as a whole in the twenty-first century: to forge unity behind the principle that massive and systematic violations of human rights – wherever they may take place – should not be allowed to stand.'[18] He called for a new type of national interest, that of pursuit of democracy, human rights and the rule of law, and reforms of the Security Council so that it can perform its role. It is unacceptable to stand by and watch massive human rights violations – that undermines the whole idea and spirit of the UN.

In an article in *The Economist* Annan speaks about two concepts of sovereignty,[19] one old-fashioned and static, the other that of the state that respects human rights and serves its people. Clearly the implication is that only the latter type of states – democracies – are legitimate in the eyes of the world community, and in an important address to the international peace conference in The Hague he put in a nutshell what the debate of human rights vs. state sovereignty is about: 'unless the Security Council can unite around the aim of confronting massive human rights violations and crimes against humanity on the scale of Kosovo, then we will betray the very ideals that inspired the founding of the UN'.[20]

In sum, the practice of hard power intervention has relied on humanitarian and human rights reasons in recent years. This has not been 'window dressing' in order to justify wars, however: when applying alternative explanations to these interventions we find that they do not fit. Neither economic nor traditional security-based explanations suffice to explain why Western states have risked both lives and credibility in undertaking interventions such as Kosovo. But we have also seen that Bosnia, with its atrocities, did not easily get the response of a hard power intervention. This indicates that Western states initially resisted getting involved, and shied away from intervention. Only when the media coverage became intense was there a response with air power. The sequence of events in Bosnia suggests that the logic and pressures of public diplomacy explain why the intervention finally came. Similarly, in Kosovo the reaction was quicker because the unpleasantness of inaction in the Bosnian case was fresh in the memory. Also the Kosovo case was well covered by Western media, and remained at the top of the Western political agenda in 1999 and 2000.

What about values? Was the motivation instrumental or 'really' value-based? Did they intervene because they felt a moral duty to do so? As stated in Chapter 4, we think that political action can and is really motivated by values in many cases, but we also think that instrumentality plays a major role as a motivating factor. If the values of the human rights regime really motivated hard power intervention, we should have expected the Rwanda case to be treated somewhat like that of Kosovo. This was not so. From this we cannot draw any substantive conclusion, however, simply note that there is no consistency in interventions and that this is an indication of instrumental cost/benefit calculations at work. But it is also true that peoples and problems closer to home matter more.

The major difference between Rwanda and the Balkans also lies in the extent of media coverage: Rwanda did not mobilise the forces of public diplomacy in any way like the conflicts in the Balkans. The political elites in Europe were forced to deal with Kosovo because it remained at the top of the public agenda.

9
Conclusions

In this study we have confined ourselves to the Western world and public diplomacy, but with the assumption that the new dynamic of public diplomacy would also spread to other parts of the world. We introduced three hypotheses about regime impact: that regimes would have an *independent impact* if embedded in IOs with strong powers and/or with regime-specific tools; that *'shaming'* would work in states close to the European and Western public sphere and public diplomacy, and that *instrumentality* would be the main motivation for adopting the human rights regime. Instrumentality could be in the form of responsivenes to 'shaming' because loss of reputation means increasingly more to those who partake in Western public diplomacy, and instrumentality is also seen in responses that move on the incentive/punishment logic. Here we expected states further away from Europe to follow this latter behavioural logic.

Most of this study has concerned the human rights regime and its importance. Another study is needed in order to study the receiving end, the state that adapts to the regime, in a systematic manner.

The findings of this study

Abbot et al. (2000) operate with a useful classification for regimes and their strength. Noting the increasing legalisation of world politics, they use three variables to define regime strength: *precision, obligation* and *delegation*.

Precision refers to the degree of detail in the specification of the regime. Here the OSCE ranks highest and the EU lowest among our three regime forms. The EU has a very vaguely stated regime for human rights, although the newly adopted human rights charter improves on this.

Obligation refers to the type of regime: is it legally binding or not? How are states bound by it? Among our three regime forms, the ECHR ranks highest on this variable, while the OSCE ranks lowest with its explicitly non-binding stipulation for the regime.

Delegation refers to the regime-specific tools: how is the regime 'equipped' in terms of tools? Here the ECHR has its own supranational court, while the EU has a 'quasi-legal' tool in the way the ECJ has judged on human rights. The OSCE naturally has no court, but has other regime-specific tools.

A fourth variable, not suggested by Abbott et al., is that of an *embedding IO* and its general strength. This variable may be more important than any of the others, because the strength with which a regime is promoted is largely determinative of its impact. We have analysed the EU and found that its general strength far surpasses that of the other two IOs in this study, but the human rights regime is so new to the EU that its major impact probably lies in the future. After the EU, the OSCE has more strength in the new states in and around Europe, whereas the COE is weak in this field but strong in its human rights 'guardian' role in Western Europe.

The empirical material used in this study is not exhaustive, as discussed in the empirical chapters. The historical *newness* of the human rights regime in the EU explains why there are relatively few cases as yet; while the fact that a new type of state now makes up 50 per cent of the COE's membership – the state that was formerly communist and has little or no democratic tradition – explains why the new tools of the COE in promoting human rights are not yet fully explorable. There are not enough case studies that can be followed over many years as of yet. It is only the OSCE which has a longer record in imposing the human rights regime on member states. But the membership here is also largely affected by the newness of all the states of the former Soviet Union. We must therefore conclude at the outset that a study like this must remain quite tentative due to the fact that the states under study are *historically new as democracies,* dating from 1990 onwards. In some years' time we will be able to study the longer-term effects of Western impacts of the human rights regime, especially how these values are internalised in each state, and the differences between the states in this respect. This will enable us to see which effect the external imposition has had beyond learning to 'talk the talk' and formally setting up democratic institutions in order to satisfy Western conditionality. The deeply interesting question concerns how and how fast democratic values are replacing old authoritarian ones. On this question this study must remain silent.

What can we conclude, albeit in tentative fashion, from this study?

States, IOs and hard power intervention

We concentrated on one set of actors, the IOs. The direct role of states was discussed regarding hard power intervention, however, as both NATO and the UNSC are intergovernmental bodies. The states are the clear actors in both these organisations, with the qualification that the intergovernmental and consensual decision-making mode of NATO masks the inequality of the actors: the USA is by far the most important one, and when joined by the UK and perhaps a few others in a potential 'coalition of the willing', the costs of resisting or even abstaining from participation in a proposed decision or action is high indeed. Thus, some states have much power in NATO, while others are followers.

In the UNSC, it is also the USA, along with the other four veto powers, that has most say. The other member states can exercise agenda-setting and brokerage power, among 'soft power' instruments, but their influence is limited. Thus, when discussing *hard power intervention it makes most sense to talk about states as the main actors*.

In the study of 'soft power' intervention we chose to look at the three IOs: the EU, the OSCE and the COE. We could also have studied bilateral national policies, but found the interesting issue to be that of regime impact through non-state actors. But in focusing on these IOs we also had to delineate the sphere of state decision-making in each one.

We proposed the hypothesis that states are motivated by various types of interests, based on security, economic factors, but also on values. But we also insisted that the value motivation could not be expected to be dominant, and that it is virtually impossible to ascertain what the real actor motivation is in a given case. What was important to point out, however, was that prima facie we should not shut out such motivations, as the mainstream IR theories of neo-realism and neo-liberalism do. As Max Weber said, both ideas and material factors explain human action.

We further insisted on the assumption that values matter even if actors move on an instrumental logic. The reason for this choice is twofold: first, we see relatively little evidence, also based on our own experience, of value-based action in the larger picture of international politics; and second, it seemed important to show that even on this assumption, values play an increasing role.

One could term it 'values as *Realpolitik*': this means that the logic of public diplomacy makes it impossible to disregard the values of the human rights regime: media and voters demand action in terms of justice and human rights, and they demand it fast, in the form of soft or hard power intervention, often in faraway places. This logic made it extremely painful to be a Western politician during the Bosnian war, when nothing effectively was done to stop atrocities; and it largely explains why Kosovo had its hard power intervention.

In addition to pressures on politicians to act, there is also the ability for them to profile themselves as 'do-gooders' on the international scene: public diplomacy requires visibility, that one works for a good and just cause, dealing with the real problems where they are. Much rivalry over visibility and roles has taken place in the Balkans over the last decade, both among politicians as well as among IOs. This is an aspect that is important as an explanatory factor in value politics. It is not necessarily a negative feature, but a factor inherent in public diplomacy: visibility is of the essence.

'Values as *Realpolitik*' has its similar equivalent in the business world, where 'values' are rapidly becoming a necessary investment and normal business risk area. New stakeholders such as consumers, shareholders and NGOs demand ethical accountability and human rights standards, and owners have to hedge against reputational risk which may ruin them in extreme cases. *The logic here is the same as in the political arena:* transparency, stakeholder demand, globalisation in real-time reporting, and increased power to international human rights instruments.

In assuming instrumentality as we have done – knowing that values also act many times as real motives – we also aimed at discussing and criticising mainstream IR theory on its own terms by showing that one need not be motivated by values to promote them.

Did states promote these values? The actors that imposed the human rights regime – the states – were found to be reluctant to use hard power, not surprisingly. However, they intervened in Kosovo, Somalia and Haiti for such reasons. As Richard Caplan puts it, 'These interventions are part of a larger trend that has seen states give increased weight to human rights and humanitarian norms as matters of international concern, to the extent that the UNSC may now choose to characterise these concerns as threats to international peace' (Caplan, 2000: 27). He also adds that 'we may well be witnessing a right of humanitarian intervention, but it seems too soon to say that such a norm has been established' (ibid.). The initial interest in intervention can safely be assumed to be non-existent on the part of any state, given the cost and risk of such political action. But once an internal conflict escalates, there is a consideration of which national interests are involved. The USA took a major economic and security interest in the Iraq case. But in most other interventions in the 1990s there was no such material interest to be found. The pressures for intervening rose with the media and public attention given to the conflict: Rwanda, despite its extreme degree of actrocities, received less attention because it was an African conflict. The conflicts in Europe received enormous attention from all Western states. Two consecutive US presidents called for intervention when 'ethnic cleansing' in Bosnia came onto the agenda in 1992: outgoing President Bush as well as incoming President Clinton made it clear that this was not an internal Bosnian affair. Thereby the commitment to act was made, for human rights reasons. Such a commitment would not have been forthcoming in a conflict no one knew much about, despite the same kind of 'abuse level'.

It therefore seems a plausible conclusion that the states as actors are reluctant to use hard power to promote value-based interests, but that the logic of public diplomacy puts major pressure on them to do so.

States, IOs and soft power intervention

But states were much more willing to promote the human rights regime in soft power intervention around the world. Here we have recorded major and increasing use of political conditionality on the part of both states and IOs. The USA plays a leading role as a state actor using such conditionality, as evidenced in the successful demand for Milosevic's arrest. Smaller states cannot easily employ this tool on a bilateral basis.

But these states use conditionality in multilateral fashion, through IOs such as the World Bank, the IMF, the whole UN system as well as through the IOs in this study. Here we see a clear increase in the use of both economic and political conditionality in the 1990s, and the specification of the goals of this action to be the human rights regime: human rights, democracy and the rule of law. Whereas formerly aid was apolitical in the sense of not being tied directly to political conditions, this is now the very opposite: internationally the trend is very clear that all aid, apart from humanitarian aid, must be tied to 'good governance' criteria. Long-term development aid is also increasingly integrated with these goals as well as security policy in the sense of creating human security on the ground as a precondition for sustainable development.

States are thus both willing and eager to intervene with soft power tools, but cannot be assumed to be redefining national interests from the primacy of security and economic interests to value-based interests. The motivation of the values of the human rights regime is probably real enough, but when it comes to the real commitment of resources, there will be competition with other, traditional interests. The 'donor fatigue' of Western states is a case in point: poverty increases while Western aid decreases.

Again the logic of public diplomacy puts pressure on states: the focus on the Balkans has led to major political attention and resources to both Bosnia and Kosovo, while equally poor and deserving states on the edges of the European region – in the Caucasus and in the former Soviet Union – are 'forgotten' because they do not figure in the media. Moldova is an extremely poor state which receives virtually no Western attention or resources, to mention one among many examples.

Thus, we assume that although the value-based interest is a real one for Western states, it is not strong enough in competition with other material and short-term interests to play any major role. However, once the value-based issues are on the public agenda, there is pressure for action as well as the opportunity for playing a visible role. Thus, the attention on the Balkans can be explained by these factors in combination: the wish to implement the human rights regime, but also the need to be visible and to play a role, as well as the necessity to respond to pressures from public opinion and the media.

When we turn to the IOs, however, we must modify the assumption made about value-based interests. The IOs as such have the human rights regime as their primary *raison d'être*, unlike the states. Only the EU among the IOs in this study has a much larger portfolio. Both the OSCE and the COE are human rights and democracy organisations, and therefore must promote these values as their main task, both because they stand for these values, but also because this is the venue to continued existence and expansion. The instrumental motives here cannot be separated from the value-based motivation.

What did we find regarding the impact of the human rights regime? Did the IOs play roles independent of the states, or were they simply arenas for the latter? Was the shaming of public diplomacy the key explanation for adoption of the human rights regime, or was there a need for direct conditionality?

We found that the IOs wielded various kinds of independent impact on states that wanted membership in them. There were *regime-specific* powers in all three IOs. The COE has its own supranational court, and the secretary-general of the COE can use his own power of initiative to make inspection visits and propose policy. Further, the Parliamentary Assembly (PA) of the COE has its own human rights monitoring procedure, which is public; this allows the PA to eventually suspend the voting rights of a member state under scrutiny. The PA is also independent in its acceptance or rejection of new members. Further, the new office of high commissioner of human rights is also independent of the member states, although it is dependent on economic contributions from member states and still does not have a satisfactory budget.

In the COE case, all these tools are both regime-specific and independent. The member states can only 'sanction' the COE's work through the annual budget allocations and through the decisions in the Committee of Ministers, which is intergovernmental. The latter two 'sanction' possibilities are important enough, but it remains a reasonable conclusion that the COE can wield important independent impact through its regime-specific tools. It can be an actor in its own right in the human rights area, with the court as its main tool, but also with new tools from the late 1990s still largely unused.

The OSCE also has independent actor impact in the human rights regime. It has several regime-specific tools: the high commissioner for national minorities, the ODHIR office, the ombudsman for free press and media, the missions themselves and their mandates which are independent of the member states of the OSCE; the review conference where NGOs are also full participants, and the power of agenda-setting and initiative of the chairman-in-office. As we saw in the analysis above, the latter can set the agenda. But he or she also has to consult the major states on important moves. These states include first of all the USA, then the major European states and Russia. The other member states are seldom consulted informally, prior to decisions being taken.[1]

The OSCE works independently in day-to-day politics, but when major political questions are at stake, there is always consultation and decisions on whether the issue should be handled by the OSCE or some other IOs or perhaps by some states themselves. The major member states clearly decide on the degree of involvement of the OSCE. The secretariat in Vienna is small, consisting of around 250 personnel only, and the budget is small. In the missions, it is national personnel, funded by the home government, which is seconded. This creates weak loyalties to the OSCE as an organisation. However, given these major restrictions on the OSCE's own regime-specific tools, it remains true that the various OSCE institutions act on their own.

Regarding the EU, we found that both *general* policy tools were important for the impact in human rights, as well as *regime-specific* ones. The general tools include the weight EU foreign policy has acquired in recent years, by expanding its policy scope to security and defence as well as human rights, and by integrating foreign policy with foreign economic policy where the EU has supranational competence. This makes the Commission a major actor, and increases the independence of the EU from the direct control of the member states. Further, we found that human rights conditionality has been integrated with both foreign policy and foreign economic policy in a comprehensive and consistent manner from around the mid-1990s, something which made for a major impact of the former. Specifically, the accession strategy for Eastern states in the first enlargement round contains detailed conditionality within the human rights regime as well as in economic and market terms. The Commission is the key actor here which *defines* the criteria for conditionality, which also *implements* them, and finally, which *evaluates* candidate state performance towards meeting them. This places the Commission, beyond direct state control, in a uniquely powerful position in terms of impacting on candidate states in the human rights regime field.

Another EU actor independent of the control of member states is the ECJ. The court has ruled on a human rights basis, akin to a constitutional court, for decades, but has recently acquired a stronger basis for so doing through the various amendments of the EU treaty. The values of the human rights regime have been included in the treaty from 1992 onwards (TEU), and have been expanded upon in small steps. The high point in this regard is the adoption at Nice of the EU Charter on Human Rights, which is not legally binding, but which is nonetheless invoked both by the court and by EU representatives as authoritative. Being based on the major legally binding human rights texts, such as the ECHR, the charter already plays a key role as the foundation for EU policy in this area.

The *regime-specific* tools of the EU include the charter and the treaty basis of the foreign policy, as well as the suspension clause art. 7 of the Nice Treaty, which specifies how a state can be suspended for breaches of human rights. They also include the pre-accession strategy, which contains detailed assessments of how a new member state must meet the criteria of human rights and democracy, as well as the PHARE programme's democratisation funding and the twinning mechanism. The effect of the regime-specific as opposed to the general policy tools is hard to separate. *It remains, however, a conclusion that the general importance of the EU towards these states lends weight to its regime-specific tools.* The insertion of the human rights regime into the general enlargement process, including substantial PHARE funding, is a case in point.

In conclusion, we have found that all three IOs have independent actor roles in the human rights area, albeit with important limitations. We also found that the impact wielded in this area was greatest for the EU, as its general impact was greater. The case of Turkey illustrates this: while seemingly oblivious to COE demands and court decisions, it responded to EU conditionality in the pre-accession strategy.

What impact from the human rights regime?

Now we shift the focus to the states that are being impacted on. What impact was in fact wielded? Further, did the states react to shaming or conditionality, or perhaps both?

We noted that all three IOs made use of a combination of conditionality and teaching: they placed clear demands on the states, while also helping them to comply with these demands. Further, the IOs also used a combination of shaming – making their policy and demands public – and discreet processes of trying to ensure compliance. For instance, the OSCE makes extensive use of press releases and webpages, and the COE seeks public attention by on-site visits and highly publicised meetings with state leaders, often in their home country. Also the EU uses public diplomacy *in extenso*: its web-page contains all the reports on compliance and progress by candidate states, and the Commission arrives in the country in question to launch these reports. There is hardly any more public and anticipated event than the periodic assessment of a state's progress report.

Shaming alone seemed to work best in the states close to the core of Europe, in this study, the Central European states. The states further away with less of a democratic tradition – here the cases of Turkey, Azerbaijan, Ukraine and the Balkans – did not respond well to shaming. They also ignored written commitments such as the abolition of the death penalty in the Ukrainian case, and the some of the sentences of the European Court of Human Rights. We should add that the cases studied are not exhaustive, only indicative.

We cannot conclude on the issue of whether learning and internalisation of human rights norms occurs from the findings of this study.

We assumed that instrumentality was the basic reason for compliance, but this is, like Risse's assumption of the same, an obvious choice for the first stages of regime impact (Risse et al., 1999). Only in-depth studies of domestic compliance can yield conclusions here.

In concrete terms, the COE effected changes in national legislation and legal institutions in Central Europe, the Balkans, and in the former CIS states discussed here. The most significant example of this is in Bosnia, where the ECHR was transposed directly into national legislation and where the COE appointed judges.

The OSCE expanded its number of missions in 2000, and carried out major democratisation work in all its aspects through these and the regime-specific tools of the organisation. It was able to use shaming constructively in the Balkans, but not in the Caucasian member states. But the work of the EU has had the most impact and was clearly the most publicised. Both Central European states and Turkey, as well as Slovakia, responded swiftly to human rights criticism. In the Central European cases, fully fledged accession programmes imply deep-seated institutional changes in the regime components, such as legal and executive organs. In the cases of Slovakia and Turkey, the public criticism by the EU led to major efforts to respond. The EU combined shaming and conditionality: Slovakia was suspended from the candidate process as long as Mechiar remained in power, to be readmitted in 1997 with a change of government. Turkey, which had resisted all efforts by the COE and the OSCE to discuss rights of minorities and the role of the military in politics, turned around in March 2001 after extensive criticism by the Commission, which demanded a programme for changes in these areas. At first the Turks responded with their usual indignation, but later there was a willingness to design such a pre-accession programme.

The EU's major role in world politics explains this result. The incentive for EU membership is a major one, and candidate countries have little choice but to go along with the pre-accession demands specified by the EU. But membership in good standing in the COE as well as in the OSCE matters as well, especially that of the COE. This acts as a 'legitimacy test' of democracy for a new state that wants to enter fully into the European political and economic sphere.

The IOs under study here have the human rights regime as their main 'interest', if one can use this term. Also the EU is now rallying around this regime as its main goal, although the EU is still most effective as an economic actor. The focus on the human rights regime entails increased weight for the IOs in question: whereas a state must attend to all sorts of national interests, first and foremost security and economic, these IOs can devote their full attention to promoting the human rights regime.

The salience of soft power in international politics today helps them in this endeavour. The need for both governments and businesses to at least appear to honour the values of the human rights regime, greatly help both IOs and NGOs that promote them. The websites of all the three IOs under study are also clearly developed to be of use in shaming, formulated positively as often as possible, but also to create pressures on actors through the method of public diplomacy.

Theoretically this study suggests that value-based interests be given serious attention as a normal and very important part of a state's foreign policy, because a good standing and a good record in public diplomacy – promoting just such interests – are essential to any modern government. Participation in common problem-solving is a must for the states that want to be counted, and that includes all but a few rare pariah states today.

Regime theory should also be developed in this respect. We support the interest-based regime theory, but add value-based interests. But such interests are very different from economic and security interests in that they may be formed through persuasion, learning, scientific knowledge, NGO activity and so on. They may thus be formed in international arenas and through international influences. The theory of interest formation and change for value-based interests is probably very different from what is true for the other types of interest. This aspect needs further work.

Also, the role of IOs as well as that of other non-state actors such as NGOs is probably greater with regard to value-based interests than in other cases. The evidence from this study is that the IOs wield important powers, partially because the human rights regime is well embedded and developed as a legal regime. The trend towards legalisation and institutionalisation of human rights and human security strengthens the regime and regime powers. Other types of regimes are also part of this trend, but not to such an extent. The human rights regime and its impact should therefore be studied much more as being in the forefront of a general development in international politics. For instance, what impact is wielded by the IOs of the 'UN family' in their various human rights fields? And what impact do we see when the IOs cooperate? Is political conditionality an overall trend in international affairs, ranging from economic IOs such as the World Bank and the IMF to bilateral development aid?

This study has been but a first foray into this empirical field, suggesting an important trend and themes for further theoretical as well as empirical work. As conjectured at the outset, sovereignty is changing. Barker and Cronin point out that the 'understanding of legitimacy tends to change from era to era . . . the political legitimation of the nation-state changes over time' (1994: 108). Here we have sought to show empirically how the criterion of legitimate governance in a state today is changing into being the values of the human rights regime: to create or restore democracy and human rights have become reasons for intervention, even for hard power intervention such as in Haiti, Somalia, Bosnia and Kosovo.

Epilogue

On 1 April 2001, former president Milosevic of the FRY was arrested on charges of corruption and war crimes. He gave himself up when he no longer had the loyalty of the army, which he thought he commanded until the late evening before. Then it seemed that the democratically elected government of the FRY would be overthrown in a *coup d'état*. Now not only rule of law prevailed, but the last dictator of Europe was also extradited to The Hague in June of the same year, under heavy American pressure. This was a case of very clear political conditionality – the application of 'hard power' for 'hard values'.

The Serbs had come full circle in a year, from being a pariah nation in Europe based on weapons power only, to becoming a democracy cooperating with the international community. But the US pressure in the form of conditionality played the key role in the arrest of Milosevic. The US ultimatum was simple: arrest him before 31 March, or lose USD 100 million and our goodwill. He was arrested some hours after midnight that day.

On 26 February of the same year, two prominent Croats, a HDZ politician and a general, were sentenced by the ICTY in The Hague for war crimes and crimes against humanity. They had taken their orders directly from the late president Tudjman of Croatia, and were found guilty of massacres, rapes and torture. They were sentenced to 25 years in prison. The week before a Serb commander of the paramilitary forces was also sentenced in The Hague, receiving the same long sentence. His crimes also included systematic rape and torture of Muslim women. It was the first time rape was the basis of such a verdict, having recently been defined as a war crime in the statutes of the ICC as well as the ICTY.

The former president of Republica Srpska, Biljana Plvasic, with whom the international community, including myself, cooperated much and well in the implementation of the Dayton agreement, is awaiting her trial in The Hague. She gave herself up willingly when she no longer had the physical protection of bodyguards and police.

While this was going on in The Hague, the court system in Chile was preparing the case against former president Pinochet, and China was hosting a delegation to compete for the summer Olympics. When such a delegation visited China a year before, officials were angry at the human rights groups and the demand that human rights be put on the agenda. This year, however, the authorities welcomed the topic, stating that 'By applying for the Olympics, we want to promote not only the city's development, but the development of society, including democracy and human rights', to quote Bejing's deputy mayor.[1] The same day the large oil company Shell confirmed that it had made a major turn towards embracing human rights and democracy as company goals after its experience in Nigeria in 1995, when Ken Saro-Wiwa and nine others were executed. Although the company had no direct role in this, Shell stated that 'Ken Saro-Wiwa's death definitely forced a change'.[2]

The international law on war crimes and crimes against humanity has made major advances in the last few years, as have the instruments of law enforcement. State sovereignty no longer protects dictators, be they Milosevic, Tudjman or Pinochet. Even China has now started to 'talk the talk' of human rights, and international companies are starting to take human rights and democracy seriously as company concerns. It is no longer sufficient to relegate those values to governments and human right groups. Companies are expected to have policies on them, and to promote them.[3] This is a major normative shift.

States and companies are thus expected to have a stance on human rights, and not to remain neutral. The have to care about their reputation in this field. Even if they could not care less about such values, they must be promoters of them. *This is the effect of the new logic of public diplomacy.*

This study has also noted that it is in Europe that the human rights regime is mostly developed. By this we mean that the tools for implementation are most developed here. They include the court of the COE and the ECJ, both supranational, the major transformations of new European states through the EU's enlargement process, and the extensive bilateral human rights policies of European states not studied here.

Globally the trend is moving in the same direction. The establishment of the ICC and the tribunals for Rwanda and Yugoslavia are creations of the UN. The widespread use of truth commissions in states with armed conflicts and human rights abuses testifies to the universal recognition of the importance of these values. It is therefore interesting to study the European experience in order to see if any lessons can be learned. This is hopefully not Eurocentrism, but universalism.

Notes

1 Towards a New Type of Sovereignty in Europe

1. www.unglobalcompact.org
2. Report on Corporate Social Responsibility by the Norwegian Federation of Business, Oslo, 2001.
3. I was state secretary of foreign affairs in the Norwegian government (representing the Christian-Democratic Party) from 1997 to 2000, *inter alia* during the Norwegian chairmanship of the OSCE.
4. The term 'intervention' has no precise definition, but should not be used only to denote the use of hard power in aiming to change the government of another state. On our definition, the intrusion into another state's political sphere with the aim of undermining the government represents intervention. Thus, the EU states' political boycott of Austria in 1999 was an intervention because it rejected the democratically elected FPÖ and the Austrian government. Likewise, the massive money and expert aid to the Serbian opposition during the Milosevic years, launched in large part by Norway, was an intervention because its expressed aim was to enable the opposition to overthrow the government. See discussion of the concept of 'intervention' in A. McDermott (ed.), *Sovereign Intervention,* Prio Report no. 2/99, Oslo.
5. *Annual Report on Human Rights*, MFA, Oslo.
6. Kofi Annan's speech at The Hague Peace Conference, 18 May 1999.

2 Human Rights and Democracy: Driving Forces and Policy Tools

1. I followed the ICC negotiations in Rome in June 1998 very closely as Norwegian state secretary. It was clear that the USA opted out of the regime formation on traditional sovereignty grounds – that US soldiers should never accept to be sentenced in a non-American court. This was the view of the Pentagon, not of the State Department, but in this case the Pentagon's view prevailed. Despite US opposition, the new regime was established. I think a reasonable prediction is that the USA will have to join the court once it is in operation.
2. Official visit to Mexico, January 1998.
3. 'Ethical Business', editorial in *Financial Times*, 8 November 2000.
4. *Aftenposten*, 19 January 2001.
5. Judge Richard Goldstone headed the South African truth commission, and put major emphasis on the acceptance of the findings of the commission by all sides to a conflict. A truth commission usually has a more difficult job than a court because it has to interact with, and operate within, a state where atrocities were committed. Meetings with Goldstone in Oslo, June 1999.

6. *International Herald Tribune*, 22 February 2001.
7. Norwegian MFA, *Menneskerettigheter 1999*, årsrapport om norsk innsats for menneskerettighetene, Oslo.
8. *International Herald Tribune*, 'Beijing is an Eager Suitor' , 22 February 2001.

3 The Formation of the European Human Rights Regime

1. S. Krasner (ed.), 'Structural Causes and Regime Consequences', in *International Regimes* (New York: Ithaca, 1983).
2. Humphrey, quoted in Sikkink (1993: 147).
3. Universal Declaration of Human Rights, WWW.UNHCHR.CH/UDHR
4. The Commission on Human Rights was abolished in 1993, in the reform of the court, which now itself decides on which cases to admit. Earlier this work was done by the commission.
5. Art. 34 allows the court to receive petitions from 'any person, NGO, or group of individuals claiming to be the victim of a violation by one of the high Contracting parties'.
6. COE publication 18/11/99, *Secretariat of the European Social Charter.*
7. *The Prevention of Torture at the Dawn of a New Millennium*, CPT/inf/E (99)1.
8. *Preventing Ill Treatment*, H/Inf (99)6, COE.
9. Framework Convention for the Protection of National Minorities, Collected Texts, COE, May 1999.
10. The so-called 'Blue Book' – the agenda for the Helsinki conference.
11. The official term for a section of the Act, which contains four 'baskets'.
12. A condition for a rule to be counted as 'customary law' is that its practitioners believe it to be legally binding (Buergenthal, 1990). This condition does not obtain in this case.
13. Letter from Pope John Paul II to Leonid Brezhnev, 16 December 1980.
14. Copenhagen Concluding Document, preamble.
15. Para. 17, Moscow Concluding Document, 1991.
16. *EU Annual Report on Human Rights* (2000), p. 10.
17. Adopted at Nice, December 2000.
18. Conversations with top officials at the COE, November 1999.
19. In both these cases the charter was invoked first as the most authoritative. I am indebted to professor of EU law, Agostin Menendez, ARENA, for pointing this out to me. The BECTU case is C.173/99, delivered on 8 February 2001.

4 The Impact of International Organisations and Regimes

1. The only way to test this empirically is by in-depth interview and/or by positing the opposite situation, which in this case is instrumental interest pursuit. However, both these methods are difficult to employ. For instance, if one wants to find out whether the Serbs accept international human rights due to pressures or persuasion, one could interview Serb leaders. But the expected answer would be that of persuasion: who would admit to being a non-democrat? Likewise, the absence of pressure for adoption of democracy could indicate persuasion and learning if democracy nonetheless is adopted, but there are few if any such cases.

5 The Impact of the Council of Europe

1. The Former Yugoslav Republic of Macedonia – the Greeks have opposed the use of the simple denomination 'Macedonia'.
2. The Former Republic of Yugoslavia, today consisting of Serbia, Montenegro and Kosovo.
3. The 'twinning' programme under PHARE is a system whereby an EU member state assumes responsibility for developing a democracy/rule of law institution in a candidate state. The member state seconds personnel who work directly with locals in the institution in question, for instance a ministry. The period of secondment has to be at least a year.
4. Meeting in Strasbourg with the president of the Venice Commission, Professor Bocquiquio, March 1999.
5. Meetings in Budapest October 1998 and Strasbourg 1999.
6. The former foreign minister Prlic asked me on several occasions why Croatia could be admitted and not Bosnia, and for Norwegian support for his cause. It is admittedly hard to see clear criteria for admission, although Bosnia is still not a 'normal' state.
7. Meetings with the president of the court, judge Luzius Wildhaber, in Oslo in April 1999 and in Strasbourg, October 1999.
8. Judgement Loizidou against Turkey, 28 July 1998.
9. Council of Ministers' Interim Resolution DH (99) 680.
10. I have myself voiced the Norwegian government's acceptance of such a negative judgement. But of course there is much discussion about the effects of the judgement behind closed doors. Several judgements where one's own government loses certainly places a burden on the government. It is a strong signal that one is out of step with European practice.
11. Meetings with Schwimmer, October–November 1999.
12. Speech at human rights conference, Dublin, 1999.
13. Meetings in Strasbourg, November 1999, just prior to a second visit to Moscow in connection with this.
14. Mandate, resolution (99)50.
15. Sources from the Norwegian MFA.
16. *Bulletin Quotidien Europe*, 21 March 2001 reports on the national programme adopted by the Turkish Council of Ministers for adapting to the EU *acquis* in their pre-accession strategy. It is the first such acceptance on the part of Turkey of the human rights discourse, and makes concessions in important areas.
17. 'Visit to Ukraine ... ' (1999), report from the fact-finding mission.
18. Hans Wilhelm Steinfeld of Norwegian national TV news sent back several field reports from Grozny and from military exercises in Russia during 2000 and 2001. In his interviews on 1 April 2001, he engaged Russian generals of the FSB (formerly the KGB) in discussions of whether Russia is violating human rights in this theatre.
19. Interview with the chairman of the ODHIR, ambassador Gerard Stoudman, Warsaw, 9 November 2000.
20. Russia is clearly not only a European state, but it is nevertheless also a European state west of the Urals. There is no need to go into the debate, an unending one, over this classification here.

6 The Impact of the OSCE

1. www.osce.org/
2. Personal experience while being a Norwegian delegate to the review conference.
3. *OSCE Yearbook*, 1998: 492.
4. The attempt for a '*demandeur*' state to ask for help or support from various IOs at the same time, also making it possible to create dissension among them. For instance, in the case of putting pressure on Milosevic over Kosovo, it was imperative to keep a united Western front.
5. The so-called Lysøen process, led by Norway and Canada, has been instrumental in this process. The foreign ministers of these two countries started a process in 1998, engaging 12 other states in setting the agenda at the UN and in general on these issues. Now there are several projects under the 'human security' umbrella, and the UNSC works on many of them, such as the role of civilians in armed conflict, which was a result of Canada's agenda-setting while chairman of the council. Norway is now a member of the UNSC from 2001 to 2003, and may thus follow up on this work, which stems from the need to develop a security policy for the 'modern war', typified by internal conflicts and civilian participation and casualties.
6. Art. 39, Chapter VII, UN Charter.
7. This is allowed under the so-called Moscow mechanism from 1990, and the Prague meeting of 1992 adopted the consensus-minus-one procedure. It is usually difficult to achieve a mission in a state without its cooperation, however, but the possibility of such extreme measures may act as pressure on such states. During the Kosovo crisis the Norwegian chairmanship had to negotiate with President Milosevic about the establishment of the KVM and its terms. Sending in the KVM without his approval would have led to an unacceptable security situation for the mission and would have been impossible given Milosevic's physical control of the FRY.
8. US statement, 23 September 1999.
9. EU and US statements, 1999 review conference.
10. Speech given to the Oslo Military Society, 4 October 1999.
11. 1999, Brussels.
12. The major reason why both Milosevic and Plavsic gave themselves up to be arrested is that they lost their 'hard power' support base: Plavsic lost her bodyguard when she was not re-elected president in Srpska; Milosevic lost the support of the JNA army in the end.
13. www.osce.org./
14. Meetings and conferences with the Albanian president, PM, and foreign minister in Tirana on several occasions during 1998 and 1999; also with head of mission and staff at the OSCE.
15. Press conference in Tirana, 8 February 2001.
16. Meeting with Stoudman, Warsaw, 9 November 2000.
17. Issued in FYROM in 1999 over the tense situation regarding the Albanian minority.
18. Conversations with the HCNM during 1999.
19. See discussion in Chapters 3 and 5.

20. The main source of income for many rebel groups in Dagestan, Chechnya and Ingushetia is kidnapping of foreigners. The price per person in ransom is said to be around USD 1 million, but details of ransoms are of course never divulged publicly.
21. *Kosovo/Kosova*, report by the ODHIR.
22. Interview with Hans Wilhelm Steinfeld on Norwegian NRK news, 4 February 2001.
23. Interview with Stoudman in ODHIR, Warsaw, 9 November 2001.
24. OSCE press release from Baku, 6 November 2000, p. 1. See also the detailed OSCE/COE report of 5 November 2000.
25. Statement of the Central Election Commission of the republic of Azerbaijan, 6 November 2000.
26. *Menneskerettighetene i Norge*, Annual Human Rights report by the Norwegian Ministry of Foreign Affairs, Oslo, 2000, pp. 54–5.
27. Inter-office memo on Macedonia trafficking case, 15 November 2000. 'Trafficked Women Freed in Rescue Operation after ODIHR Intervention', undated OSCE press release.
28. ODHIR, 'Implementation Meeting on Human Dimension Issues', Consolidated summary, 17–27 October 2000, Warsaw.
29. Mission temporarily withdrawn due to the precarious security situation.

7 The Impact of the EU

1. He worked in the Commission during these years.
2. Case 26/62 Van Gend en Loos vs. nederlandse administratie der belastungen.
3. Austria was one of the driving forces behind this amendment after its own extensive 'shaming' by EU states.
4. Meetings with secretary-general Walter Schwimmer, and deputy secretary-general Kruger of the COE, September 1999.
5. *The European Parliament and the Defence of Human Rights*, p. 11, publication from the EP.
6. The chairmanship of the OSCE was held by Austria in 2000, after Norway.
7. The Commission's publication on enlargement, *European Union Enlargement: a Historic Opportunity*, undated, p. 21.
8. Ibid., pp. 22–3.
9. *Bulletin Agence Europe*, 21 March 2001.
10. Regular Report from the Commission on Progress Towards Accession, 13 October 1999, quoting the 1998 report.
11. Interviews with higher officals of the MFA, Warsaw, 9 November 2000.
12. Interviews with Hungarian policy-makers and higher civil servants, Budapest and Oslo, 2000.

8 Human Rights and Hard Power: a New Norm for Intervention?

1. Geneva Conventions of 12 August 1949.
2. Charter of the United Nations, 26 June 1945.

3. The use of force without a UNSC mandate is only possible under international law in cases or self-defence or when an attacked state asks for assistance against an aggressor. This was the case of Kuwait, thus there was no need for an explicit mandate from the UNSC. However, it is assumed that the USA and the other participants wanted to have UN legitimacy for their engagement, something which signals the importance of legitimacy in contemporary international politics (Cortrell and Davis, 1996).
4. DUPI report, 1999, p. 69.
5. Statute of the International Criminal Tribunal for the former Yugoslavia, 25 May 1993. The tribunal is mandated as a supranational tribunal, to judge in cases of human rights violations, war crimes, genocide and crimes against humanity.
6. Art. 43, Ch. VII, UN Charter.
7. Eighteen US marines were ambushed in a fight with the warlord Aidid in Mogadishu, and their bodies were mutilated and drawn through the streets. This was shown on TV, and incited a debate on the 'body bag' issue in the USA. The common view is that US interventions after this have to be risk-free and thus only employ air force.
8. NATO web page, www.nato.int/docu(facts/2000/Kosovo
9. They include the UDHR, the 1966 Convention on Civil and Political Rights, the OSCE documents discussed above and the ECHR, all of which define the right to individual security – 'security of person' – as a basic human right.
10. *The Economist*, 18 September 1999, lead article by Kofi Annan.
11. Today such a procedure would not have succeeded in getting a majority for any kind of intervention, given the large group (G-77, now 144 states) sceptical of such policies. But in 1955, when 'Uniting for Peace' was adopted, the UNGA only had 46 member states.
12. Memo by the UK FCO, 7 October 1998.
13. The Holiday Inn on 'Sniper's Boulevard' in downtown Sarajevo hosted journalists throughout the whole siege, 1991–95.
14. Speech to the House of Commons, 25 March 1999.
15. As was the case with the massacres at the Markala market place in Sarajevo in August 1994, it was alleged that Bosniacs themselves – in the Rajak case, the KLA itself – were behind the massacres in order to trigger Western intervention. In both these cases there are inconclusive investigations on this point, but the major evidence suggests that this 'conspiracy' theory is false. See OSCE documentation from the KVM and the findings of Finnish forensic experts on the Rajak case, also reported by the OSCE.
16. Quoted in Lapidus (1998: 141).
17. Report of the Secretary-General, 1999.
18. Kofi Annan's intervention, 20 September 2000.
19. Ibid., 18 September 1999, p. 49.
20. The Hague speech, 18 May 1999.

9 Conclusions

1. This information is *inter alia* based on my own experience during Norway's chairmanship.

Epilogue

1. *International Herald Tribune*, 'Beijing is an Eager Suitor to Host Olympic Games', 21 February 2001.
2. *Financial Times*, 'Shell Takes Action to Counter Criticism', 22 February 2001.
3. *Human Rights and the Oil Industry*, eds Eide, A. et al. (Intersentia: Oxford, 2000).

Bibliography

Abbott, K.W. and Snidal, D. (2000) 'Hard and Soft Law in International Governance', *International Organization*, 54 (3)

Abbott, K.W. et al. (2000) 'The Concept of Legalization', *International Organization*, 54(3), Summer

Alter, K. (2000) 'The European Union's Legal System and Domestic Policy: Spillover or Backlash?', *International Organization*, 54(3), Summer

Barbe, E. (1998) 'Balancing Europe's Eastern and Southern Dimensions', in Zielonka, J. (ed.), *Paradoxes of European Foreign Policy*, Kluwer Law International, The Hague

Barker, J.S. and Cronin, B. (1994) 'The State and the Nation: Changing Norms and the Rules of Sovereignty in International Relations', *International Organization*, 48 (1), Winter

Bergesen, H.O. and Lunde, L. (2000) *Petro-States: Predatory or Developmental?* FNI-Report no. 62/2000, Oslo

Biersteker, T. (1993) 'Constructing Historical Counter-Factuals to Assess the Consequences of International Regimes: the Global Debt Regime and the Course of the Debt Crisis in the 1980s', in Rittberger, V. and Mayer, P. (eds), *Regime Theory and International Relations*, Clarendon Press, Oxford

Black, D. (1999) 'The Long and Winding Road: International Norms and Domestic Political Change in South Africa', in Risse, T. et al. *The Power of Human Rights: International Norms and Domestic Change*, Cambridge University Press, Cambridge

Blair, P. (1993) *The Protection of Regional or Minority Languages in Europe*, Institut du Fédéralisme, Fribourg, Switzerland

Bloed, A. (1990) *From Helsinki to Vienna: Basic Documents of the Helsinki Process*, Martinus Nijhoff Publishers, Dordrecht, The Netherlands

Bloed, A. (1993) *The OSCE: Basic Documents, 1972–1993*, Kluwer Academic Publishers, Dordrecht, The Netherlands

Bloed, A. (1997) *The OSCE: Basic Documents, 1993–1995*, Kluwer Academic Publishers, Dordrecht, The Netherlands

Bloed, A. et al. (eds) (1993) *Monitoring Human Rights in Europe: Comparing International Procedures and Mechanisms*, Martinus Nijhoff Publishers, Dordrecht, The Netherlands

Bothe, M. et al. (eds) (1997) *The OSCE in the Maintenance of Peace and Security*, Kluwer Academic Publishers, The Hague

Breitmeier, H. and Wolf, K-D. (1993) 'Analysing Regime Consequences: Conceptual Outlines and Environmental Explorations', in Rittberger, V. and Mayer, P. (eds), *Regime Theory and International Relations*, Clarendon Press, Oxford

Brinar, I. (1999) 'Slovenia: from Yugoslavia to the European Union', in Henderson, K. (ed.), *Back to Europe: Central and Eastern Europe and the European Union*, UCL Press, London

Buergenthal, T. (1990) 'Copenhagen: a Democratic Manifesto', *World Affairs*, 153(1)

Buergenthal, T. (1991) 'The CSCE Rights System', *George Washington Journal of Law and International Economics*, 25

Burg, S. and Shoup, P.S. (1999) *The War in Bosnia-Hercegovina. Ethnic Conflict and International Intervention*, M.E. Sharpe, Armonk, NY

Burli, A-M. and Mattli, W. (1993) 'Europe before the Court: a Political Theory of Legal Integration', *International Organization*, 47(1), Winter

Buzan, B. (1991) *Peoples, States, and Fear: an Agenda for International Security Studies in the Post-Cold War Era*, Harvester Wheatsheaf, Hemel Hempstead, UK

Calmfors, L. et al. (1996) *EMU. A Swedish Perspective*, Kluwer Academic Publishers, Amsterdam

Cameron, P. (1992) 'The 1992 Initiative: Causes and Consequences', in Sbragia, A. (ed.), *Euro-Politics: Institution and Policy-Making in the 'New' European Community*, Brookings Institution, Washington, DC

Cameron, P. (1997) 'Economic and Monetary Union: Underlying Imperatives and Third-Stage Dilemmas', *Journal of European Public Policy*, 4

Caplan, R. (2000) 'Humanitarian Intervention: Which Way Forward?', *Ethics and International Affairs*, 14

Chayes, A. and Chayes, A. (1995) *The New Sovereignty: Compliance with International Regulatory Agreements*, Harvard University Press

Checkel, J. (2000a) 'Why Comply? Social Norms and the Study of International Institutions', draft, Oslo

Checkel, J. (2000b) 'Compliance and Conditionality', Working Paper, ARENA, no. 18, September

Chopra, J. (1994) 'Enforcement Mechanism for Humanitarian Crimes', in Eknes, Å. and McDermott, A. (eds), *Sovereignty, Humanitarian Intervention and the Military*, UN programme, WUPI, Oslo

Clapham, A. (2000) 'On Complementarity: Human Rights in the European Legal Orders', *Human Rights Law Journal*, 21(8), November

Coleman, J. (ed.) (1999) *The Conscience of Europe*, Council of Europe Publishing, Strasbourg

Convention for the Protection of Human Rights and Fundamental Freedoms (1950) Council of Europe, ets. no. 5, Rome, 4 November

Cornett, L. and Caporaso, J. (1992) 'And Still it Moves! State Interests and Social Forces in the European Community', in Rosenau, J. and Czempiel, E-O. (eds), *Governance without Government: Order and Change in World Politics*, Cambridge Studies in International Relations, Cambridge

Cortrell, A. and Davis, J.W. (1996) 'How Do International Institutions Matter? The Domestic Impact of International Norms and Rules', *International Studies Quarterly*, 40, pp. 451–78

Cowles, M. (1995) 'German Big Business and Brussels: Learning to Play the European Game', Working Paper for the American Institute for Contemporary German Studies, Johns Hopkins University, Baltimore

Croft, S. et al. (2000) 'Nato's Triple Challenge', *International Affairs*, 76, 3

Daalder, I. (1996) 'The United States and Military Intervention in Internal Conflict', in Brown, M.E. (ed.) *The International Dimensions of Internal Conflict*, MIT Press, Cambridge, Mass.

Daalder, I. and Froman, M. (1999) 'Dayton's Incomplete Peace', *Foreign Affairs*, Nov./Dec.

Daftary, F. (1998) 'The Third OSCE Implementation Meeting on Human Dimension Issues in Warsaw, 1997', in *OSCE Yearbook*

Dahl, R. (1961) *Who Governs? Democracy and Power in an American City*, Yale University Press, New Haven

Donnelly, J. (1988) 'Human Rights: the Impact of International Action', *International Journal*, XLIII, Spring

Donnelly, J. (1995) 'State Sovereignty and International Intervention: the Case of Human Rights', in Lyons, G. and Mastanduno, M. (eds), *Beyond Westphalia: State Sovereignty and International Intervention*, Johns Hopkins University Press, Baltimore

Drzemczewski, A. (1999a) 'The Prevention of Human Rights Violations: Monitoring Mechanisms of the Council of Europe', Athens, 24–25 May, Panteion University

Drzemczewski, A. (1999b) 'The Human Rights Convention: Protocol no. 11, Entry into Force and First Years of Application', San José, 23–24 November, Seminar by the Inter-American Court of Human Rights

Drozdik, E. (1998) 'The Difficult Business of Perception – the OSCE in Croatia', in *OSCE Yearbook*

DUPI (Danish Foreign Policy Institute) (1999) *Humanitær intervention. Retlige og politiske aspekter*, Copenhagen (No specific authors, study presented by DUPI itself)

Dyson, K. (1994) *Elusive Union. The Process of Economic and Monetary Union in Europe*, Longman, London and New York

Eide, A. et al. (eds) (2000) *Human Rights and the Oil Industry*, Intersentia, Oxford, Groningen, Antwerp

Eknes, Å. (1994) 'Humanitarianism and the Military: the UN and Humanitarian Intervention, in Eknes, Å and McDermott, A. (eds), *Sovereignty, Humanitarian Intervention and the Military*, NUPI, Oslo

Finnemore, M. (1993) 'Constructing Norms of Humanitarian Intervention', in Katzenstein P. (ed.), *The Culture of National Security: Norms and Identity in World Politics*, Columbia University Press, New York

Finnemore, M. (1996) *National Interests in International Society*, Cornell University Press, Ithaca

Finnemore, M. and Sikkink, K. (1998) 'International Norm Dynamics and Political Change', *International Organization*, 52, 4, Autumn

Flynn, G, and Farrell, H. (1999) 'Piecing Together the Democratic Peace: the CSCE, Norms, and the "Construction" of Security in Post-Cold War Europe', *International Organization*, 53(3), Summer

Friis, L. (1996) 'When Europe Negotiates: from Europe Agreements to Eastern Enlargement', Ph.D. thesis, University of Copenhagen, Institute of Political Science

Forde, S. (1995) 'International Realism and the Science of Politics: Thucydides, Machiavelli, and Neorealism', *International Studies Quarterly*, 39

Fossum, J.E. (2000) 'Constitution-Making in the European Union', in Eriksen, E-O. and Fossum, J.E. *Democracy in the EU: Integration through Deliberation*? Routledge, London

Fox, G. H. (1997) 'New Approaches to International Human Rights: the Sovereign State Revisited', in Hasmi, S. (ed.), *State Sovereignty. Change and Persistence in International Relations*, Pennsylvania State University Press.

Gartner, H. et al. (2001) *Europe's New Security Challenges*, Lynne Rienner, Boulder, London

Ghebali, Victor-Yves (1996) *L'Osce dans l'Europe post-communiste, 1990–1996*, Emile Bruylant, Brussels

Ginsberg, R. (1989) *Foreign Policy Actions of the EU*, Lynne Rienner, Boulder, Colo.

Glendon, M-A. (2001) *A World Made New: Eleanor Roosevelt and the Universal Declaration of Human Rights*, Random House, New York

Goldmann, K. (1989) 'The Line in Water: International and Domestic Politics', *Cooperation and Conflict*, XXIV

Goldstein, J. et al. (2000) 'Introduction: Legalization and World Politics', *International Organization*, 54, 3, Summer

Goldstein, J. and Keohane, R. (eds) (1993) *Ideas and Foreign Policy: Beliefs, Institutions and Political Change*, Cornell University Press, Ithaca and London

Gourevitch, P. (1978) 'The Second Image Reversed: the International Sources of Domestic Politics', *International Organization*, 32(4)

Gow, J. (1997) 'Shared Sovereignty, Enhanced Security: Lessons from the Yugoslav War', in Hasmi, S. (ed.), *State Sovereignty. Change and Persistence in International Relations*, Pennsylvania State University Press

Gow, J. (1999) 'Security and Democracy: the EU and Central and Eastern Europe', in Henderson, K. (ed.), *Back to Europe: Central and Eastern Europe and the European Union*, UCL Press, London

Grabbe, H. (1999) 'A Partnership for Accession? The Implications of EU Conditionality for the Central and East European Applicants', EUI Working Paper, Florence

Granzer, S. (1999) 'Changing Discourse: Transnational Advocacy Networks in Tunisia and Morocco', in Risse, T. et al. (eds), *The Power of Human Rights: International Norms and Domestic Change*, CUP, Cambridge

Graver, H-P. (2000) 'Normative mønstre i EU-retten', ARENA Working Paper no. 13

Grubmayr, H. (1998) 'Problems and Difficulties of the OSCE's Long-Term Missions', in *OSCE Yearbook*

Guzzini, S. (1991) 'Structural Power: the Limits of Neo-Realist Power Analysis', paper from the European University Institute, Fiesole

Haas, E.B. (1990) 'Why Collaborate? Issue-Linkage and International Regimes', *World Politics*, 43

Haas, P.M. (1992) 'Introduction: Epistemic Communities and International Policy Coordination', *International Organization*, 46, 1, Winter

Haas, P.M. (1993) 'Epistemic Communities and the Dynamics of International Environmental Cooperation', in Rittberger, V. and Mayer, P. (eds), *Regime Theory and International Relations*, Clarendon Press, Oxford

Haggard, S. and Simmons, B. (1987) 'Theories of International Regimes', *International Organization*, 41, 3, Summer

Haller, G. (1998) 'Human Rights Protection in the Field of Action of the Council of Europe and of the OSCE', in *OSCE Yearbook*

Hanrieder, W. (1978) 'Dissolving International Politics: Reflections on the Nation-State', *American Political Science Review*, 72

Hanssen, G. and Stenelo, L-G. (eds) (1990) *Mak toch internationalisering*, Carlssons, Stockholm
Harris, J. (ed.) (1995) *The Politics of Humanitarian Intervention*, Pinter, London
Haufler, V. (1993) 'Crossing the Boundary between Public and Private: International Regimes and Non-State Actors', in Rittberger, V. and Mayer, P. (eds), *Regime Theory and International Relations*, Clarendon Press, Oxford
Henderson, K. (1999) 'Slovakia and the Democratic Criteria for EU Accession', in Henderson, K. (ed.), *Back to Europe: Central and Eastern Europe and the European Union*, UCL Press, London
Herd, G.P. (1999) 'The Baltic States and EU Enlargement', in Henderson, K., (ed.), *Back to Europe: Central and Eastern Europe and the European Union*, UCL Press, London
Herz, J. (1957) 'The Rise and Demise of the Territorial State', *World Politics*, IX
Heuser, B. (1997) 'Sovereignty, Self-Determination, and Security: New World Orders in the 20th Century', in Hasmi, S. (ed.), *State Sovereignty. Change and Persistence in International Relations*, Pennsylvania State University Press
Holsti, K.J. (1992) 'Governance without Government: Polyarchy in 19th Century European International Politics', in Rosenau, J.N. and Czempiel E-O. (eds), *Governance without Government: Order and Change in World Politics*, Cambridge Studies in International Relations, Cambridge
Hopkins, R. (1976) 'The International Role of "Domestic" Bureaucracy', *International Organization*, 30(3)
Hopmann, T. (2001) 'An Evaluation of the OSCE's Role in Conflict Management', in Gartner, H. et al. *Europe's New Security Challenges*, Lynne Rienner Publishers, Boulder and London
Huber, D. (1999) *A Decade which made History: the Council of Europe, 1989–1999*, Council of Europe Publishing, Strasbourg
'Human Security: Safety for People in a Changing World', Canadian MFA, no date, Ottawa
Hurd, I. (1999) 'Legitimacy and Authority in International Politics', *International Organization*, 53 (2), Spring
Ingebritsen, C. (1999) 'Scandinavia's Influence on International Norms: the Cases of Environment, Security and Welfare', unpublished paper
International Crisis Group (1999) *Is Dayton Failing? Bosnia Four Years after the Peace Agreement*, Brussels
Jackson, R.H. (1995) 'International Community beyond the Cold War', in Lyons, G. and Mastandano, M. (eds), *Beyond Westphalia: State Sovereignty and International Intervation*, Johns Hopkins University Press, Baltimore
Jacobs, D. and Stewart-Clark, J. (1990) *Competition Law in the EU*, Kogan Page, London
Jerneck, M. (1996) 'Democracy and Interdependence', in Stenelo, L-G. and Jerneck, M. (eds), *The Bargaining Democracy*, Lund University Press, Lund
Jerneck, M. and Gidlund, J-E. (1996) *Svenskt EMU-medlemskap som pro-aktiv strategi och integrationsdilemma*, Fritzes, Stockholm
Jervis, R. (1976) *Perception and Misperception in International Politics*, Princeton University Press, Princeton, NJ
Jetschke, A. (1999) 'Linking the Unlinkable? International Norms and Nationalism in Indonesia and the Philippines', in Risse, T. et al., *The Power of Human Rights: International Norms and Domestic Change*, CUP, Cambridge

Kahler, M. (2000) 'Conclusion: the Causes and Consequences of Legalization', *International Organization*, 54 (3), Summer

Kamarck, E.C. and Nye, J. (1999) *democracy.com? Governance in a Networked World*, Hollis Publishing Company, Hollis, NH

Katzenstein, P. (ed.) (1993a) *The Culture of National Security: Norms and Identity in World Politics*, Columbia University Press, New York

Katzenstein, P. (1993b) 'Conclusion: National Security in a Changing World', in Katzenstein (1993a)

Keck, M. and Sikkink, K. (1999) *Activists beyond Borders. Advocacy Networks in International Politics*, Cornell University Press, Ithaca, NY

Kelstrup, M. (1992) *European Integration and Denmark's Participation*, Copenhagen Political Studies Press, Copenhagen

Keohane, R. (1990) 'Empathy and International Regimes', in Mansbridge, J. (ed.), *Beyond Self-Interest*, University of Chicago Press

Keohane, R. et al. (2000) 'Legalized Dispute Resolution: Interstate and Transnational', *International Organization*, 54(3), Summer

Keohane, R. and Nye, J. (1972) *Transnational Relation and World Politics*, Harvard University Press, Cambridge, Mass.

Keohane, R. and Nye, J. (1989) *Power and Interdependence*, Little, Brown, and Co., Boston

Klotz, A. (1995) 'Norms Reconstituting Interests: Global Racial Equality and US Sanctions against South Africa', *International Organization*, 49(3), Summer

Koh, H. (1997) 'Why Do Nations Obey International Law?', *Yale Law Review*, 106(8), June

Koh, H. (2000) 'Complementarity between International Organizations on Human Rights: the Rise of Transnational Networks as the "Third Globalization"', *Human Rights Law Journal*, 21(8), November

Krasner, S. (1982) 'Structural Causes and Regime Consequences: Regimes as Intervening Variables', *International Organization*, 36, 2

Krasner, S. (1993) 'Sovereignty, Regimes, and Human Rights', in Rittberger, V. and Mayer, P.(eds), *Regime Theory and International Relations*, Clarendon Press, Oxford

Krasner, S. (1995) 'Sovereignty and Intervention', in Lyons, G. and Mastanduno, M. (eds), *Beyond Westphalia: State Sovereignty and International Intervention*, Johns Hopkins University Press, Baltimore

Krasner, S. (1999) *Sovereignty: Organized Hypocrisy*, Princeton University Press, Princeton, New Jersey

Kratochwil, F. (1982) 'On the Notion of "Interest" in International Relations', *International Organization*, 1, 36, Winter

Kratochwil, F.G. (1991) *Rules, Norms, and Decisions: On the Conditions of Practical and Legal Reasoning in International Relations and Domestic Affairs*, Cambridge University Press, Cambridge

Lapidus, G. (1998) 'Contested Sovereignty: the Tragedy of Chechnya', *International Security*, 23(1), Summer

Laursen, F. and Vanhoonacker, S. (eds) (1992) *The Intergovermental Conference on Political Union*, Nijhoff, Maastricht

Levy, M. and Young, O. (1994) 'The Effectiveness of International Regimes', Paper presented at the annual convention of the International Studies Association, Washington, DC, March

Lodgaard, S. (2000) 'Human Security: the Concept and Operationalisations', unpublished paper, NUPI, Oslo

Lodge, J. (ed.) (1989) *The European Community and the Challenge of the Future*, Pinter, London

Louis, J-V. (1990) *The Community Legal Order*, Commission Publication, Brussels

Ludlow, P. (1991) 'The European Commission', in Keohane, R. and Hoffman, S. (eds), *The New European Community: Decision-Making and Institutional Change*, Westview Press, Oxford

Lutz, D. (1998) 'Strengthening the OSCE – the Strengths of the OSCE', in *OSCE Yearbook 1998*

Lyons, G. and Mastanduno, M. (1995) 'Introduction: International Intervention, State Sovereignty, and the Future of International Society', in ibid. (eds), *Beyond Westphalia: State Sovereignty and International Intervention*, Johns Hopkins University Press, Baltimore

MacManus, C. (1998) 'Poland and the Europe Agreements: the EU as a Regional Actor', in Petersen, J. and Sjursen, H. (eds), A *Common Foreign Policy for Europe? Competing Visions of the CFSP*, Routledge, London and New York

Malnes, R. (1994) *National Interests, Morality, and International Law*, Scandinavian University Press, Oslo

Mansbridge, J. (ed.) (1990) *Beyond Self-Interest*, University of Chicago Press, Chicago, Ill.

March, J. and Olsen, J.P. (1989) *Rediscovering Institutions: the Organizational Basis of Politics*, The Free Press, London and New York

Maresca, J.J. (1987) *To Helsinki. The Conference on Security and Cooperation in Europe, 1973–1975*, Duke University Press, Durham

Marks, G. et al. (1996) 'European Integration from the 1980s: State-Centric vs. Multi-Level Governance', *Journal of Common Market Studies*, 34

Matláry, J.H. (1997) 'The Role of the Commission: a Theoretical Discussion', in Nugent, N. (ed.), *At the Heart of the Union: Studies of the European Commission*, 2nd edn, Macmillan – now Palgrave, Basingstoke, UK

Matláry, J.H. (1998a) 'The OSCE's Role in European Security – a Norwegian View', in *OSCE Yearbook 1998*

Matláry, J.H. (1998b) 'Challenges Facing the OSCE in the Field Operations in Albania, Bosnia-Hercegovina, Croatia, and Kosovo', speech, 11 December, Oslo

Matláry, J.H. (2000) 'Between State Security and Human Rights: Challenges to Security Policy', Guest lecture at the John F. Kennedy School of Government, Harvard University, 6 November 2000

Matláry, J.H. (2001) 'Norme internazionali per il diritto dell'uomo. Strategie di promozione del diritto naturale', *Vita et pensiero*, no. 1

Matveeva, A. (2000) 'Missed Opportunities', *New Routes: Journal of Peace Research and Action*, 5 (1–2), Uppsala

Menneskerettighetene i Norge (2000) Annual human rights report, MFA, Oslo

Millard, F. (1999) 'Polish Domestic Politics and Accession to the EU', in Henderson, K. (ed.), *Back to Europe: Central and Eastern Europe and the European Union*, UCL Press, London

Minear, L. (1994) 'Humanitarians and Intervention', in Elenes, Å. and McDermott, A. (eds), *Sovereignty, Humanitarian Intervention and the Military*, NUPI, Oslo

Moravcsik, A. (1993) 'Preferences and Power in the European Community: a Liberal Intergovernmentalist Approach', *Journal of Common Market Studies*, 31

Morgan, R. and Evans, M. (1997) 'Preventing Torture and Protecting Prisoners', *Interights Bulletin*, 11

Morgan, R. and Evans, M. (1999) *Protecting Prisoners: the Standards of the European Committee for the Prevention of Torture in Context*, Oxford

Muller, H. (1993) 'The Internalization of Principles, Norms, and Rules by Governments: the Case of Security Regimes', in Rittberger V. and Mayer, P. (eds), *Regime Theory and International Relations*, Clarendon Press, Oxford

Noelle-Neumann, E. (1993) *The Spiral of Silence: Public Opinion, Our Social Skin*, University of Chicago Press, Chicago

'Norway–Canada Partnership for Action: the Lysøen Declaration' (1998) Bergen

Nuttal, S. (1994) 'The Commission and Foreign Policy-Making', in Edwards, G. and Spence, D. (eds), *The European Commission*, Longman Current Affairs, Harlow

Nye, J. (1995) *Bound to Lead: the Changing Nature of American Power*, Basic Books, New York

Nye, J. (1999) 'Redefining the National Interest', *Foreign Affairs*, 78 (4), July/August

Nye, J. and Owens, W. (1996) 'America's Information Edge', *Foreign Affairs*, March/April

Oudraat, C. de J. (1996) 'The United Nations and Internal Conflict', in Brown, M.E. (ed.), *The International Dimensions of Internal Conflict*, MIT Press, Cambridge, Mass.

Our Global Neighbourhood (1995) Report from the Commission on Global Governance, UN

Patten, C. (1999) 'The Future of the ESDP and the Role of the European Commission', speech at Berlin, 16 December

Patten, C. (2000) 'The Protection of Human Rights in the 21st Century', conference speech, Dublin, 3 March

Petersen, J. (1996) 'The European Union as a Global Actor', in Petersen, J. and Sjursen, H. (eds), *A Common Foreign Policy for Europe? Competing Visions of the CFSP*, Routledge, London and New York

Pierson, P. (1996) 'The Path to European Integration: a Historical Institutionalist Analysis', *Comparative Political Studies*, 29

Polakiewicz, J. (1999) *Treaty-Making in the Council of Europe*, Council of Europe Publishing, Strasbourg

Price, R. (1998) 'Transnational Civil Society Targets Land-Mines', *International Organization*, 52 (3)

Putnam, R. (1998) 'The Logic of Two-Level Games', *International Organization*, 42 (3)

Reuter, J. (1998) 'Kosovo 1998', in *OSCE Yearbook 1998*, Nomos Verlag, Baden-Baden

Risse, T. and Ropp, S.C. (1999) 'International Human Rights Norms and Domestic Change: Conclusions', in Risse et al. (eds), *The Power of Human Rights: International Norms and Domestic Change*, CUP, Cambridge

Risse, T. and Sikkink, K. (1999) 'The Socialization of International Human Rights Norms into Domestic Practices: Introduction', in Risse, T. et al. (eds), *The Power of Human Rights: International Norms and Domestic Change*, CUP, Cambridge

Risse, T. et al. (eds) (1999) *The Power of Human Rights: International Norms and Domestic Change*, CUP, Cambridge

Risse-Kappen, T. (1995) *Bringing Transnational Relations back in: Non-state Actors, Domestic Structures and International Institutions*, Cambridge University Press, Cambridge

Rittberger, V. and Mayer, P. (1993) *Regime Theory and International Relations*, Clarendon Press, Oxford

Roberts, A. (1995) 'From San Francisco to Sarajevo: the UN and the Use of Force', *Survival*, 37 (4)

Roberts, A. (1999) 'NATO's 'Humanitarian War over Kosovo', *Survival*, 41 (3)

Rønnfeldt, C. et al. (1999) *Preventive Action in Theory and Practice: the Shopfe Papers*, NUPI, OSLO

Ropp, S.C. and Sikkink, K. (1999) 'International Norms and Domestic Politics in Chile and Guatemala', in Risse, T. et al. (eds), *The Power of Human Rights: International Norms and Domestic Change*, CUP, Cambridge

Rosas, A. (1993) 'The Decline of Sovereignty: Legal Perspectives', in Iivonen, J. (ed.), *The Future of the Nation State in Europe*, Aldershot, UK

Rosas, A. (1995) 'State Sovereignty and Human Rights: Towards a Global Constitutional Project', *Political Studies*, XLIII

Rosenau, J.N. and Czempiel, E-O. (eds) (1992) *Governance without Government: Order and Change in World Politics*, Cambridge Studies in International Relations, Cambridge

Rosenau, J.N and Czempiel, E-O. (1995) 'Sovereignty in a Turbulent World', in Lyons, G. and Mastanduno, M. (eds), *Beyond Westphalia. State Sovereignty and International Intervention*, Johns Hopkins University Press, Baltimore

Ruggie, J.G. (ed.) (1993) *Multilateralism Matters. The Theory and Praxis of an Institutional Form*, Columbia University Press, New York

Rupp, M.C. (1999) 'The Pre-Accession Strategy and the Governments Structures of the Visegrad Countries', in Henderson, K. (ed.), *Back to Europe: Central and Eastern Europe and the European Union*, UCL Press, London

Sandholz, W. (1993) 'Choosing Union: Monetary Politics and Maastricht', *International Organization*, 47

Sandholz, W. and Zysman, J. (1989) '1992: Recasting the European Bargain', *World Politics*, 42

Schierbeck, J. (2000) 'Operational Measures for Identifying and Implementing Human Rights Issues in Corporate Operations', in Eide, A. et al. (eds), *Human Rights and the Oil Industry*, Intersentia, Oxford, Groningen, Antwerp

Schimmelfennig, F. (1999) 'The Double Puzzle of EU Enlargement: Liberal Norms, Rhetorical Action, and the Decision to Expand to the East', ARENA Working Paper, no. 15, June

Schmizt, H.P. (1999) 'Transnational Activism and Political Change in Kenya and Uganda', in Risse, T. et al. (eds), *The Power of Human Rights: International Norms and Domestic Change*, CUP, Cambridge

Schwimmer, W. (2000) 'The Protection of Human Rights in the 21st Century: Towards Greater Complementarity within and between European Regional Organisations', speech, Dublin, 3 March

Seidelmeier, U. (2000) 'Eastern Enlargement and the EU as an Actor in European Security: the Interplay between the EU's role and Policy', *Redefining Security: the Role of the EU in European Security Structures*, ARENA Report 7/2000, Oslo University

Sikkink, K. (1993) 'The Power of Principled Ideas: Human Rights Policies in the US and Europe', in Goldstein, J. and Keohane, R. (eds), *Ideas and Foreign Policy: Beliefs, Institutions, and Political Change*, Cornell University Press, Ithaca and London

Slaughter, A-M. (1995) 'International Law in a World of Liberal States', *European Journal of International Law*, 6 (4)

Smith, K. (2000) 'The EU, Human Rights, and Relations with Third Countries', *Redefining Security: the Role of the EU in European Security Structures*, ARENA Report 7/2000, Oslo University

Smith, D. (1997) 'Interventionist Dilemmas and Justice', in McDermott, A. (ed.), *Humanitarian Force*, PRIO Report No. 2, Oslo

Smith, D. (1999) 'Sovereignty in an Age of Intervention', in McDermott, A. (ed.), *Sovereign Intervention*, PRIO Report No. 2, Oslo

Smith, M. (1994) 'The Commission and External Relations', in Edwards, G. and Spence, D. (eds), *The European Commission*, Longman, Harlow

Solana, J. (1999) 'NATO's Success in Kosovo', *Foreign Affairs*, Nov./Dec.

Sosialt ansvarlige bedrifter (2000) Report by the Norwegian Federation of Business, Oslo

Steil, B. and Woodward, S. (1999) 'A European "New Deal" for the Balkans', *Foreign Affairs*, Nov./Dec.

Stevens, T. (1997) 'CPT – Past and Present', speech at a Human Rights Conference, London

Tarzi, S. (1998) 'The Role of Norms and Regimes in World Affairs: a Grotian Perspective', *International Relations*, XIV (3)

Thomas, D.C. (1999) 'The Helsinki Accords and Political Change in Eastern Europe', in Risse, T. et al. (eds), *The Power of Human Rights: International Norms and Domestic Change*, CUP, Cambridge

Thune, H. (1998) 'Westfalerfreden og "humanitær intervensjonisme" – individ vs. stat i internasjonal politikk', *Internasjonal politikk*, 56 (4)

Timmermann, H. (1998) 'The OSCE Representation in Belarus', in *The OSCE Yearbook 1998*, Nomos Verlag, Baden-Baden

Tonra, B. (1997) 'Practitioners' Assessment of Political Cooperation: Denmark, Ireland, and the Netherlands', in Jørgensen, K-E. (ed.), *Reflective Approaches to European Governance*, Macmillan – now Palgrave, Basingstoke

Underdal, A. (1992) 'Arena or Actor? The Role of IGOs in International Environmental Management', CICERO Working Paper, Oslo University

Underdal, A. (1998) 'Explaining Compliance and Defection: Three Models', *European Journal of International Relations*, 4 (1), March

Universal Declaration of Human Rights, 1948

Usher, H. (1994) 'The Commission and the Law', in Edwards, G. and Spence, D. (eds), *The European Commission*, Longman, London

Van Ham, P. (1995) *The EC, Eastern Europe and European Unity*, Pinter, London

Vetschera, H. (1998) 'The Role of the OSCE in the Military Stabilisation of Bosnia and Herczegovina', in *OSCE Yearbook*

Wallensteen, P. and Sollenberg, M. (1998) 'Armed Conflict and Regional Conflict Complexes, 1989–97', *Journal of Peace Research*, 35 (5)

Waltz, K. (1979) *A Theory of International Politics*, Addison-Wesley, Reading, Mass.

Weber, M. (1968) *Economy and Society*, University of California Press, Berkeley

Weiler, J.H.H. (1996) 'European Neo-Constitutionalism: in Search of Foundations for the European Consitutional Order', in Bellamy, R. and Castiglione, D. (eds) *Constitutionalism in Transformation: European and Theoretical Perspectives*, Blackwell, Oxford

Weiler, J.H.H. (1999) *The Constitution of Europe: Do the New Clothes Have an Emperor?*, Cambridge University Press, Cambridge

Weiler, J.H.H. (2000) 'Federalism and Constitutionalism: Europe's "Sonderweg"', Harvard Jean Monnet Working Paper, 10/00

Weiss, T. and Chopra. J. (1995) 'Sovereignty under Siege: from Intervention to Humanitarian Space', in Lyons, G. and Mastanduno, M. (eds), *Beyond Westphalia: State Sovereignty and International Intervention*, Johns Hopkins University Press, Baltimore

Woodward, S.L. (1995) *Balkan Tragedy: Chaos and Dissolution after the Cold War*. Brookings Institution, Washington, DC

Yost, D. (1998) 'The New NATO and Collective Security', *Survival*, 40 (3)

Young, O. (1992) 'The Effectiveness of International Institutions: Hard Cases and Critical Variables', in Rosenau J.N. and Czempiel, E-O. (eds), *Governance without Government. Order and Change in World Politics*, Cambridge Studies in International Relations, Cambridge

Young, O. (1994) *International Governance: Protecting the Environment in a Stateless Society*, Cornell University Press, Ithaca, NY

Zacher, M. W. (1992) 'The Decaying Pillars of the Westphalian Temple: Implications for International Order and Governance', in Rosenau, J.N. and Czempiel, E-O. (eds), *Governance without Government: Order and Change in World Politics*, Cambridge Studies in International Relations, Cambridge

Zanger, S. (2000) 'Good Governance and EU Aid: the Impact of Political Conditionality', *European Union Politics*, 1 (3)

Zellner, W. (2001) 'The High Commissioner on National Minorities', in Gartner, H. et al., *Europe's New Security Challenges*, Lynne Rienner, Boulder and London

Council of Europe documents

'Methodology for Implementing Mechanisms for Monitoring Commitments by Member States of the Council of Europe and the OSCE', Strasbourg, 1997

'Compliance with Commitments Entered into by Member States: Development of the Committee of Ministers' Monitoring Procedure', Strasbourg, 1998

'Compliance with Member States Commitments: "Decisions" taken within the context of the Commitee of Ministers' Monitoring Procedure', Strasbourg, 1999

'Monitoring of Compliance with Commitments entered into by the Council of Europe Member States: an Overview', Strasbourg, 1999

'Report to the 104th Session of the Committee of Ministers on the Implementation of the Action Plan and the Follow-up to the Final Declaration', Budapest, 6–7 May 1999

'Stability Programme for South-East Europe', 23 April 1999

'Preventing Ill-treatment. An Introduction to the European Committee for the Prevention of Torture and Inhuman or Degrading Treatment or Punishment (CPT)', 1999

'A Visit by the CPT – What's it all about? 15 Questions and Answers for the Police', 1999

'The Prevention of Torture at the Dawn of a New Millennium: Substantive Sections of the CPT's General Reports', 1999

'Framework Convention for the Protection of National Minorities. Collected Texts', Strasbourg, 1999
'Introduction to the Framework Convention for the Protection of National Minorities', Strasbourg, October 1999
'The Advisory Committee on the Framework Convention for the Protection of National Minorities', Strasbourg, 1999
'The European Charter for Regional or Minority Languages: Outline for Periodical Reports to be Submitted by Contracting Parties', Strasbourg, 1999
'European Charter for Regional or Minority Languages. Treaties and Reports', Strasbourg, 1993
'International Conference on the European Charter for Regional or Minority Languages', Strasbourg, 26–27 March 1998
'Implementation of the European Charter for Regional or Minority Languages', Conference, 14–15 December 1998
'The Council of Europe and Minorities', Strasbourg, 1994
Short Guide to the ECHR, Strasbourg, 1991
Council of Ministers, concerning the European Court of Human Rights, judgement of 28 July 1998, in the case of Loizidou against Turkey (Interim resolution DH (99) 680)
'Visit to Ukraine by the Chairman of the Committee of Ministers, Mr. Halldor Asgrimsson' (1999) Kiev, 18–19 October, SG/inf (99), 16, revised

EU documents

Draft Charter of Fundamental Rights of the European Union, 28 September 2000, Brussels (http://db. consilium.eu.int)
'Enlargement and Civil Society', 1999 Conference Proceedings, Brussels, October
'Enlargement of the European Union: a Historic Opportunity', DG Enlargement
'Enlargement: Twinning', Information Package, EU Commission, 1998
EU Annual Report on Human Rights, 2000
The European Parliament and the Defence of Human Rights, Office for Official Publications of the EU, 16 July 2000
PHARE Multi-Beneficiary Programmes, Number three, EU Commission, 30 November 2000
'Towards Greater Economic Integration', Central and Eastern Europe: trade, investment and assistance of the EU, EU Commission, 1999

OSCE documents

ODIHR (Office for Democratic Institutions and Human Rights), *Semi-Annual Report, autumn, 1998*
ODIHR, 'Kosovo/Kosova: as Seen, as Told: an Analysis of the Human Rights Findings of the OSCE KVM, October 1998 to June 1999, Warsaw, 1999
OSCE Handbook, 1999, Vienna
OSCE International Election Observation Mission, Republic of Azerbaijan, Election to the Milli Majlis, 'Statement of Preliminary Findings and Conclusions', 5 November 2000

OSCE, 'Elections in Azerbijan Mark Progress, though Falling Short of International Standards', press release, 6 November 2000
OSCE, 'International Election Observers in Azerbaijan Welcome CEC Decision to Investigate Allegations of Fraud', press release, 7 November 2000
OSCE, 'Statement by the Central Election Commission of the Republic of Azerbaijan', 6 November 2000

UN documents

UNSC res. 221/66
UNSC res. 418/77
UNSC res. 678/90
UNSC res. 688/91
UNSC res. 733/92
UNSC res. 757/92
UNSC res. 770/92
UNSC res. 794/92
UNSC res. 827/93
UNSC res. 918/94
UNSC res. 940/94
UNSC res. 995/94
UNSC res. 1160/98
UNSC res. 1199/98
UNSC res. 1199/98
UNSC res. 1244/99

Norwegian parliamentary reports

Stortingsmelding nr. 34 (1998–99) *Norges deltagelse i Europarådet i 1998*
Stortingsmelding nr. 40 (1999–2000) *Om samarbeidet i OSSE i 1998-99 og Norges OSSE-formannskap*

Newspaper articles

Aftenposten, 'Russland gikk mot Vesten i splittet OSSE', 29 November 2000
Aftenposten, 'Borodin arrestert', 19 January 2001
Aftenposten, 'Milosevic nærmere rettssak', 8 February 2001
Financial Times, 'Ethical Business', 8 November 2000
Financial Times, 'Shell Takes Action to Counter Criticism', 23 January 2001
International Herald Tribune, 'International Law is Dissolving the World's Borders', 3 July 1999
International Herald Tribune, 'Beijing is an Eager Suitor to Host Olympic Games', 21 February 2001

Index